ADVANCE PRAISE

This is a book that challenges the Church's notion of canonized saints, and asks the question, "Who are the true followers of Jesus?" You may love it or you may hate it, agree with it or dispute nearly every word of it. But you will not be unmoved by Eileen DiFranco's truth-telling about some of the Roman Catholic Church's most beloved icons. Pages pulsate with the author's intent to expose the need for clerical power and political control that has driven the Church's canonization machine over the centuries. Grounded in scripture, theology, and pastoral care, as well as in Eileen's personal experience, the book is a must-read for those who are brave enough to pull the curtains back on one of the Church's deepest hypocrisies.

— Gloria Carpeneto, Ph.D.

Sometimes you don't know what you don't know until someone points it out. In Taking Out the Saints, Eileen McCafferty DiFranco focuses our attention on all we do not, but should, know about some the Catholic Church's most venerated saints, ancient and modern. A compelling storyteller, she applies her diligent research and extensive fact-finding to highlight egregious behavior on the part of such luminaries as Augustine, Athanasius, Ambrose, Jerome, Thomas More, and others. She also illuminates the truth behind the Church-manipulated sainthoods of Joan of Arc, Catherine of Siena, Theresa of Avila, the virgin martyrs, and many more. As she makes compelling arguments for those to be left out, she presents equal justifications for those throughout history who should have been, and could still be, included and venerated as true followers of Christ. A stunning, engrossing, inspiring read.

— Ellie Harty is an emeritus educator, current co-editor and writer for a Catholic feminist newsletter and has published articles for the Women's Ordination Conference website and the *National Catholic Reporter*'s "Earthbeat".

DiFranco is relentless in her efforts to deconstruct and debunk of the "official" saints of the Roman Catholic Church. Chapters are organized around themes, only loosely in chronological order; this works well, as each chapter coheres around a key point that the author wishes to drive home. Each begins with a brief autobiographical prelude—the author shares an experience from her own Catholic upbringing and education that anticipates the chapter's focus--she then continues on for a set of saints sharing the common theme (examples), taking care to provide context and plausible evidence driving home the fact that many of the selections for sainthood are motivated by a desire by the wealthy and powerful to maintain wealth and power and to denigrate and control women. Her account is very well-researched (there is a n extensive reference list at the end for anyone driven to "check facts"); at the same time, it is not academic or dry, but conversational. The book is long, but the stories shared engage the reader to the end.

Her account has an edge to it, but most readers (those who continue seeking more) will find that the "sting" gradually subsides; not all saints are debunked. Each chapter ends with a summary of which saints "are not saints. Some chapters include a few for whom the jury is "still out" and about whom the reader is left to make personal judgement. All chapters end with the names of "non-saints" who probably should have been so named.

Throughout the book, the author underlines questions that were not asked, as well as questions that beg asking. I found myself asking the very fundamental question, "in the end, what constitutes sainthood"? The author rightly, I think, through her inductive building of a definition through examples and non-examples, points to compassion, healing, love. In this emphasis, her book provides a valuable counterpoint to the complicated, implicit rubrics that the Roman Catholic Church might be accused of using through the centuries.

— Frank Bernt, Ph.D.

The author has done very thorough research and has laid out an impressive wealth of information on the true meaning of sainthood. She has succeeded in taking us on a perilous and exciting journey through the history of saints, sinners and martyrs. Among the martyrs we meet individuals, religious groups and indigenous nations of different faiths who were victimized for reasons the author will uncover. Her enthusiasm for learning and sharing her knowledge is contagious, and the result is a true page turner.

— Ida Trilnick, M.D.

The Cost of Sainthood

The Cost of Sainthood

Questioning the moral, financial, and spiritual cost of the
historical saint's designation within the Catholic Church

EILEEN MCCAFFERTY DIFRANCO

EMERGENCE EDUCATION

Philadelphia, Pennsylvania

ISBN: 978-1-954642-56-0

Emergence Education Press
P.O. Box 63767
Philadelphia, PA 19147
emergenceeducation.com

Interior design by Sophie Peirce.

Printed in the United States of America.

DEDICATION

I have dedicated this book to the millions of people who have lost their lives due to the deeply held religious beliefs of others. Their blood cries out to us from their graves. We must humbly listen to these voices, we must repent, and we must change. Or the bloodshed will continue.

CONTENTS

INTRODUCTION

"Moral law must lie at the root of all sound historical judgment.
Failing this, the historian, in trying to apply different standards to
different epochs will confuse everyone by taking the explanation for
the conduct for the justification of it."

C.V. Wedgewood

During a 2015 visit to a group of islands off the coast of North Carolina called the Outer Banks, I attended an outdoor theater presentation called "The Lost Colony." Designed to celebrate the courage and determination of the proper, stalwart, and thoroughly Christian British in the face of native violence and intransigence, advertisements for the show included the promise of epic battles, haunting Indian dances, and beautiful costumes. The play certainly delivered these things to a large and attentive audience who clapped appreciatively as the swashbuckling colonists battled the toma-hawk-wielding native people.

While the play did provide drama, it did not portray history. Yet, it is this well-attended and well-liked play first performed in 1937 that declared the Roanoke Colony "lost" (McLerran, 2020.) Despite archeological evidence to the contrary, the play with its persistent myth of brave settlers combatting ignorant savages imbued the story with what pundit Stephen Colbert labels "truthiness." The play annually repeated the fictitious scenario of endemic indigenous violence that morphed into fact, finding its way into school history curricula, including mine. Used in a narrative that justified the elimination of violent native people by Christian colonists, several generations of students, including me, learned in history class that the intrepid little colony disappeared without a trace, likely massacred by heartless, savage Indians.

The truth is very different.

This colony, called Roanoke by both the indigenous people and later by the colonists, was founded in 1587 by an experienced explorer named Sir John White. Backed by both Sir Walter Raleigh and Queen Elizabeth I, White and another one hundred and seventeen people, including White's pregnant daughter and son-in-law made the perilous journey across the Atlantic Ocean to establish what they hoped would be the first permanent English settlement in North America. English settlers would not accomplish this feat for another twenty years in another place called Jamestown, Virginia.

The "lostness" of the colony is augmented by pathos. Virginia Dare, dubbed the first English child born in North America, was White's newborn granddaughter. White had to leave baby Virginia, his daughter, son-in-law, and his compatriots behind on the island and set sail for England to replenish supplies a mere six weeks after their arrival. White left clear instructions with the tiny, vulnerable colony. If the settlers needed to move to a different place, they were to carve their new location into a tree or post. If they encountered trouble, they were to include a Maltese cross.

Unfortunately, a war between England and Spain delayed White's return for three years. When White returned and found the site empty, he did not surmise that the native inhabitants had massacred the colonists since they had followed his instructions, carving the word "Croatoan" on a fence post and "Cro" on a tree. There was no Maltese Cross or sign of distress, and the village was dismantled rather than destroyed. Croatoan was the name of the Indigenous people in the area. It was also the native name of Hatteras Island. It was clear to White where the colonists had gone.

Under the threat of mutiny, White was not able to sail to Hatteras and search for his family and fellow colonists. He was not alarmed. Unlike the war-like natives portrayed in the play, White had had a very different experience with the native people and knew their chiefs Manteo and Wanchese. He expressed his comfort with the native people writing, "I greatly joyed that I had safely found a certaine token for their safe being at Croatoan, which is the place where Manteo was borne, and the savages of the islands are friends" (White, 1590).

White was never able to return to Croatoan and never learned the fate of his family. He later described the voyage as "luckless to many and sinister to myself" (White, 1590).

What happened to the settlers? The evidence lies in what they took with them as they dismantled and then abandoned the little settlement on Roanoke Island. Archeologists have found sixteenth century British artifacts mixed in with native ones in digs along the Outer Banks. In the early eighteenth century, explorer John Lawson encountered blue-eyed native people who told him that their ancestors "spoke out of a book." If Virginia Dare survived into adulthood, she might have lived out the remainder of her life among those her grandfather had regarded as "friends."

Despite White's letters and archeological evidence to the contrary, the tale of brutal Indians maliciously and wantonly attacking and killing courageous, Christian colonists persists in the yearly reenactment of a lie.

Unfortunately, myths, legends, and fables tend to be a common way of understanding history. The emotion evoked by lost colonies, missing babies, the treachery of enemies, and the stubbornness and ignorance of those who refuse to share the dominant culture's beliefs nudge out reality, enabling human beings to believe the worst about those they label enemies. What people feel and believe about the past becomes more important than what happened.

Myths and legends also form the basis of many established religious traditions. When these traditions are dipped into the noxious cauldron of power and privilege, once innocent, meaningful, and life-giving beliefs can become a set of alternative facts that become baptized as the truth. As the complex relations between the colonists and native Americans prove, the influence of traditional stories is hardly neutral and can inflict damage unto the generations.

Christian theology is based upon the purported disobedience of a mythical couple named Adam and Eve. The church has designated Eve as its official theological villain whose disobedience and pride caused the fall of a once sinless, immortal humanity. Eve's brash defiance and indifference to divine commands stands in stark contrast to Mary, the church's meek, obedient, humble, and virginal heroine who said, "Let it be done to me according to your word."

Like the mythology surrounding Eve, the church has surrounded Mary with "mansplainations" that have become religious truth, effectively removing her from the human realm and fashioning her into a demi-god. A fixation upon Eve's disobedience and Mary's virginal humility has led to the denigration of women by religious authorities for millennia.

For many believers, these myths are divine truth.

While writing in a parish e-group some years ago, I tried to give Mary a human face by exploring what she might have experienced giving birth to her first child in a strange city far away from the comfort of her village midwife and her mother in a barn surrounded by animals.

As a former labor and delivery nurse, I had accompanied women who sweated and groaned and screamed their way through labor. I saw birth waters and blood stream from the mother's body as she pushed her baby out through a gaping vagina. How could Mary be any different from other women? How could she be honored as a universal mother if she did not experience the pangs of childbirth? Why did the mother of Jesus have to be rendered almost unrecognizable as a normal human woman and mother to be considered holy?

One of the members of the e-group, an elderly priest had a very different point of view.

"That's not how Mary gave birth!" he almost yelled through an email. Using a collective "we," he informed me that "we know" that Mary was so holy by age sixteen, mind you, that God spared her from experiencing any pain during childbirth. In addition, he claimed that angels delivered Jesus, swooping down from heaven and dropping him into the waiting feeding trough that served as his crib. In his celibate opinion, Mary's holy body simply could not have delivered Jesus' holy body in a completely human (aka profane) way, through her vagina. The thought that Mary even had a vagina repelled him. For him, birth was a revolting enterprise. Another priest asked me why I chose to "ruin" what was for him a beautiful story by mentioning pain, blood, and women's body parts.

What is the harm, the churchmen implied, in accepting traditions from which millions of people have derived comfort? Likewise, why not continue to believe that savage Indians wantonly murdered

Baby Virginia Dare and her brave family if it inspired patriotism? Why allow fact to ruin faith and tradition?

Because myths baptized as doctrine have harmed people, we need to question and challenge foundational stories that have become entrenched as deeply held beliefs. The romantic idealization of a blurry and morally complicated past has served no one well. The myth of the savage Indian led to the oppression and slaughter of native peoples in the Americas by devout Christians who believed that they were chosen to spread their faith by any means necessary, including the sword. The ancient myth of virginity as a criterion for holiness led to the millennia-long denigration of women.

Like Eve and Mary, a cast of characters regarded as saints has been handpicked by the church over the millennia to prove the truth of dogma and doctrine, concretize metaphors, promulgate the party line, and to serve as poster girls and boys for an institution that aligned itself with reactionary secular forces that have served as the church's enforcers. The opposite is also true. Truly holy and admirable people were not canonized because they did not reflect the values of the institutional church.

Thus, the title of "saint" is morally compromised by a church that has repeatedly failed to muster up enough humility to confront and reject the unsavory parts of its history, practices, and deeply held beliefs. While some of the recent popes have offered apologies for the egregious sins committed under the church's watch, its examination of conscience has not gone far enough. Rather than changing its triumphalist patriarchal outlook and practices, the church has expected the world to change and conform to its often-blinkered views, rendering their apologies moot. Its ongoing understanding of itself as the spotless bride of Christ has sidelined the virtue of humility and its glib reliance upon original sin as an excuse for bad behavior hides the painful truth that the Christian churches bear a moral responsibility for how they and their adherents have behaved.

It is time to examine the church's approved cast of sainted characters. Who does the church truly admire? Royalty? Priests and bishops? Nuns? Mythological characters from a murky past? Politicians? Apologists? Wealthy donors? Defenders of the status quo? Those who believe that giving up sex for Jesus will make them holy? Those who starve and disfigure their bodies? Or those who follow the gospel, an act that might be in direct contradiction to the institutional church and the socio-political status quo? The priest sexual abuse scandal, the Black Lives Matter and the MeToo# movements have exposed the morally complicated and unexamined lives of heroes. Likewise, the lives of the saints are due for a moral reckoning. Confederate statues have lost their pedestals. It is time for quite a few saints to lose their halos.

This book is a counter-narrative to the hagiography of the institutional church. It is time to end the silence surrounding the violent, militant aspects of the church and its favored ones who deliberately chose to ignore the mandate of the gospel to love, to show mercy, and treat all people as Jesus himself commanded. Members of the faithful deserve to know that there were always saintly people outside of traditional hagiography who did not sink to the lowest common denominator of human behavior and persecute their neighbors.

Throughout the book, I remove the halos from saints who not only neglected the gospel mandate to love, but also failed to fulfill the basic standards of human decency and dignity proclaimed by Jesus. I remove those blinded by piety, their own self-regard, culture, economics, and empire, those who have been canonized to make a political point, and those who fulfilled gender or ethnic stereotypes. I put to rest the myth that virginity, especially female virginity, equals holiness or proximity to God.

I also add individuals throughout history whose efforts to improve humanity were censored by the church and consigned to oblivion for not fitting into the ecclesial idea of holiness. This is not revisionist history or cancel culture. Many of the canonized were not respected by their contemporaries. It was the churchman who canceled their debts to society and retrofitted them with a sanctity they might not have shown during their lives. In doing this, I shall surely "ruin" some beautiful stories for some true believers.

It is my belief, however, that these stories deserve to be ruined.

Chapter 1:
SETTING THE STAGE

"In judging human beings and things,
ethics go before dogma, politics, and nationality."

Lord Acton

Like all good Catholic children in the 1960s, I said my fair share of prayers in school. The prayers that we memorized as homework just rolled off our collective tongues like endlessly recited times tables and spelling words. Prayer provided the framework for the school day at our local parish school where Roman Catholicism defined our lives. We memorized questions from the *Baltimore Catechism* each night for homework. Each afternoon after lunch, we read something called Bible history, which reduced all of scripture to a war between the good guys and bad guys where the former always won due to the intervention of God. We prayed the Morning Offering when we arrived at school and the Act of Contrition before we left lest we die unforgiven and spend eternity in hell. We went to Mass on Friday and Sunday mornings, had hymn practice on Wednesday afternoons, and went to confession on Saturday afternoons. We abstained from sweets during Advent and in Lent and "adopted" pagan babies. In March of my fourth-grade year, our teacher, Sister V.I., decided that a practice called Blessing the Hours would give us yet another opportunity to pray to and honor God. She directed a quiet girl named Rosemary who wore a usually forbidden watch to school to stand up each hour right in the middle of whatever we were doing to remind us to stop our lessons and pray.

Each day, a different student was to be responsible for the prayer, "Let us come into the presence of God," to which the class would respond, "And let us adore his divine majesty." Then the assigned student would ask the saint of the day to pray for us.

We got off to a good start on March 1. Rosemary dutifully, if shyly, stood up and we put down our pencils as the student began the prayer. The saint of that first day was St. Albinus. In a class filled with nine-year-old Marys, Kathys, Pattys, Johns, Joes, and Jims, "Albinus" jarred our very parochial ears. Some of us snickered as we asked St. Albinus to pray for us. The student designated to pray on March 1 could barely get the name out without laughing. St. Heraclius was the saint for March 2. There were more laughs.

March 3 was my day to pray. I recall looking at the calendar provided by the local funeral director that hung on our refrigerator door at home. With great dismay I noted that my saint of the day was Cunegunda. St. Cunegunda: how was I ever going to use that name in prayer? In all my books of saints that were filled with recognizable and pronounceable names like Mary, Barbara, Cecilia, Dorothy, Catherine, and Agnes, there was no mention of a Cunegunda. I tried to practice saying "St. Cunegunda, pray for us" at home with my mother, who would laugh hysterically each time I said it. Although I was a quiet, obedient child, I simply could not say "Cunegunda" without laughing. My mother was no help.

March 3 arrived and my debut at blessing the hour quickly approached. At nine a.m., Rosemary steadfastly stood up. The first part of the prayer just rolled off my tongue. But I simply could not get St. Cunegunda out of my nine-year-old mouth. Instead, I burst out laughing. So did the rest of the class. In disgust, Sister handed over my job to the student who sat behind me—who also burst out laughing. Perhaps it was the hourly disruption of our lessons or our irreverent laughter, but the Blessing of the Hours ended on St. Cunegunda's feast day in our fourth-grade classroom.

Despite my laughter that day, by age nine I was a confirmed saintaholic. Who wouldn't be in those thrilling pre-Vatican II days of Christendom when we were preparing for martyrdom by the godless Russian Communists whose conversion we prayed for every Sunday after every Mass? Like the caped crusaders who marched into battle against the infidel with the cross of Jesus emblazoned upon their shields, we too were proud members of the Church Militant, directed by our faith to conquer the world for Jesus. Armed with the deeply held beliefs of our faith, we were ready to accompany the saints into the valley of death to protect our faith from faithless Communists, Protestants, Jews, and atheists.

From an early age, the lives of the saints inspired my Catholic fervor. My aunt had bought fake gilt-edged pamphlets for me. Before I could read, I looked at the pictures of haloed figures in robes holding the instruments of their torture and death. How brave they were: a handsome, blonde, partially clad St. Sebastian with his eyes rolled up to heaven, tied to a tree and shot through with arrows, one in a very muscled pectoral; St. Helen, the mother of the emperor Constantine, holding the one true cross she miraculously uncovered during on a trip to the Holy Land; and a buxom Mary Magdalene with signature red hair dressed in a form-fitting, push-up green bodice and kneeling before a skull, repenting for her sin of fictitious whoredom. To a little girl hungry for tales of strong women, my favorite saint was Joan of Arc who stood amid plumes of smoke, her long blonde hair flowing over form -fitting armor. I prayed to her for courage in the face of the persecution to come before going to bed.

The Catholic world has had a love affair with saints from its inception. The saints are quintessential Catholic role models who have exorcised their demons and won their race, attaining holiness at great cost to themselves. The Catholic Church rewarded their hard-won holiness with a halo, an august title, and a place in heaven near the throne of God where they intercede for the faithful still slogging through their vale of tears on earth. Faithful Catholics adorn their homes and churches with paintings and statues of the saints. Babies are named for them and cities are placed under their protection.

But are these people truly worthy of our emulation? Were they paragons of sanctity? Were all the stories about them true?

Throughout the millennia, thousands of (mostly) men and (some) women were canonized by the institutional church as saints. Many of these people were, indeed, holy people, faithful to the gospel, who deserved canonization and the respect of their fellow Catholics. However, the calendar of saints is also graced by any number of cranks, thugs, sexual voyeurs and perverts, tricksters, hypocrites, misogynists, and egotists. Some were violent men (and some women) who preached crusades and pogroms, ordered executions and persecutions, approved the Inquisition, sponsored witch hunts, and relegated women to permanent second-class status.

Athanasius and Cyril of Alexandria, for instance, were redeemed by the title of saint and Doctor of the Church although they engaged in violent pogroms against those they designated as heretics. Augustine, Jerome, and John Chrysostom were overt misogynists who created an atmosphere of gender intimidation and oppression. Their theological heirs, Albertus Magnus and Thomas Aquinas taught that women were defective and misbegotten. The anti-woman diatribes of these churchmen have sunk deeply into ecclesiastical policy, impeding, and preventing the full flourishing of women in the church.

Those dubbed "apologists" wrote in defense of the church, even when dogma and doctrine did not cohere with the gospel. Many were caught up in a dualistic universe that oftentimes condemned "the other" to persecution, ostracism, or genocide. John Paul II covered up child abuse and conflated the teachings of Jesus with Marxism. Members of the royal class were canonized for empowering the clergy or for merely supporting the activities of the pope or the local bishop. St. Cunegunda and her husband, the sainted emperor Henry II of Germany, are prime examples of this practice.

The less than stellar behavior of the canonized is too often glibly dismissed by churchmen and members of the faithful who shrug their shoulders and ignore or defend the shadow sides of the sainted. Because of Adam and Eve, everybody sins. God uses both saints and sinners to accomplish the divine will. All eventually work for the glory of God. However, these stories of perceived holiness handed down through the generations too often merge complex moral issues with triumphalism— as did the fable of Roanoke Island. Too often, they inspire sympathy and identification when they should evoke horror.

Thus, the elevation of people into paradise has not been without consequences centuries later. The words of sainted fourth-century heresy-hunters were used as a battle cry by medieval crusaders and Inquisitors as they massacred those the church identified as heretics. Both Catholic and Protestant Europeans used these same words to destroy Indigenous life and culture in the Americas. Twenty-first century right- wing Catholics and evangelicals label their inability to persuade their fellow Americans to follow their anti-abortion, anti-LGBTQ policies as religious persecution. It is only in the very recent past that a pope has stated that religions other than Roman Catholicism are viable pathways to God. So, it is important that we choose our heroes wisely and disassociate them from sympathy, admiration, and unquestioned belief.

While few may know the names or history of St. Cunegunda (975–1033) and her sainted husband, Henry (973–1024), they serve as a prototype for misguided canonization.

Cunegunda and Henry filled in all of the boxes that guaranteed canonization; their childlessness was attributed to a sexless marriage, and they made large donations to the church, so large that that the clergy needed to establish a bureaucracy to deal with their newly acquired wealth. Missing from the story of saintliness is that the treasure they amassed resulted from the taxation of serfs and wars against fellow Christians. Unfortunately, the vast amounts of money Cunegunda and Henry donated to the church was not shared to ease the poverty of the serfs who had produced the wealth through their labor but rather to enrich bishops and increase church land holdings. Church hagiography suggests that the royal couple's real vocation was to religious life. Henry purportedly renounced his aspiration to become a monk after an abbot advised the ambitious scion of the imperial dynasty that his vocation lay elsewhere. Once Henry died, Cunegunda retired to a Benedictine monastery, the practice of many royal widows. Their reported religious vocations to religious life coupled with their childlessness proved the validity of their pre-nuptial agreement to remain celibate. So, the story goes.

What are the facts? According to historian and prince-bishop Thietmar of Merseburg (975–1018), Henry, called "the exuberant" by his contemporaries, was on a mission of conquest rather than on a quest for personal holiness. Unmoved by the death of his king, Henry began his quest for power by angling for the crown of Germany during his predecessor's funeral procession, demanding that the bishop hand over the regal insignia while the prelate was enroute to the late king's burial. The bishop refused, fearing Henry's obvious ambition. Incensed, Henry imprisoned him and instead persuaded another bishop to anoint him king in 1002 without asking for the expected support from the German nobles. Two years later, he was crowned King of Italy, and in 1014, Holy Roman Emperor. Cunegunda, far from isolating herself from the attractions of the world, was one of his closest advisors, supporting his drive for power, wealth, and prestige.

Henry was a savvy political ruler who unified his empire by playing a medieval game of moneyball. As he encouraged the church to buy into his drive for power by bequeathing generous gifts of money, land, and royal titles to bishops, he simultaneously sidelined fractious nobles who might have disagreed with his politics. According to Thietmar, the imperial couple bought their way right into the heart of the church, making the two entities a seamless garment. Wedded by bands of gold to the secular mission of the emperor, the churchmen abandoned the Prince of Peace and followed Henry into his many battles for territorial acquisition against fellow Christians in southern Italy and Poland.

One of Henry's many pro-church actions was to restore Pope Benedict VII to the papal throne after a two-year eviction by an antipope. It was the grateful Benedict who repaid Henry by crowning him Holy Roman Emperor in 1014. Dissatisfied with this august tile, Henry needed more adulation and insisted that he was king by divine right, the first king to make such a claim.

After claiming a plentitude of power in the western secular domain, Henry used his prestige with the church to delve deeply into time-honored religious sensibilities and promulgate a change in an article of faith. The fourth century Nicene Creed, a declaration of faith hammered out by an ecumenical council comprised of diverse bishops, had been recited without incident by Christians in both the East and the West for almost seven hundred years. A local variation to the creed called the "filioque" had arisen in Spain in the sixth century to combat the Arian heresy which disputed the eternal nature of Christ's divinity. This local variation in the creed, made without the approval of the whole church, claimed that the Holy Spirit proceeded from the Father and the Son rather than from the Father alone. Although Charlemagne, crowned the first Holy Roman Emperor in 800, approved of this addition of the creed, most men of the church, including the pope who crowned him emperor, disagreed with the unlawful tampering of an article of faith. Some eastern theologians considered the alteration outright heresy and a sin against the unity of the whole church. Despite these warnings, Henry persuaded the pope to use what the East considered to be a heretical creed at his coronation as Holy Roman Emperor in Rome in 1014 (Galli, 1997).

The controversy over the filioque was just one of several issues that slowly dissolved the tenuous bonds of unity between the East and the West. As the two entities grew theologically and philosophically apart throughout the centuries, what began as differences resolved with tact and diplomacy, eventually became insurmountable chasms. After a series of misunderstandings augmented by the mutual deposing and excommunication of emperors and bishops, the church fell into schism in 1054. A hundred and fifty years later, crusaders enroute to the Holy Land sacked Constantinople and usurped the throne. The Byzantine Empire would never recover. It was not able to defend southeastern Europe from Muslim inroads and fell to the Ottoman Empire in 1453.

As I researched Henry and Cunegunda, I was struck by the failure of the Catholic resources to mention the inconvenient facts of the couple's many wars of conquest or Henry's devious route to kingship. These resources literally gushed over the alleged holiness of two monarchs who wore imperial crowns and engaged in active warfare against fellow Christians when it is quite obvious that their Christianity rested as lightly upon them as does a slice of lemon upon a dinner plate. The factual accounts of their generosity and military support of the Roman Church overshadowed and excused anything else they might have done. The sources also never challenged the ancient assumption that their childlessness resulted from a vow of celibacy rather than from the ancient curse of barrenness aka infertility. The presumption of celibacy added another layer of unfounded holiness to the couple that survives almost a thousand years later.

Pious Catholics celebrate the feast days of Saints Henry and Cunegunda on July 15 and March 3 respectively. Unless they probe deeper into the lives of this royal couple, however, they will never learn the inconvenient truth that while the two might have been successful monarchs who won their many wars for territorial conquest, they surely were not saints.

The intensifying entanglement between church and state that emerged after Constantine created strange bedfellows. Bernard of Clairvaux (1090–1153), founder of the Cistercian order, was a zealous advocate of papal power who insisted upon the divine right of popes to control both the spiritual and the political lives of European Christians. One of the most famous people of his time, the austere Bernard liked to hobnob with twelfth-century power brokers as much as he liked to pray and engage in ascetic practices. His association with the wealthy and the powerful influenced his rejection of self-rule by citizen communes in some Italian cities.

The papacy was one of the most powerful political offices of the time. Factions of wealthy Italian families pursued it in a most unholy manner via intrigue and murder. The winners of these iniquitous contests, in league with the college of cardinals who had repudiated their pastoral duties to become members of the papal court, were entrusted with teaching faith and morals to the faithful. The number of popes, anti-popes, deposed popes, violent and immoral popes did not arouse cognitive dissonance in this apostle of orthodoxy. Because of his stellar reputation, rich and powerful church rulers and princes enlisted Bernard to decide the worthiness of the candidates who were lobbying to become pope in 1145. It was hardly happenstance that the College of Cardinals elected one of Bernard's former pupils. The new pope asked Bernard to drum up military support for the second crusade called by the church to retake the Holy Land from the Muslims. A renowned and powerful preacher, Bernard did this with skill and gusto. His oratorical skills were enough to inspire thousands of men to don the cross of the crusader and march off to war to commit unspeakable violence in the name of God. Bernard promised potential crusaders that their sins could be expiated by "victories over the infidel" and issued the ominous warning, "cursed be he whose sword is not dripping in blood" (Quoted in Michaud, 2015).

Bernard also whipped up violence against the unconverted western Slavs, urging crusaders to battle until their pagan foe was either converted or deleted (Quoted in Christensen, 1997).

Although Bernard also preached against the Crusaders' penchant to purify local communities by massacring Jews enroute to their mission against the Muslims, he used his considerable voice to condemn the Jewish people as venomous evil doers whose deliberate blindness caused the death of Jesus. Regarded as the holiest man of the time, Bernard intensified and spread anti-Semitism proving the blunt warning of nineteenth-century religious critic Elizabeth Cady Stanton that what is preached from the pulpit is carried out by the man (and woman) in the street (Stanton, 1895).

In 1121, Bernard trained his fanatical eye and considerable oratory skills upon Peter Abelard (1079-1142) and Arnold of Brescia (1090-1155) after orthodox churchmen reported the two to the crusading monk.

Abelard was a famous and well-regarded French scholar with a large following that included the revolutionary Italian priest, Arnold of Brescia. Although Abelard regarded himself as a loyal son of the church, his insistence upon using reason to understand faith put him in opposition to the church as did his support of personal inquiry into scripture and theology without the mediation and interpretation of the clergy. In a time before transubstantiation became an article of the Catholic faith, Abelard believed that Jesus became present in bread and wine when any believer recited the words of institution. Abelard's teaching that faith is a private determination alarmed Bernard who was not above making ad hominem attacks against his theological foes. He publicly called Abelard a heathen.

Both Bernard and the church were alarmed by what appeared to be Abelard's theological and philosophical declaration of independence from ecclesiastical control. The irritating presence of Arnold, a monk as austere and ascetic as Bernard who relentlessly criticized the wealth and power the institution had painstakingly accumulated over the centuries, augmented their alarm.

Arnold believed that owning property disqualified the clergy from administering the sacraments. He accused the College of Cardinals of being a place of shame and a den of thieves marked by pride, avarice, and hypocrisy rather than gospel values. The pope, he said, was "a man of blood who maintained his authority by fire and sword, a tormentor of churches and oppressor of the innocent, who did nothing in the world save gratify his lust and empty other men's coffers to fill his own." For his part, Bernard called Arnold "the incorrigible schismatic, the sower of discord, the disturber of peace and the destroyer of unity." Arnold minced no words about his persecutor. According to his contemporary John of Salisbury, Arnold described the famous Bernard as "a man puffed up with vainglory, jealous of all those who have won fame in letters or religion." (John of Salisbury, 1163)

After being expelled from Italy and declared a schismatic by the pope for leading a revolt against the bishop of Brescia, Arnold arrived in France and attached himself to Abelard. It remains unclear if Abelard knew of Arnold's revolutionary teaching. For Bernard and the bishops of France, however, even the hint of association indicated guilt. The two needed to be silenced.

Desperate to clear his name, Abelard summoned Bernard to a public debate to refute the latter's accusations of heresy. At first Bernard demurred, fearing the skill of a well-liked man who had never lost a debate. Under pressure from powerful bishops and abbots, Bernard led Abelard to believe that the two would publicly debate theological points in good faith. Instead, Bernard, whose religious sensibilities were not offended by prevarication, convened a kangaroo court to try Abelard for heresy. When Abelard arrived at the proposed site for the debate, he found an assembly of bishops and nobles along with a man who was to be his inquisitor rather than his sparring partner. Recognizing that the saintly Bernard had set him up, Abelard left and announced that he was going to plead his case before the pope.

Before Abelard was able to leave France, Bernard began barraging the pope with letters condemning him of heresy. Abelard never had a chance to clear his good name. The pope who Bernard helped place upon the throne of Peter condemned Abelard as a heretic and silenced him without reading his works or listening to his point of view. Abelard's books were burned, and his health ruined.

The same tribunal also silenced, condemned, and banished Arnold. While Abelard accepted papal discipline, Arnold continued his relentless campaign against church wealth and temporal power. Arriving in Rome in 1145, he found that the citizens had revived the ancient Roman senate, expelled the pope, and declared Rome a republic. Moving from the religious to the political sphere, Arnold joined the insurgents, collaborating with the citizens to consolidate their power over the pope and the curia. The pope excommunicated Arnold for his efforts.

When a new pope invited the Holy Roman Emperor to take Rome by force and return it to papal control, Arnold accused the pontiff of seizing power through "homicide." The emperor's forces seized Arnold, condemned him of treason against the papal state, and hanged him, fulfilling Bernard's dictum that those who do not respect authority cannot be forgiven. His ashes were thrown into the Tiber.

Arnold never recanted or apologized. His recalcitrance earned him the titles, "forger of heresies," "sower of schism," "enemy of the Catholic faith," and "the father of political heresies" from various churchmen. Arnold was not without admirers. Many of his contemporaries admired a man who practiced his faith by standing with the poor as Jesus did rather than with the powerful and wealthy. His very public condemnation of clerical excess and wealth exposed the ecclesiastical and political entanglements that underpinned medieval life. Arnold's contemporary, historian John of Salisbury (1120–1180) described the clarity of Arnold's vision in his work *Historical Pontificals*:

> *"He said things that were entirely consistent with the law accepted by Christian people, but not at all with the life they led. To the bishops he was merciless on account of their avarice and filthy lucre; most all because of stains on their personal lives, and their striving to build the church of God in blood."*

Church officials burned all of Arnold's works. John of Salisbury recorded his words and deeds. When the Papal States were dissolved after the unification of Italy in 1871, the people of Brescia erected a statue in their famous native son's honor. The English historian Edward Gibbons (1737–1794) wrote in *The History of the Decline and Fall of the Roman Empire* that Arnold of Brescia was the first to sound the trumpet of Roman liberty. Despite his prophetic stance, Arnold was never canonized.

On the other hand, Bernard of Clairvaux, a defender of the wealthy church, was canonized a mere twenty years after his death despite the violence emanating from both his mouth and his pen. This rapid canonization signaled that the bishops and cardinals, the popes and abbots wanted other churchmen to emulate a man like Bernard who could neatly mix religious faith with politics while wearing a monk's robe. As heresy hunter, papal elector, and crusade enthusiast, Bernard of Clairvaux willingly served as the church's poster boy for unity at all costs. Bernard's reputation remains untarnished today. He is revered as a saint and a Doctor of the Church, a title that grants special and timeless authority to his words and endows them with truth.

The bloodshed and violence preached by those considered to be redeemed is perceived to be different from the violence preached by the local politician or the village bully. Bernard's biographers have been careful to absolve him of wrongdoing, claiming that he was neither a bigot nor a persecutor. How could Bernard who wrote poems about loving God and Mary, who ravaged his body by engaging in severe ascetic practices, who was the loyal servant of the pope, and who loved God and practiced contemplation, not be a saint? Surely, the death and destruction resulting from his preaching the second crusade was nothing but a series of unfortunate events over which he had no control!

Bernard of Clairvaux might have been a mystic. He might have been a loyal servant to both the papal and secular courts. He might even be a Doctor of the Church. But is he a saint? Should a man who preached pogroms against his fellow human beings be raised to the heights of holiness?

As you can see from this brief portrait of one of the church's most favored saints, holiness tends to reflect the religious culture that defines it. A church that ruled by fiat canonized the powerful and the obedient. A church that regarded suffering as a path to holiness admired severe asceticism, self-inflicted pain, suffering, and isolation. Where modern people might regard the ascetic practices of the past as a sign of mental illness, churchmen and many of the faithful perceived sanctity and heroic virtue. Many still do.

For instance, St. Antony abandoned his family so he could sit upon a pillar and pray to God in the heat of the Egyptian desert. St. Rose of Lima threw acid on her hands to make herself unappealing to men. St. Catherine of Siena is one of many female saints who starved themselves to death to please God. St. Paula left behind her minor children to follow Jerome and thereafter, never bathed or washed her face. St. Jane de Chantal stepped over her fifteen-year-old son, who had lain down across a doorway to prevent her from leaving the family to follow Christ. No one told her that she could love Jesus and her family simultaneously.

Of course, sainthood has always been a difficult title to bear. The bestowal of saintliness adds another layer of complexity to an already complicated human being. Human nature itself seems to preclude a seamless garment of lifelong individual holiness. Even a cursory examination of our fellow travelers indicates that life is pretty much a mess, and even the most sainted usually have to make deals with themselves and others in order to live in a challenging world with other problematic human beings. In addition, every human being is a product of all he or she has met and experienced. Consequently, like Bernard, Cunegunda, and Henry, no human being leaves the world unscarred by life.

But do the good deeds of the saints absolve them of the evils that they inflicted upon others? Do redemption and transformation erase unworthy deeds or put them into a pardonable dimension? As the modern clergy sexual abuse scandal has proven, it was once an easy task to excuse evil in those declared holy and redeemed, as if their bad behavior was a minor aberration in an otherwise stellar career or part of a journey to a higher plane of existence.

Allow me to put this idea into perspective. Augustine of Hippo (354–430) lived with a woman for thirteen years. Although they had a son together, he did not marry her because she was of a lower caste. When his mother arranged a marriage for him with a wealthy Christian woman of a higher class, Augustine had to send away his long- time companion whom he purported to love and kept their thirteen- year- old son with him. As a result, Augustine's compan-ion lost both her partner and her son. Their son later died, adding yet another layer of misery upon this poor woman, whose name Augustine never bothered to share.

Augustine seemed genuinely upset by the loss of his unofficial family, but it did not stop him from pursuing a promising future that could only happen without the woman he purported to love—who was good enough for sex— but not good enough to be his wife. Furthermore, after his son's mother went away, Augustine took another mistress while waiting to get married. Once, as the saying goes, he "got religion," Augustine sent both his mistress and his fiancée packing, deeply hurting two more women.

Augustine was a Manichean before he converted to Christianity. Manicheans believed in a dualistic world of light and darkness, good and bad, body and soul. The soul, the spirit, and the intellect belonged to the light while evil, ignorance, and the body were relegated to the dark side. Although Augustine understood how badly he had treated his faithful companion of thirteen years, he could neatly tuck himself inside his intellect where the light covered up and eventually excused the dark and cruel things he had done. Augustine, and the Christian world that came to revere him as a saint, never looked back. The women were merely steps he had to climb as he made his way into the rosy glow of holiness.

Augustine avidly studied scripture and wrote faith- filled treatises on a multitude of Christian concepts, including Christian charity. His words were remarkable: whoever thinks that they know scripture but then fails to build a life upon the love of God and neighbor does not understand scripture at all. Augustine, however, failed his own test. His goal of church unity mattered far more than did the exercise of the cardinal virtue of charity. Like many church fathers, Augustine wrote screeds against the unorthodox and advocated the use of force to enforce belief, rendering his fellow Christians into enemies of the faith. Violence disguised as original sin deformed Christian charity for the next fifteen hundred years.

Augustine also saddled Christianity with the unbiblical and unchristian idea of original sin because of his own sexual proclivities. Someone had to be responsible for his sex drive, which he could not seem to control, and it was not he, the great Augustine! Augustine went back to the beginning and found that the real culprits who ruined the early part of his life were Adam and Eve, two characters as mythical as Pandora and Hercules, who transmitted sin through sexual relations. Thus, original sin, a concept that neither Jesus nor any of the authors of scripture knew anything about, has come down to us as one of Christianity's most basic doctrines.

The priest sexual abuse scandal and the #MeToo movement should lead to a reexamination of the sexual peccadillos of those who appear to have been transformed sufficiently to be canonized or considered for canonization. The spiritual transformation of brilliant and inspiring men (and women) is not always victimless. Human beings should not be used and abused to perfect another's understanding of God.

Twenty-first-century culture has allowed space for questions that were rarely asked in the past, when churchmen lifted their institution and themselves above the common bonds of Earth into the rarified atmosphere of self-declared and unchallengeable holiness. To challenge the church in the past was to court death. Even in the present, those who disagree with church teaching sometimes find themselves marginalized and excommunicated. Despite the threats and fulminations of a mostly defanged institution, Catholics can now wonder publicly about saints—and other things—that might have made sense in the fifth century, but now make us scratch our heads.

We ask for the blessings of St. Arnold of Brescia as we begin our journey..

Augustine, Bernard of Clairvaux, Cunegunda, and Henry used violence to accomplish their goals. Violence is not an indication of holiness.

Follower of the Way of Jesus
Abelard
Arnold of Brescia

Chapter 2:
IN THE BEGINING

"History is written backwards and it cleans up the mess."

Richard Reeves

When I was a little girl, one of my favorite places in the world was the Port Richmond branch of the Free Library of Philadelphia. As I approached the large stone building set in a park amidst the almost treeless, narrow streets of my neighborhood, I always felt excited. My lot was the dull and boring life of an urban schoolgirl, quite unlike the life of pioneer girl Laura Ingalls Wilder, creator of the *Little House* books, and one of my favorite authors. How could anything I would do in my life compare to a life like Laura's in her many little houses? It seemed to me that the places in the exciting times in world history had already been taken. I found solace in books.

Inside the library, the dark paneling and dim lighting played with the sunlight from the large windows, creating an aura of mystery and anticipation. I was happiest there, walking slowly past every single book, choosing new stories, rereading the familiar ones to the point that I knew the next line in each story. The choices were all mine and I could read them on my own time. The library endowed me with a sense of power. That little library taught me that I could learn anything I chose to.

An archetypical older lady librarian with her hair pulled back into a bun and glared at me over wire-rimmed glasses presided over the circulation desk. Since I liked to read, you would think that she would have been friendly to me. But she never was. All business-like, she stamped the card with the return date and stuck it in a flap at the back of the book, never once cracking a smile or engaging in conversation. I never figured out if she was mean, bored, or just plain unhappy, although I could never imagine being unhappy working among books.

One particular section of the children's library always attracted me: the biographies, a set of light blue books, each dedicated to a famous person. I turned the pages of these books filled with wonderment. It was here that I learned the marvelous story of Nathan Hale, who regretted that he had but one life to give for his country, of Paul Revere, who warned his fellow patriots of the approach of the British, and of George Washington and Abraham Lincoln, who each led our country through difficult times. The set also included the scientist Marie Curie and Susan B. Anthony, who, along with Elizabeth Cady Stanton, worked for women's suffrage. At about age nine or ten, I had as yet no idea that there had been a time when women could not vote or be scientists. The biographies both inspired me and outraged me. I wanted to be a hero working for justice or a scientist discovering something that would help the world. Those stories provided important guidance that regular people like me could accomplish great things if given the chance. All a person had to do was be brave and stand up for what was right. It seemed both daunting and possible. I wanted to be ready. All of the exciting places in history had not been taken after all!

I did not know at the time that most of the authors had glossed over or omitted crucial details like the fact that Thomas Jefferson and George Washington had owned slaves. I did not know that the teenaged Sybil Ludington rode twice as far as Paul Revere through the night to warn the militia that the British were going to attack Danbury, Connecticut. What a difference that story would have made to me and generations of girls! Regardless of the omissions and the bungling of facts, the stories of these great people remained with me throughout adolescence, sustaining and inspiring me during the turbulent times of the 1960s which provided its own set of heroes and anti-heroes.

At the Catholic school I attended, there was a different slate of heroes: the saints. The most famous and most honored were the martyrs, especially the women martyrs who were beaten and tortured and burned and beheaded to give glory to God. The female saints seem to be repenting for something: their beauty, their lack of humility, or their desire to be educated. Many of them lost body parts in the process: St. Lucy, her eyes, and St. Agatha, her breasts and St. Agnes, her head. Our teachers, all religious sisters, presented these ascetic women to us as role models even as we desperately tried to make ourselves beautiful and appealing, qualities the saints eschewed. I recall thinking that it was far less dangerous to be a hero like Betsy Ross and sew a flag.

After the second Vatican Council (1962—1965) called by St. John XXIII who tried to move the creaky and cumbersome Vatican machinery into the twentieth century, the church began to remove perennial favorites from the calendar of the saints. To the chagrin of automobile drivers who relied upon a St. Christopher medal hanging from the dashboard to protect them from harm, the church declared that the saint who carried Christ upon his shoulders was a legend. This de-sanctification process was not a new phenomenon. After the upheaval caused by the sixteenth-century Protestant Reformation which criticized the Catholic fixation on saints and martyrs, a group of Jesuit priests had sifted through the annals of martyrs that had accumulated across the centuries. The Society of Bollandists had decided after reviewing thousands of stories that only a small handful of the early saints and martyrs really existed (Moss, 2003).

This de-sanctification did not cause the pious to throw out all of their St. Christopher medals. Nor did it put a damper on the ongoing pious veneration of saints.

How, why, and where did the passionate Catholic veneration of holy people begin?

The answer remains shrouded behind a screen of triumphant church history that insists upon an unbroken tradition of divine origin. This history, renamed the deposit of faith, is supposedly confirmed by scripture, revelation, and the magisterium. It cannot be challenged or questioned, even two thousand years later. When Christians say, "As it was in the beginning, is now, and ever shall be," they aren't kidding.

The reality is of course, very different. To understand how the concept of sainthood developed, it is important to situate it in its very ancient beginnings, a place obscured by the patina of age, faith, assumptions and presumptions, mistranslations, and cultural and religious appropriation. Sainthood, like Christianity itself, did not just spring up in full bloom in the days and months or even years after Jesus died because in the beginning, Christianity had no organization, no structure, no theology, no churches, no set liturgy, and, of course, no saints—not even John the Baptist or the proto-martyr Stephen. In fact, the faith that grew up slowly around Jesus was Judaism— with a twist. The followers of Jesus remembered him during the sabbath meal.

Acts of the Apostles (2:46-47) describes the followers of Jesus "worshipping in the temple each day." On Sunday, they shared the Lord's supper together "with great joy and generosity." They had no idea that they were founding a new religion. In fact, the tiny group of proto-Christians was just one of the Jewish sects that existed in first-century Judea along with the Pharisees, the Scribes and Saduccees, the Essenes, and the Zealots. The followers of Jesus were not referred to as Christians until the beginning of the second century. Even then the line of demarcation between Christian and Jew was not clearly recognizable to sizable numbers in the ancient world.

As it gradually separated from Judaism, Christianity retroactively inserted creeds, dogma, doctrine, miracles, and wonder workers into its developing faith to prove the truth of what it was teaching many years and iterations later. The four canonical gospels, written in the last two decades of the first century C.E., are documents of faith, not history, and record what believers were experiencing at the time they were written and not in the time they were describing.

Consider the implausible story of the martyrdom of Stephen in Acts of the Apostles (6:8-7:60). The arrest, trial, and execution of Stephen follows that of Jesus. Like Jesus, Stephen performed great signs and wonders that drew a large following. Concerned with his teaching and miracle working, naysayers secretly plot to trap him. Brought before the scribes and elders, Stephen is accused of blasphemy by bogus witnesses. Unlike Jesus, Stephen has quite a bit to say at his trial, delivering a three- page theological thesis on salvation history, complete with citations from the psalms. Borrowing a line from the prophet Nathan, he drops a bombshell accusation of unfaithfulness and murder upon his judges at the end of his discourse.

They, not Stephen, are the blasphemers. They are the ones who have killed the prophets.

The mood of the scribes and elders changed. They could no longer see the "angelic face" they saw at the beginning of Stephen's trial. Now they were enraged. They gnashed their teeth and called for his death by stoning. After his sentencing, Stephen calmy looked up to heaven and announced that he saw the glory of God with Jesus standing at the divine right hand, as if waiting for him to enter. As he lay dying, he asked Jesus to "receive his spirit,' like Jesus did on the cross. And like Jesus, he asked God to forgive his executioners.

Stephen's vision was confirmed by his heroic death. It would later become a statement of belief in the Nicene Creed. Jesus, as Christ, sits at the right hand of God.

However, it is important to remember that Stephen was not executed because he was a Christian any more than Jesus was. Those who stoned him viewed him as a criminal, a blasphemer, and a faithless Jew.

The early followers of Jesus had also found motivation in the heroes of the Jewish faith recorded in the Old Testament or Hebrew Bible, the only scriptures the early Christians had until the gospels began circulating late in the first century. The deeds of Moses, Elijah, who raised a boy from the dead, Daniel, who repelled a den full of hungry lions, and the Maccabee family, who demonstrated exemplary fortitude during their gruesome martyrdom, foreshadowed later Christian heroes. Christians co-opted Jewish archangels and canonized them as Christian saints.

The ancient Jewish writers were not the only ones who recorded the mighty deeds of healers. Pagans had their share of renowned miracle workers as well. One of the most well-known was Apollonius of Tyana whose auspicious birth, life, miracle working abilities, and after-life, like Stephen's, resembles that of Jesus.

The realm of the miraculous always lies before humanity as a fertile field of imagination. Who or what can save me and my family during perilous times? Will my side be victorious? How can I insure my health and that of my family? Will God punish me and my dear ones for our sins? How best can I insure God's favor? Can I appease the divine and deflect punishment? How can I live forever?

Unlike modern people, who know that they live in an immense, expanding, thirteen-billion-year-old universe filled with black holes, whirling galaxies, and exploding supernovas, our ancestors lived in a universe that resembled the little transparent globe that one must shake to simulate falling snow. The world and the visible planets and stars were all tucked neatly into the dome of the sky. From that blue dome of the sky, God or the gods, depending on what one believed, directed the operations of the world through signs and portents interpreted by divinely chosen people. The ancient world shared its existence with the presence of beings who were as real to people as were members of their own families, so few found contacts with the supernatural either uncommon or impossible. Few doubted that these unseen beings from the netherworld determined the progress of life on earth. Charms and amulets devoted to these beings, like Christian medals and scapulars, warded off disaster.

Like us, the ancients worried about their health and the health of their families. and illness and sometimes sought out the power of holy people to heal them. Shamans promised magical cures in the ancient world just as hucksters on television promise to magically cure anything from baldness to midriff bulge. Miracles obviously did not cure everyone, but if a miracle appeared to cure just one, God and the people who performed these services were powerful and worthy of honor.

Like pagans and Jews, early Christians were anxious to show off their miracle-working abilities to potential converts. Christianity's adherents began to record the stories of their wonder workers in the four canonical gospels that were written in the latter part of the first century C.E. as if to say, "Look what we Christians can do in the miracle department!" Peter's reported parting words to his followers in the Apocryphal Acts of Peter were not, "Remember that Jesus came to proclaim liberty and set the captives fee," but rather, "Remember the miracles you have seen!"

What miracles the early Christians would share about Jesus in the cities throughout the empire! While walking the dusty roads of Palestine, this Jesus healed the sick, raised the dead, and fed the multitudes just like the Old Testament and pagan prophets, only better, because Jesus was the promised Messiah and the Son of God.

This divine wonder worker bequeathed the power to heal to his disciples, allowing the miracles to continue after his death. In Acts of the Apostles, people are described as being converted en masse because of the many miracles performed by Peter and later, by Paul. Believers spoke in tongues and yet everyone could understand them. Both Peter and Paul were miraculously freed from jail by angels, the chains dropping from their wrists.

While some church historians attribute the rise of Christianity to their members' virtuous living and concern for the poor, Bart Erhman (2018) has posited that it was the miraculous deeds of Jesus and his followers that eventually caused what became Christianity to knock the Roman gods out of the pantheon and install the Roman pontiff in Caesar's palace as the Vicar of Christ. The church would continue to use miracles performed by members of its Communion of Saints for the next two millennia to repeatedly shore up its fortunes and vindicate church dogma. Miracles performed by the church's poster children would deflate or deflect the actual harm perpetrated by an imperial, authoritarian church. The church still requires miracles— that is, events that fall outside of scientific laws— to justify membership in that august group.

The elaboration of the miraculous and God-besotted wonder workers never did convince many Jews to convert despite the stories of mass conversion in Acts of the Apostles. To the consternation of the earliest Jewish-Christians, most Jews did not believe that Jesus was the Messiah. Nor did they believe that they needed to be saved from their sins. Theological disagreement led to animosity between the two groups. This mutual hostility is expressed in the dialogue between Jesus and the scribes and the Pharisees in the gospels.

Jewish people did not view their scripture as a precursor to Christianity. They did not believe that the ancient Hebrew prophets predicted Jesus. The young woman bearing Immanuel, the stump of Jesse, the rose of Judah, and the suffering servant were Jewish, not Christian tropes. Expressed in the words of Stephen, Jewish followers of Jesus felt that their fellow Jews were being stubborn and stiff— necked, deliberately ignoring the clarity and truth of Christian beliefs. By the 80's and 90's C.E., the Jews were described by the evangelists as saying, "Let his blood be upon us and upon our children," and "Crucify him, we have no king but Caesar." (Matt. 27:28 and John 19:15) Upon the malignant disappointment of the early followers of Jesus rests two thousand years of persecution and pogroms.

The early Christian missionaries had more luck within the Greek-speaking Jewish diaspora and among Gentiles who lived on the fringe of Judaism. The reality is that in the beginning, the number of those who believed in Jesus was very small. Except for the vastly overstated claims of Peter and Paul and their adherents in Acts, there is no historical record of major conversions impressing people to the point of instant baptism and conversion in great numbers. While Acts describes an exponential growth of immediate converts in the months after Jesus rose from the dead, many biblical historians posit something very different. Sociologist Rodney Stark (1996), along with many biblical scholars, historians, and archeologists, has proposed that there might have been just 1,000 proto-Christians by the year 60 C.E. scattered throughout the entire Roman Empire, which was then comprised of 60 million people, an unrecognizable drop in a bucket of thousands of faiths. In his 248 C.E. tract "Against Celsus," second-century apologist Origen seems to agree with Stark's finding: "Let us admit that the Christians were few in the beginning." Like any new faith, it took a while to catch on.

Catch on it eventually did, of course. Miracles remained the most important selling point of Christian missionaries, who traveled east as well as west to preach the good news, fleshing it out with stories of miracles and miraculous human beings from both the Jewish scriptures and the Christian gospels that were now being written down.

When the earliest missionaries brought their gospel to the capital city of Rome in the 40's C.E., they found a deeply conservative, religious people who loved and honored their gods. Like Christians who venerated the saints by kneeling before their statues and praying for special favors, the Romans prayed for good fortune and good health. Pagan Romans celebrated the gods' feast days with the same gusto and religious fervor that Christians used to celebrate Christmas and Easter. They dedicated cities to specific gods as Christians placed cities under the protection of patron saints. Excavations of some ancient cities have unearthed temples as numerous as Christian churches indicating the deeply religious nature of their inhabitants. Ancient cities throughout the empire hosted shrines visited by observant pilgrims.

Romans also honored their ancestors. In fact, they were often less devoted to the gods of Rome than they were to their household gods: the *Lares*, the spirit of their dead ancestors, and the *Parentes*, the spirits of their immediate family, who protected them from harm and guided them along the path of righteousness. The Romans made statues of the *Lares* and *Parentes* and prayed to them before leaving the house and upon their return. These beings were believed to watch over them throughout their lives, so the Romans took the statues with them when they changed residences. Thus, connecting the dots between the *Lares* and *Parentes* with Catholic patron saints does not require much imagination.

Nor does it take a leap of faith to believe that what grew to be Catholic fascination with and dedication to the saints is based upon the understanding that God, like the emperor, was unapproachable. The ancient Christians believed that the order in heaven mirrored the order on Earth. Thus, God was the undisputed king of heaven who lived in a court surrounded by his minions of angels and saints, just like the Roman emperor sat upon his throne on Earth surrounded by the nobility. People prayed for favors from the lower echelon of heavenly society occupied by the saints just as they begged for patronage from wealthy and favored people in Rome because God and his counterpart, the emperor, were beyond the reach of common people.

Some might regard the premise that Christians adopted pagan, Roman, and Jewish ideas and renamed them as articles of faith to be sacrilegious. Members of the faithful may prefer to believe that their faith is pure and unadulterated, a direct revelation from God. However, Christianity is unimaginable without Judaism and church governance flowed directly from Roman law.

Apologists from all faiths are often quick to charge competing faiths and their followers with all sorts of crimes and misdemeanors. Other faiths worship false gods or idols. They participate in barbaric and inhuman practices. They are unsophisticated, demonic, and silly, worthy only of rejection and condemnation. The Jews who seemed to "reject" Jesus despite the "proof" provided by Christians seem to be rejecting reason, reality, and God. These charges were, of course, also leveled against Christians before they came to occupy the throne of Caesar in the Lateran Palace.

Few to none of the charges leveled against those perceived as "the other" are ever true. Most, in fact, are ad hominem attacks, a failure in logic where opponents fail to discuss points of disagreement and instead choose to heap disgraceful and usually unfounded charges against their opponent's reputation to discredit those they regard as enemies. Thus, the basis for religious persecution is laid. When a faith reaches a critical mass, too often it forcibly converts or murders those who disagree with them. Many existing religious faiths have engaged in this heinous behavior.

However, the beliefs of a conquered faith do not disappear just because the triumphant declare them dead. In fact, pagan beliefs remained so strong after Christianity grew ascendant that Christian emperors after Constantine had to destroy pagan temples in order to prevent believers from worshipping in them. Some pagan beliefs persisted in Christianity, rising from oblivion with new names and new understandings to disguise their origins.

The Oracles of Delphi, for instance, which predicted the future, and the Vestal Virgins of Rome, who were believed to have kept the national hearth fires burning, were banned by triumphant Christians. However, Christians never did reject the practice of soothsaying. The art of prophesying, touted by Paul in 1 Corinthians, was the province of those who would build up the church— the saints. Like the Vestal Virgins of Rome, consecrated Christian virgins prayed for the safety of their community. A Vestal Virgin who engaged in sexual activity resulted in her immediate execution. The Christian virgins were believed to incur the wrath of God if they reneged on their promise to remain celibate and married.

Virginity was not just the province of Christians. The ancients regarded the perpetual virgin Athena as the goddess of wisdom. Statues of Athena are impressive. She is depicted as a large woman with rows upon rows of teats, which questioners suck to gain wisdom. The great cathedral Hagia Sophia (or Holy Wisdom) in Istanbul is built atop an ancient temple dedicated to the goddess.

The Virgin Mary has a long string of titles more indicative of a goddess than a woman who was the human mother of Jesus. Along with Athena, Hestia, Cybele, and Artemis, she too is ever-virgin. Like the Egyptian goddess Isis, she also lost a son who was later resurrected. Hymns refer to Isis as God's mother and Queen of Heaven. So do hymns to Mary. John Paul II understood Mary as co-redemptrix with Jesus, making her divine.

Like the Romans, who believed that the gods protected their Empire, Christians placed their cities and what became their countries under the protection of patron saints. The life of St. Genevieve (419–502), the patron saint of Paris, follows a pattern that many canonized women would follow: a commitment to virginity at an early age, a life devoted to prayer and penance, and a starvation diet. When Attila ravaged the French countryside in the fifth century, Genevieve told her fellow Parisians not to flee because God would protect them. Providentially, Attila was defeated at the Battle of Chalons by a Roman-Germanic tribal alliance and withdrew from France, never reaching Paris. During a twelfth century plague, desperate citizens carried a statue of St. Genevieve through the streets. If she protected the city once, she could do it again. Miraculously, people were said to be healed as the statue passed them by. Thus, Genevieve's designation as the patron saint of Paris appears to be well-earned on two counts, especially if one fails to consider the role of military might and strong immune systems.

By the year 100 C.E., there were sixty million people living in the Roman Empire. A mere 1/60 of 1 percent were Christians (Ehrman, 2018). The new faith remained a mishmash of ideas held together by the belief that Jesus rose from the dead, the most important miracle of all time. As the new century unfolded, those on the path to orthodoxy began to teach that the risen Jesus gave explicit directions on founding his new church to his hand-picked cadre of apostles. Miracles solidified belief.

Chapter 3:
APOSTLES

"Religious groups in their earliest stages have an informal, spontaneous, charismatic leadership. If these groups survive, this is inevitably institutionalized, formalized, and professionalized at some point."

Denis R. Janz

In my twelve years of Catholic school education, I never read even one verse from the Bible in any of my classes. In elementary school, we studied Bible history, a made-up subject where all of scripture was reduced to a safe, theologically correct narrative. My pseudo-scripture lessons led me to believe that everything the church taught was accurate because it was "history" easily proven by facts laid out in our textbooks, just like American history.

We did not read scripture at home either. My family of origin had no Bible in the house. My maternal grandmother's Bible sat ceremoniously on the coffee table, its pages fresh and shiny. As a small child visiting my grandmother, I would page through it, looking at the pictures. I recall the seraphim standing outside the Garden of Eden with a flaming sword, Cain standing over the dead Abel with a bloodied knife, and desperate people grabbing fruitlessly for the Ark as Noah sailed safely away, leaving the dying people in his wake. The terror on the drowning faces disturbed me. I would ask my grandmother to read me the stories. I wanted to learn why Noah refused to help the drowning people.

My grandmother steadfastly refused to read anything from the Bible. Even my aunt, who always read to me, refused to read from the holy book. Why, I asked? The priests, she said, told them not to read anything from the Bible at home. I asked why anyone would say such a thing. Because, she replied, they worried that we might get the wrong idea.

It was not until my first theology class at a Catholic college that I learned why some priests might have thought that parishioners might get the wrong idea if they tackled scripture on their own.

The cognitive dissonance begins in the first two chapters of the very first book in the Bible where there are two completely different versions of creation. In chapter one, God sat down after a week of hard work, looked around at the splendor unfolding before the Divine, said, "This is really good!" and blessed it. The first version of creation required no atonement for sin, no banishment from a mythological garden, no death or destruction, and no need for a savior. It was the re-write in the second chapter that got humanity into trouble. The author of chapter two did not like God's original blessing and transformed it into a primordial curse. Christian theology is based upon the second version. The sin of the first two people doomed all of humanity to physical death. Their sin closed the gates of heaven to all who followed them. Humanity now required a savior who would redeem them from the sin committed by Adam and Eve and re-open the gates of heaven. Which version is right? Christians are taught to believe that it is the re-write, the only creation story that is read during Mass. Many Catholics do not know that there are two completely different versions of creation in their Bible.

The discrepancies in the various gospels perplexed me as well. For Mary to remain a perpetual virgin, she could not have had any other children so Jesus' "brothers and sisters" in scripture were explained away as being cousins or step— siblings, children of Joseph by a previous marriage. My first theology professor, who was fluent in both Latin and Greek, told us that Jesus really did have siblings. The Greeks, he explained, used precise words for specific relationships, just like English speakers did. Paul, the earliest New Testament scribe does not know much about the mother of Jesus except that she is "a woman," a normal one rather than a virginal one. However, he does know that Jesus has a brother named James.

There were other inconsistencies. The names of the apostles are different in the four gospels. The arrest of Jesus and the stories of the resurrection are all different as are the names of the women at the foot of the cross. These irregularities occurred, the professor told us, because the evangelists—who were anonymous and not Matthew, Mark, Luke, and John—did not know Jesus and wrote decades after he had died. This knowledge was so shocking to one of my classmates that she had to leave the course. For me, who as a second grader compared God to a mean teacher who punished the entire class for the misdeeds of one student, the discrepancies in scripture finally had an explanation.

My grandmother and my aunt were wrong about being forbidden to read scripture. Pius XII encouraged biblical study and reading in his 1943 encyclical *Divino Afflante Spiritu*. However, this encouragement to read scripture never reached the pulpit in my working-class neighborhood parish church. Others never got the message either as Catholics continue to lag significantly behind their Protestant sisters and brothers in their knowledge of scripture. The 1983 *Revised Common Lectionary* did not help expand biblical knowledge because it failed to offer a wide variety of readings to a community long starved for scripture. Instead, the same stories are read repeatedly over a three- year cycle. As a result, Catholics never hear Romans 16 where Paul calls Phoebe a deacon and Junia an apostle proclaimed during Mass because these women leaders do not fit into the institutional narrative of Jesus' choice of all male leaders from the beginning.

Not only are Catholics largely unaware that lectionary readings are picked through, sorted, and chosen carefully to preserve the institutional company line, but they are also unaware that there once existed thousands of holy books that faithful early Christians with wide— ranging and deeply held beliefs regarded as "scripture." While the canonical gospels have always been regarded as the "Word of God," the institutional Church dismissed the non-canonical gospels as examples of hearsay or heresy. Heresy hunters like Athanasius of Alexandria had these unauthorized gospels destroyed.

Monks under duress during epidemics of book burnings lovingly wrapped up and buried their holy books in caves in the Egyptian desert to protect them from zealots. In the last century, archeologists unearthed these jars containing fragments of these books in Nag Hammadi, Egypt. By piecing fragments of the lost works together, scholars have learned that early Christianity was much more diverse than had been previously believed. "As it was in the beginning" took on a new meaning.

Other non-canonical books survived intact because they contained elements that later became doctrine, dogma, and tradition. The same orthodox Church that destroyed allegedly heretical books regularly used concepts and fanciful stories put forth in non-canonical gospels if they promoted the institutional story line. This is true of the Apocryphal Acts of Peter, the Gospel of James, and the Apocryphal Acts of the Apostles.

In the Apocryphal Acts of Peter, written at the end of the second century after the characters in the story were long dead, the careful reader must tease out the very fine difference between magic, which the church regarded as demonic, and miracles, which are the work of God, although both may accomplish the same thing. Like his mentor, Jesus, the angelic Peter healed large numbers of the blind, the deaf, and the lame. Likewise, Simon, dubbed a magician by Christians, had the same type of power. Although his fellow citizens called Simon's abilities the "Great Power of God," Peter was not persuaded. (Acts 8:10) While the circumstances surrounding his putative request are lost, Acts 18 describes Simon asking the apostles if he can purchase the power of the Holy Spirit. This request is the origin of simony, the purchasing or sale of holy objects or ecclesiastical office.

Despite a magnetic personality that drew both prominent and lowly citizens to him and baptism and membership in the early church, Simon's ideas differed from those of Peter. For these differences in opinion, Simon was placed outside the pale of orthodoxy and labeled a "Magus" or magician. He remains a villain.

Some of the stories in the Apocryphal Acts of Peter are silly. Along with his many cures, Peter is recorded as bringing a sardine back to life. Peter and Simon have a miracle duel in the forum. Simon flies high above the skies of Rome for all to see until Peter's prayers bring him crashing to the ground, the Divine orchestrating Simon's demise to prove Peter's power.

After Simon succumbs to his injuries, Peter convinces the wives and concubines of prominent Roman citizens to "love the word chastity" and leave their husbands' beds. This leads the prefect Agrippa to seek Peter's arrest. Warned by a female convert, Peter flees certain capture. On his way out of Rome he meets Jesus who was going in the opposite direction. Peter asks Jesus in surprise, "Que Vadis" or "Where are you going?" "I am going back to Rome to be crucified," Jesus replied. In shame, Peter returns to Rome to be crucified by the Roman authorities.

Although there is no other record of Peter's martyrdom, the apocryphal acts describe him as being crucified upside down. While few remember the resurrected sardine and the flying contest, the legend of Peter's upside-down crucifixion in Rome was soon baptized as truth.

Written around 145 C.E., the Gospel of James contains the first assertion that Mary remained a virgin when her midwife discovered an intact hymen after delivery. The book also proposes that Joseph was an old man not capable of or wanting sexual relations and, therefore, a caretaker husband whose children from his first marriage were Jesus' frequently mentioned "brothers." The Gospel of James is the only place we hear the names of Mary's parents, Joachim and Anne who purportedly placed Mary in the temple at age three specifically to preserve her virginity, a concept that would be perplexing to a toddler separated from her parents. The couple, especially Anne, has received a great deal of devotion over the years although she did not raise her daughter past the age of three.

It was the author of the non-canonical Gospel of James who solidified Mary's perpetual virginity as a cornerstone of the Christian faith. Unlike other non-canonical gospels that were burned or rejected out of hand for presenting unbiblical ideas, the Gospel of James remained in circulation in the ancient world, giving life to a myth. Churchmen preserved over a hundred Greek copies and translated it into Coptic, Syriac, Ethiopic, Arabic, Armenian, and Latin, disseminating belief in Mary's perpetual virginity throughout the Roman Empire.

The Apocryphal Acts of the Apostles, written in the late second century C.E. laid the foundation for the Christian myth of constant persecution. The apostles —whose names differ in the four canonical gospels– follow the command of Jesus to baptize all nations by going to the ends of the known world and founding churches. Like Jesus, they meet unjust rulers and are martyred for their faith. There is no historical evidence that justifies this belief despite what is called the constant tradition of the church.

Consider the story of the evangelist Mark, Peter's alleged traveling companion and the purported author of the first gospel. Mark is believed to have brought Christianity to Alexandria, Egypt and served as its first bishop. He is believed to have been martyred there for his faith.

Alexandria was one of the largest, most important cities in the Roman Empire and the site of a large Jewish community. With its close links to Jerusalem, it is not surprising that some of the early followers of Jesus, who did not yet self-identify as Christians, would travel to this great city, bringing with them their good news about Jesus. Their journey would have been dangerous. Political unrest was widespread in first-century Alexandria and parts of Palestine as Jews tried to shake off their Roman overlords.

Riots broke out in 40 C.E. in Alexandria because pagans believed that their fellow Jewish citizens were not honoring the emperor. Keeping the arithmetic growth of Christianity in mind with Christians numbering 1,000 in the entire Roman Empire in the year 60 C.E., Alexandrians who followed Jesus in the year 40 C.E. would be a miniscule and undetectable percentage of the population and virtually impossible to single out for persecution. Mark might, indeed, have gone to Alexandria and established a small congregation of like-minded Jews who also believed in Jesus. He, like other Jews, might have been killed in the riot. It is, however, doubtful that he was martyred for the Christian faith since it did not yet exist apart from Judaism.

While the life and death of Mark cannot be proven historically, even less is known about the other apostles, except for Peter, James, and John whom Paul mentions by name in Galatians 1:19, a primary source. The fates of all remain unknown. Contrary to tradition, the fate of Peter, the figure upon whom Jesus said he would build his church, a man Jesus called "Rocky" for his obvious thick-headedness, is not known. The twelve quite obviously did not rise from the table after the Last Supper crowned with miters, holding staffs, invested by divine power to run a newly established church with all of its theological trimmings already in place.

Thus, the names and later deeds of the apostles have come down to us as a combination of memory, history, and religious beliefs held together by nuggets of truth. Whoever the evangelists were, they wrote how they *imagined* the apostles might have acted and preached in works written forty to sixty years after Jesus died because that is what they were experiencing, feeling, and believing. The authors of the gospels wrote, as the gospel of John says, "So that you will come to believe that Jesus is the Messiah, the Son of God, and that through believing you may have life in his name," and not as history.

Paul's letters remain the only primary source of information about the three apostles he knows: Peter, James, the brother of Jesus and not James, son of Zebedee, and John. Acts of the Apostles were written two generations or more after Paul's epistles and its timeline and the stories do not coincide with Paul's earlier, original works. It is from the original letters of Paul: Romans, 1 and 2 Corinthians, Galatians, Philippians, 1 Thessalonians, and Philemon that we get an inkling of the development of early Christianity and those who carried the gospel across the known world.

Paul was a zealot infused with religious fervor, first as a self-described Pharisee and then, as a follower of Jesus. He was a force of nature, a whirlwind of passionate conviction who frenetically traveled the known world preaching his apocalyptic idea of Jesus' teaching: the end is near, believe in the death and resurrection of Jesus, and you will be saved. His preaching caused riots in the streets, and he often found himself whipped and imprisoned for disturbing the peace. He often bragged about himself and his escapades in his letters, saying that God "set him apart" and "revealed" his son to him, how, we do not know, since he does not mention being thrown from his horse or being blinded in his original letters. Something did, however, change the course of his life and possibly the life of what would become the Christian church. Paul had become a new man in Christ and he wanted and fully expected that others would feel the same way. When they did not, he became irate and yelled at people who refused to follow him. Subsequent believers adopted Paul's over-zealous proselytism and often found themselves at odds with the diaspora Jews they met in other countries. These converts also sparked riots among Jewish communities, antagonizing local authorities who threw them in jail. The emperor Claudius was so annoyed, he expelled the Jews— including early followers of Jesus— from Rome.

Once converted, Paul was so sure of his calling and his gospel that he bragged that he never bothered to check out the facts of his faith with those who were intimately acquainted with Jesus during his earthly ministry. Instead, Paul's first steps were to Arabia and Syria and not Jerusalem, where the eyewitnesses lived. It took him three years to reach Jerusalem, where he finally did meet with Cephas and James, the "Lord's brother." Ever proud and assured of himself, Paul described how his influence caused the people of Syria and Cicilia to give glory to God.

Paul insisted that his gospel is the one and only gospel because it came directly to him from God and not from any human being, including those who walked and talked with Jesus and heard his voice. While Peter and James expected Gentile believers to first convert to Judaism before they could be baptized as Christians, Paul regarded this extra step as a perversion of Jesus' message.

In the fiery Paul's own words, those who preached a gospel different from his— let him or her be accursed! No wonder he found himself whipped and in chains! It is in Galatians that Peter and Paul had a huge blowout and Paul lost his traveling partner, Barnabas, to what he disparagingly called "the circumcision faction," those who believed that converts needed to be Jews before they could be Christians. Since their missions were so at odds with each other, it is difficult to believe that Peter and Paul could work together as a dynamic duo and found a church in Rome.

Paul knew nothing about the intimate details of Jesus' life except that he had a brother named James who was now the leader of the church in Jerusalem. John's name was mentioned with no further information. Paul seemed to know nothing about Mary, the mother of Jesus, who might still have been alive in the late 30s C.E. Nor does he know about Joseph, the shepherds, the star, or the Magi. He did not even know about Judas or his betrayal. All he knew, as he said himself, was Christ crucified and raised from the dead by the power of God. We might assume that Peter and the rest of Jesus' followers believed that as well since Paul described the risen Jesus first appearing to Peter, then to the twelve, then to more than five hundred sisters and brothers, then to James, and finally to him, Paul, the least deserving because of his past history of persecution, and then only in a dream. The bombastic Paul could not resist adding, "I worked harder than any of them" (1 Cor 15: 5-11).

Paul wrote his last letter to the Romans while anticipating a visit to Rome before making his way to Spain, a place where "Christ has not been named," so that he would not have to "build on someone else's foundation." We do not really know if he ever got to either Rome or Spain. We do know, however, that there was already an established church in Rome that had been founded prior to 57 C.E. because Paul addressed his epistle to the Romans to a list of that church's members. Tellingly for us, but perhaps not for him, that list did not include Peter.

At the top of the list of those Paul greeted were two prominent names: Prisca and Aquila, a married couple who are mentioned six times in the New Testament. We know from Acts that the peripatetic Prisca and Aquila were in Rome very early, sometime between 41 and 49 C.E., because they were expelled from Rome along with the Jews by Emperor Claudius (41–54 C.E.) who obviously did not detect any difference between the Jews and the early Christians. By 57 C.E. the couple was back in Rome and pastoring a church that met in their house. In his letter to the members of that church, Paul expressed his gratitude to the couple for their proselytizing activities. The early Christians clearly held this couple in high regard.

It is clear from chapter 16 of Paul's letter to the Romans that Prisca and Aquila founded the church in Rome. It is time to rename the great basilica in Rome after its actual founders.

Along with Prisca and Aquila, Paul also listed the members of the base community in Rome to whom he was indebted. Not one of them was an apostle in the classical sense. Paul, who knew at least three apostles back in Palestine, specifically cited Junia and Adronicus as being "prominent among the apostles." Paul also provided a long list of early followers of Jesus who are unfamiliar to most Christians: Epaenetus, Mary, Urbanus, Ampliatus, Stachys,

Apollos, Aristobulus, Herodion, Tryphanena, Tryphosa, Persis, Rufus, Asyncritus, Phlegon, Hermes, Patrobas, Julia, Nereus, and Olympas—people whose lives and deeds have been largely lost. In his other letters, Paul listed the founders of house churches in other parts of the empire: Chloe in Corinth, Stephanus in Achaia, Euodia and Syntyche in Philippi, Nympha in Laodicia, and James in Jerusalem. These people were the founders of the earliest church communities and not the apostles we find in the gospels. If the apostles did follow Jesus, the evangelists depict them as fearful men who ran away after the crucifixion. For all we know, those men could have returned to their lives in Galilee died there.

While most Christian churches have canonized Prisca and Aquila, they remain minor saints in comparison to the homage paid to the amorphous group of twelve, all of whom are canonized and regarded as the first bishops of the church. Junia and Andronicus have not been canonized. In fact, a later scribe at his own behest or that of a later church authority changed her name to "Junias," a nonexistent male Roman name, to support the belief that there were only twelve apostles, all of whom were male. Such editing of scriptural texts is not uncommon and often reflects the efforts of scribes to make scripture cohere with institutional beliefs (Mendenhall, 2002).

Despite Paul's letter to the church in Rome that met in the house of Prisca and Aquila, a letter dating from the earliest days of the Jesus movement, Christian tradition—without scriptural proof—has taught that Peter, along with Paul, were the founders and the first bishops of the church in Rome. Why did this happen?

The idea that Peter traveled to Rome to found a church and to be martyred by Nero appeared in the *Apocryphal Acts of Peter*, a non-canonical gospel, and in *Against Heresies* by Ireneus of Lyons, both written in the second half of the second century around the time that a Roman deacon named Gaius began reporting miraculous events at a site he claimed was the burial place of St. Peter (Lewis, 2018). Prior to Gaius, there is no indication that Christians knew or cared about the location of Peter's tomb, mainly because the idea that he founded a church in Rome was not in circulation. Jesus' bestowal of the keys of heaven to Peter did not become a part of the Peter legend until the third century. Prominent Christians such as Clement of Rome, the purported successor of Peter, and (later) Tertullian had no knowledge of the primacy of Peter or the existence of a pope in Rome (Moss, 2013). Neither did Augustine hundreds of years later. During his travels to Rome for martyrdom, Ignatius of Antioch (d 108 C.E.) mentioned the names of bishops in cities he visited along the way. He never mentioned the name of a bishop at Rome.

Justin Martyr, writing in the middle of the second century, knew that Marcion, Valentinius, and Simon Magus, who were labeled heretics by the emergent orthodox wing of the growing church, were teaching, and preaching in the capital city, but he made no mention of Peter's purported role in the founding of a church in Rome. However, the presence of popular and renowned but allegedly heretical faith leaders in Rome with large followings needed to be balanced with a figure who knew what Jesus had in mind at the beginning. That man was, or seemed to be, Peter. And so, the legend began, more than a hundred years after Peter's death. Not only did Peter come to be understood as Jesus' right-hand man and the founder of the church in Rome, but he also had to be martyred for professing the one true—and apparently only—faith that all followers of Jesus had to believe in order to be saved. Thus was Peter promoted from the rock-headed, illiterate Galilean fisherman to the lofty rank of the first imperial pope, chosen by Jesus himself to lead his church.

The problem is that just as there is no evidence of Peter's actual presence in Rome, there is no proof that Nero executed Peter and Paul in 64 C.E. In addition, the emperor Nero turns out not to be the monster Christians have made him out to be.

There was a fire in Rome in the year 64 C.E. during the reign of the emperor Nero, a ruler portrayed by Christian apologists as a psychopathic persecutor and the personification of evil. Modern historians are not so sure. Nero was not in Rome when the fire began but returned to lead firefighting efforts and provide care for the victims of the fire. There is no doubt that Nero brutally punished guilty as well as innocent souls to placate the citizens of Rome who were calling for blood after their city nearly burned to the ground. Some of the unfortunate victims caught up in the government dragnet might have been followers of Jesus. However, there is no proof that Nero singled out Christians for execution because the term "Christian" was not yet in existence (Shaw, 2015). In addition, Christians would have been difficult to identify, since there were, perhaps, one thousand Christians in the entire empire in the year 60 C.E. In the late 50's, Paul named twenty-eight of them in Romans 16. How many followers of Jesus could there have been at the time of the fire a few years later?

Shaw also wrote that Peter and Paul might have been executed by Nero as part of that round-up, although there are no definitive documents attesting to this belief anywhere in the canonical books of the New Testament. Clement's 95 C.E. letter mentions the presence of jealousy in an unnamed church community that caused problems for Peter. However, jealousy is hardly the same as persecution and execution. It is only the historian Tacitus who claimed sixty years after the fact that Nero specifically targeted a discrete group called "Christians" for execution although that term did not exist at the time of the fire. At the time Tacitus wrote, however, Christians finally *had* become a discrete minority with a name and *were* being persecuted in some areas.

Tacitus also had another reason to malign Nero, the last of the Julio-Claudian family who had founded the Roman Empire, a man who remained popular with the residents of the empire. The subsequent ruling family, the Flavians, had used the Roman legions to usurp the throne. To legitimize their position, the new imperial family needed to smooth over the unpleasant details by ruining the reputation of their predecessors, rendering them immoral and worthy of replacement. Tacitus and later Suetonius operated within this framework of character assassination. Both made Nero into a cartoon villain. Early Christians picked up this false impression. By the fourth century, the cartoon became a historical fact. The royal tutor of Constantine's son called Nero an "abominable and criminal tyrant," even though proto-Christians at the time of the fire had made no mention of Nero's alleged shortcomings.

Thus, it was second-century non-canonical gospels and their fanciful traditions that made Peter the touchstone of orthodoxy. Through them Christians came to believe that there was only one true faith that was passed on directly by Jesus to Peter and the rest of the apostles, who then passed on that one true fully formed faith to others. The rest were mere posers. No other branch of Christianity could boast of such continuity. The apostles were resurrected from Christianity's murky beginnings to become princes of a church led by the greatest prince of them all, Peter, selected personally by Jesus to guide the Church into a triumphant future. The actual leaders of the early Christian communities mentioned by Paul were condemned to obscurity by their perceived lack of connection to this framework.

The door to the mid-first century house church of Prisca and Aquila will remain forever closed to us. We do know that in the second century work, *The Shepherd of Hermas*, the author describes a council of elders presiding over the Roman Church, not a bishop. Did the church founded by Prisca and Aquila follow their conciliar model for more than a hundred years? It was not until the very end of the second century that this model was rejected by a Roman bishop named Victor who established himself as a monarchial ruler.

By the fourth century C.E., the Christian communities grew large, powerful, and rich enough to build houses of worship in the great cities of the empire. The churches that had been planted in the name of the apostles long after they had died were headed by powerful, ambitious, and wealthy men from prominent senatorial families called bishops or, in the case of Rome, Constantinople, Antioch, and Alexandria, pope or "papa." These men justified their august position by claiming apostolic succession, a power they claimed harked back to the twelve apostles. Thus was the tradition of apostolic succession born, long after the last apostle died, most likely in total obscurity.

Apostolic succession bestowed the ability to forgive sins upon, or not, as the case might be. Those whom the ecclesial successors to the apostles did not forgive remained unforgiven, often finding their way into the ranks of what would become known as heretics who were then excommunicated, shunned, ejected from religious assemblies, and prevented from visiting an orthodox believer's home. However, heretics were hardly enemies of either God or of the church. In a world where Christianity grew organically according to location and leadership, they had a different theology and a different understanding of the church that they had also grown in Jesus' name.

As the bishops ascended to thrones unimagined by their

predecessors by tapping into the putative power of the apostles, they rejected the lifestyle of the poor man of Palestine who had one robe and no place to lay his head. These men came to amass secular and spiritual power that they wielded from gilt palaces while wearing the regalia of the empire that executed Jesus.

The behavior of wealthy ordained office holders has always been a scandal to the faithful. In the Pauline tradition of mutual exhortation, prophets would arise from the masses to condemn obvious abuses of power. Rather than examining their consciences, however, popes and powerful bishops embarked upon a policy that labeled exhorters as heretics, tracking them down, torturing, imprisoning, and even killing them in the tradition of the empire they had maligned. In so doing, they became the Beast in the book of Revelation.

Like the Roman Empire, the Roman Church embarked on a journey to conquer the world, a journey approved of by a risen Jesus, who is depicted as saying in Matthew 28: 18–20, "All authority in heaven and on earth has been given to me. Go, therefore, and make disciples of all nations, baptizing them in the name of the Father, the Son, and the Holy Spirit, and teaching them to obey everything that I have commanded you." The followers of Jesus took this command to heart, much to the dismay of Indigenous peoples all over the world, who were often forcibly separated from the customs and beliefs that had sustained them for generations by the missionaries and their armed protectors.

As the centuries unfolded, the triumphal church and its militant members shed its ethical obligation to love its neighbor as it had come to love and admire itself.

We do not know if Anna and Joachim, and most of the apostles aside from Peter, James, and John existed. The evangelists were anonymous.

Followers of the Way of Jesus
Prisca and Aquila
Junia and Andronicus

Phoebe
Chloe
Apollos
Euodia and Syntyche
Nympha
Stephanus of Achaia

Those listed in Romans 16 have more of a right to be considered saints than the twelve listed in the scriptures who have been lost.

Chapter 4:
CHURCH FATHERS

"The mind at times fashions for itself false shapes of evil when there are no signs that point to any evil; it twists into the worst construction some word of doubtful meaning; or it fancies some personal grudge to be more serious than it really is, considering not how angry the enemy is, but to what lengths he may go if he is angry. But life is not worth living, and there is no limit to our sorrows if we indulge our fears to the greatest possible extent."

Seneca (D. 65 C.E.)

Aunt Nellie was my father's oldest sister, eighteen years his senior. She fell in love with Uncle Charlie who was a faithful Lutheran. To their credit, my staunch Irish Catholic grandparents did not object to their romance. In 1927, Aunt Nellie and Uncle Charlie were quickly and unceremoniously married in the vestibule of the rectory lest Charlie's Lutheran faith pollute the white marble altar and fill the parish church with whiffs of heretical Lutheranism. Aunt Nellie never forgave the church for the disrespect it showed to her loving, devout husband.

Although Aunt Nellie attended church on Sunday, she often complained bitterly about what she saw was its blatant hypocrisy. She found the church's stance on birth control particularly irksome. As the oldest of eight, Aunt Nellie had tired of taking care of little kids who arrived at regular intervals. What was the benefit in having a bunch of kids and not having enough money to feed them properly? Who enjoyed living in a tiny house where there was no privacy? During our mutual visits to my grandmother's house, Aunt Nellie would sit and pontificate in the great armchair that had belonged to my deceased grandfather. Who gave a bunch of childless, clueless priests the power to make decisions for families, anyway? Aunt Nellie had only two children. Her sisters Anna and Marie had none and one, respectively.

My feisty aunt lived to be one hundred. The Lutheran side of her family joined the Catholic side at her Catholic funeral Mass in 2005. Like a bad rerun, the priest disinvited all of the Lutherans from receiving communion, as if their faith would taint the Body of Christ. I turned to one of my cousins and commented that Aunt Nellie was rolling over in her coffin.

Aunt Nellie's two children attended public school, so they were not subjected to the pre-Vatican II tirades often made by nuns about the evil nature of Protestants, which included the children's beloved father. My friends with Protestant mothers or fathers who suffered from cognitive dissonance when they compared the upright lives of their non-Catholic parent with the diatribes they often heard in church and in the classroom. Was their beloved parent really going to hell because of their Protestant faith? It made no sense either to them or to me.

When I attended a Lutheran seminary with classmates from various denominations, I learned that what separated us Christians was so small, it was not even worth mentioning. We believed in one faith, one Lord, and one baptism. How did the small differences in dogma and doctrine become so magnified that my aunt and uncle had to be married in the vestibule of a rectory? That Europe was embroiled in religious wars and crusades that killed tens of thousands of people? That Catholic priests regularly and publicly disinvite Protestants from the table of Jesus during Mass? How could any Christian be denied communion if we are many parts of one Body? Was Jesus the son of a loving God or a mean— spirited enforcer?

The modern practice of denying communion to fellow Christians pales beside the intra-Christian religious wars that date back to the earliest days of Christianity. The first five hundred years of Christianity's existence were irreparably marred by the infighting between Christianity and its parent faith, Judaism, and then by the internecine conflicts that church historian Philip Jenkins labeled the "Jesus Wars" (2010). Driven by the obsessions of the early fathers of the church and their adherents to mold their theological narratives into doctrines of faith, these wars killed far more Christians than did any Roman persecution.

After becoming the state religion of the Roman Empire in the fourth century, the church fancied itself the successor of both Caesar and Jesus as they moved the gospel into the gold-plated imperial palaces granted to them by Constantine. Blinded by the allure of power, church leaders relinquished the mutual forbearance recommended to Christian communities by Paul. Aligned with imperial forces as recommended by Augustine, the church resorted to persecution, war, and violence to settle disputes with enemies they labeled heretics. The "other" made its appearance as the villain on the Christian stage.

The fateful union of faith with empire had significant consequences. It set the stage for future pogroms against Jews, the Crusades, the Inquisition, witch hunts, and the European colonial invasion of Africa, the Americas, and Asia. The church's reliance and insistence upon unquestioning obedience has extended into the twenty-first century as it outs and fires LBGTQ+ people, denies communion to divorced and remarried Catholics, and excommunicates anyone who supports women's ordination and abortion. The words of biblical scholar George Mendenhall are worth mentioning, "Once the exercise of coercive force is considered indispensable, people who want it will begin sacrificing most other ethical considerations in order to keep it" (2001).

But let us begin at the beginning. Most Christians prefer to believe that their forebears in faith were warm, fuzzy, and loving people like bearded hippies and flower children living peacefully in a commune. And perhaps some of them were. Acts of the Apostles describes a loving community where believers shared their goods. It also describes a community where dissent incurred instant death. When the couple Ananias and Sapphira lied to Peter, they were immediately struck dead. "Great fear seized the whole church and all who heard these things" (Acts 5:1–11). The message to the early Christian community was clear. Authoritarian rule backed by fear would supersede mutual forbearance.

The dysfunctional and destructive in-fighting continued in the epistles. The author of 1 John 4:20 insisted, "But if we say we love

God and do not love each other, we are liars. We cannot see God. So how can we love God if we do not love the people we can see?" Yet he shuns those he accuses of teaching "false doctrine," calling them the "anti-Christ," and bars them from entering his home.

The author of 1 Timothy turns over Hymenaeus and Alexander, two of his fellow Christians, to Satan for committing what he regards as blasphemy. The author of 2 Peter confidently predicts that any naysayer will be subject to the same fate as Sodom and Gomorrah: "God will condemn them to extinction" (2 Peter 2: 1–6).

Thus, the seeds of sectarian violence were sown during Christianity's beginnings making believers suspicious of everyone who did not believe the way they did. Even the whiff of heresy drove zealots to violence. Along with vituperative in-fighting, early Christians also bullied and maligned their fellow Jews who did not agree that believing in the death and resurrection of Jesus was necessary for their salvation. We can see the increasingly tense situation that existed between the Jews and the nascent Christians in the latter part of the first century C.E. reflected in the gospels, epistles, and in Acts of the Apostles.

The fighting between the sectarians became nasty on both sides. The prominent and respected rabbi Gamaliel tried to calm the Jews who threatened to kill the sectarians by saying, "Keep away from these men and let them alone; because if this plan or this undertaking is of human origin, it will fail; but if it is of God, you will not be able to overthrow them; in that case, you may even be found fighting against God!" (Acts 5:33–39). If the Christians had heeded the esteemed rabbi's advice, the world would be a different place. For his effort toward conciliation, early Christians claimed Gamaliel as one of them and canonized him, although there is no record of his conversion. The same is true of John the Baptist. Although he is portrayed as the forerunner of Jesus, John the Baptist was not a follower of Jesus. John's baptism of repentance where the axe is already laid to the root and eternal woe is the fate of unbelievers differs from the kingdom values and Beatitudes of Jesus. John's followers in Ephesus had to be converted and re-baptized in order to become "real" Christians (Acts 19: 1–7).

In the New Testament, the evangelists went to extraordinary

lengths to vilify the Jews. Matthew painted Pilate, described by his contemporaries as a violent, unfeeling man who cared only about maintaining order, as a sensitive, unwilling accomplice to the execution of Jesus. Biblical scholars believe that the stories about Pilate's hand-washing, his wife's dream, and the offer to substitute Barabbas for Jesus were largely made up by the authors of the gospels to heap additional blame upon those who chose to believe— in good faith— that the death and resurrection of Jesus, however wonderful and prophetic this might have been for Christians, did not and could not make them right with God. For faithful Jews, only the law did that.

The Jewish people also did not believe that their scriptures, appropriated by Christians, provided overwhelming evidence for the veracity and legitimacy of Christianity. Their prophets did not predict Jesus and Christian practices, manna did not prefigure the Eucharist, the virgin in Isaiah was not Mary, and the suffering servant was not Jesus, but rather figures in their own religious experience. Most renown biblical scholars would agree. Scholars like Catholic priest Raymond Brown have taught that the Hebrew Bible should not be regarded as a prophecy pointing miraculously to the founding of a new faith in the distant future, but rather as the Jewish people's attempts to confront the serious political, social, and economic problems of their own time.

As Christians grew in strength, number, and, consequently, power, they found the Jews stubborn, obnoxious, and evil. When they began to insist that God had replaced Jews with Christians as "His" chosen people, Jews became the persona non grata of the Christian world. They would eventually be regarded as Christ-killers by some leaders of the early Christian communities.

Although bishops were directed to be "meek men" in an early church document called the *Didache*, we can see from the Ananias and Sapphira story that those who bore that title began to gather and wield considerable power even while the number of Christians remained quite small. As the *imago Dei* of Jesus who sat at the right hand of God, clerics acting in his persona were more like god-men than ordinary human beings. Entitled to wealth and power as befitting sons of God and heirs of heaven, all things became possible within this model. Bishops interpreted scripture, bound and loosened sins, and established traditions that may or may not have had anything to do with Jesus. Less than one hundred years after the death of Jesus in an empire in which the Christian population might have numbered 10,000 souls, bishops like Ignatius of Antioch (d. 108) began to equate themselves with God. "Take care to do all things in harmony with God, with the bishops presiding in the place of God" (*Letter to the Magnesians*, date varies between 98 and 117). Like the author of the three letters of John, Ignatius had a keen eye for criticizing and condemning divergent views:

> *"Take not of those who hold heterodox opinions on the grace of Jesus Christ which has come to us, and see how contrary their opinions are to the mind of God... They abstain from the Eucharist and from prayer because they do not confess that the Eucharist is the flesh of our Savior Jesus Christ, flesh which suffered for our sins and which the Father, in his goodness, raised up again. They who deny the gift of God are perishing in their disputes (Letter to the Smyrnaeans 6:2-7:1)*

The sainted martyr also hated Jews. En route to his martyrdom in Rome, he wrote, "It is monstrous to talk of Jesus Christ and to practice Judaism" (*Letter to the Magnesians*, 10:3).

The anti-Jewish invective came from the top down in the writings of other church fathers. John Chrysostom, (d. 407) he with the reputation of having a "golden tongue," penned a virulent anti-Jewish screed designed for Christians who did not share his hatred of Jews. These so-called Christians, he wrote, viewed synagogues as holy places where their fellow citizens worshiped God and sometimes attended Jewish festivals and services, as friends and possibly as family and neighbors who lived together in peace and harmony. Chrysostom tried his best to destroy this harmony by delivering a tantrum full of hateful invective proclaiming that Jews were demons, their holy books, trash, and their synagogues, "houses of prostitution." Like other churchmen, Jerome helped set the stage for Christian persecution of the Jews. In the eyes of orthodox Christians both then and in the future, however, Chrysostom was a saint and the Christians who fraternized with the perceived "enemy" were heretics.

"I know that many have high regard for the Jews, and they think that their present way of life is holy. This is why I am so anxious to uproot this deadly opinion. I said that the synagogue is no better than the theater. The synagogue is a house of prostitution, a hideout for thieves, and a den of wild animals. God is not worshipped there. It is a temple of idolatry. Nevertheless, some go to these places as though they were sacred shrines" (Against the Jews).

Christian invective did not end with vilifying the Jewish people. Although the church was still in its infancy, Irenaeus of Lyons (130-202) wrote five books against those he labeled heretics even though those he condemned understood themselves to be faithful Christians. Steeped in the growing ecclesiastical nature of the church, he imagined a legalistic faith that did not align itself with Jesus' kingdom values (Frend, 1985). While Irenaeus is credited with establishing the rule of faith and the consolidation of the church under the bishops, he was more a useful rather than a saintly man.

Despite the fulminations of Ignatius, Ireneus, and Jerome the church was never monolithic. It flourished in different soils that produced diverse understandings of Jesus and his message. Church communities founded by other early followers of Jesus adapted to the local culture and grew organically rather than in opposition to a developing company line.

Once Christianity became the official religion of the Roman Empire, those that the church regards as apostolic fathers embarked on a mission to control the various narratives of Jesus and render it univocal, using the power of their office to establish and enforce a precarious thing they called unity. Under men like John Chrysostom, Athanasius and Cyril of Alexandria, and Augustine of Hippo, the gospel words of persuasion, "that all might be one" became words of coercion, "that all must be one." These are the words of a conqueror and not the Prince of Peace. The intense disagreements, mutual condemnations, denunciations, and intolerance seeped deeply into framework of the early church, controlling the narrative. Differences in opinion, in world view, and in understanding something as complex as the Almighty became an exercise in power and control. Who was in and who was out consumed Christian dialogue for almost two millennia. It still does.

By the year 312 C.E., Christians had become—by arithmetic proportion—so numerous that they were a force to be reckoned with. Wily politicians like Constantine used the idea of unity to his own advantage. While notable scholars such as Elaine Pagels and Bart Ehrman posit that Constantine was a true believer, he was also a suave and cagey politician who sought to unify a fractious empire against the inroads of the barbarians. Like many politicians, Constantine kept one eye on God and the other on the political reality that would determine his survival. Occasionally, he closed the eye watching God as he executed his ten-year-old nephew, his adult son, and possibly, his wife. Like many rulers both ancient and modern, his savagery and his grave sins were ignored by the bishops who regarded him as their most favored patron. The image of the cross leading angry men into battle replaced the Good Shepherd.

The Christian church moved into Constantine's palaces with alacrity, absolving themselves of the taint of imperialism by claiming that the church was the spotless bride of Christ that cannot sin. Churchmen still believe this.

Despite his violent streak, Constantine accomplished something that no ancient ruler envisioned. He proclaimed freedom of religion. While the Edict of Milan (313) favored Christianity by exempting clergy from outside duties, making Sunday a day of rest, and returning confiscated church property, it guaranteed freedom of religion to all people of the Roman Empire. It is important to read the wise words of Constantine on religious freedom and compare them to the vituperations of the Christian clergy.

"When we, Constantine and Licinius, Emperors, met at Milan in conference concerning the welfare and security of the realm, we decided that of the things that are of profit to all mankind, the worship of God ought rightly to be our first and chiefest care, and that it was right that Christians and all others should have freedom to follow the kind of religion they favored; so that the God who dwells in heaven might be propitious to us and to all under our rule. We therefore announce that, notwithstanding any provisions concerning the Christians in our former instructions, all who choose

that religion are to be permitted to continue therein, without any let or hindrance, and are not to be in any way troubled or molested. Note that at the same time all others are to be allowed the free and unrestricted practice of their religions; for it accords with the good order of the realm and the peacefulness of our times that each should have freedom to worship God after his own choice; and we do not intend to detract from the honor due to any religion or its followers" (Edict of Milan, 313).

The emperor Julian (330-363), labeled disparagingly "the Apostate" by contemporaries and generations of Christians to come for repudiating his Christian faith, also favored persuasion over coercion. The fact that he preferred the ancient gods of Rome to Christianity did not prevent him from allowing his subjects to practice the faith of their choice. In 362, Julian wrote pointedly of the hypocrisy of the Christian religious wars:

I had imagined that the prelates of the Galilaeans were under greater obligations to me than to my predecessor. For in his reign many of them were banished, persecuted and imprisoned; and many of the so-called heretics were executed...All this has been reversed in my reign; the banished are allowed to return, and confiscated goods have all been restored to the owners. But such is their folly and madness that, just because they can no longer be despots, or carry out their designs first against their brethren and then against us, the worshippers of the gods, they are inflamed with fury and stop at nothing in their unprincipled attempts to alarm and enrage the people. They are irreverent to the gods and disobedient to our edicts, lenient as they are. For we allow none of them to be dragged to the altars unwillingly...Men should be taught and won over by reason, not by blows, insults, and corporal punishments. I therefore most earnestly admonish the adherents of the true religion not to injure or insult the Galilaeans in any way, either by physical attack or by reproaches (Julian, On Toleration, 362).

Unlike the forbearance of the largely pagan Constantine and the apostate Julian, the sainted Christian heroes graced with the title

Fathers of the Church used their bully pulpits to shock and awe their opponents, unleashing a reign of terror upon those whose beliefs fell outside the orthodox pale. Early Christian writings by the fathers maligned and demonized their opponents. Their writings include pages upon pages of polemic language, diatribes, and ad hominem attacks against fellow Christians, Jews, and pagans that seeded the developing Christian world with intolerance and hatred. These sermons, essays, and letters often employ language that we Christians usually ascribe to fanatics of other faiths. As a result, spectacular violence erupted against their fellow citizens once Christians gained the political upper hand in 312. In a very short time, the persecuted became the persecutors.

The Syrian administrator Libanius described the behavior of Christian monks in 386 C.E., seventy-four years after Constantine's decree:

> *"This black-robed tribe eats more than elephants. They ravage fields, destroy temples, and attack fellow citizens. They strip off roofs, demolish walls, and tear down statues. This is nothing less than war in peace time waged against the peasantry. What is the purpose if while you keep external enemies away, one group of your citizens attacks another?" (quoted in Watts, 2020).*

Aggression and hostility against unbelievers became the calling cards of Christianity, especially in the great imperial cities of Rome, Antioch, Alexandria, and Constantinople. Zealots stripped the marble from pagan temples to adorn their churches, burned down synagogues and pagan temples, and smashed idols. The demands for restitution made by angry Jews and pagans over the destruction of their property by militant Christian mobs fell on the deaf ears of sainted church fathers like Athanasius, Ambrose, Cyril, and Augustine who were happy with the idea of Christian hegemony and were quite unwilling to heed the voices of their aggrieved fellow citizens. The fathers wanted all impediments to Christian universalism removed. As a result, the depredations against non-Christians and heretics continued unabated.

The post-Constantinian battle for doctrinal purity led to orgies of violence in the eastern cities of the Roman Empire that killed tens of thousands of Christians by the end of the sixth century. Impelled by incendiary language in homilies, infuriated monks poured into the churches of their enemies armed with spears and swords to murder their fellow Christians. Zealots murdered bishops in cathedrals and shattered the communion vessels that recently held the Body and Blood of Christ. Some forced the Eucharist into the mouths of dissidents. The ancient historian Ammianus described contemporary Christians thus, "No wild beasts are such enemies to mankind as are most Christians in their deep hatred of one another" (quoted in Rubenstein, 1999). Jesus would have wept at this assessment.

Christian theology justified the violence. As the fifth-century monk Shenoute wrote after destroying a pagan's home while searching for idols to smash, "There is no crime for those who have Christ," as not having Christ *had* become a crime. In a homily from the ambo of Hagia Sophia in Constantinople, the new bishop Nestorius (386-451) announced to the emperor, "Give me, my prince, a world purged of heretics, and I will give you heaven as recompense" (Socrates Scholasticus, 439).

This unchristian, uncivil, and ungodly behavior morally traumatized the seedling faith, grafting intolerance into its very roots and blinding it to the divine presence in those they labeled heretics. As ecclesiastical power grew, its wielders declared themselves immune from the ethical obligations that bound others. In one of his fights with Constantine over tolerating Arians, Athanasius announced that God would choose him over the emperor.

Ambrose of Milan influenced the emperor Theodosius (347–395) to decree:

It is our desire that all the various nations which are subject to our clemency and moderation should continue in the profession of that religion which was delivered to the Romans by the divine Apostle Peter, as it hath been preserved by faithful tradition; and which is now professed by the Pontiff Damascus and by Peter, Bishop of Alexandria, a man of apostolic holiness. According to the apostolic teaching and the doctrine of the Gospel, let us believe the one deity of the Father, the Son, and the Holy Spirit, in equally majesty and in a Holy Trinity. We authorize the followers of this law to assume the title of Catholic Christians; but as for the others, since in our judgment, they are foolish madmen, we decree that they shall be branded with the ignominious name of heretic and shall not presume to give to their conventicles the name of churches. They will suffer in the first place the chastisement of the divine condemnation, and in the second, the punishment which our authority, in accordance with the will of Heaven, shall decide to inflict. Let them be entirely excluded even from the thresholds of churches, since we permit no heretics to hold their unlawful assemblies in the towns. If they attempt any disturbance, we decree that their fury shall be suppressed and that they shall be expelled outside the walls of the cities, so that Catholic churches throughout the world may be restored to the orthodox bishops who hold the faith of Nicea" (Code of Theodosius. Xvi.i.2).

By the late fourth century, the Christian Roman Empire destroyed Constantine's and Julian's edicts of religious toleration and outlawed pagan religions. After strongarming the state to do its dirty business, the church fathers set the stage for violent destruction of those they decided were heretics.

Jenkins (2010) wrote that while the fathers won the battle over the identity of Jesus and his exalted place in the Trinity, they were hardly victorious. In fact, they lost the war. More than half the population of Christianity simply refused to abide by the Trinitarian decision made at Chalcedon in 451 and left the orthodox fold as the Roman Church declared the Syriac Orthodox, Armenian Apostolic, and Coptic Church of Egypt heretical.

Centered in Babylon, theses sects became the Church of the East. At its height, it was far more extensive than what became the Roman Catholic Church. Exhausted by the endless wars about the Trinity, the relationship of the divine persons, and the composition of their substances that few even now can fully understand, millions converted to Islam, a firmly monotheistic faith that eschewed endless debating and fighting over the finer points of Greek philosophy (Jenkins). Parsing the person of Jesus at the point of a sword did nothing to make the world a better place. Contrary to the triumphal declarations of Christians throughout the ages, Christianity did not change the world for the better. Instead, it added another level of violence to an already violent world.

Jesus has been ensconced as the second person of the Trinity, co-eternal and co-equal with God the Father for fifteen hundred years. Were the deaths of tens of thousands worth this Pyrrhic victory? Does the Prince of Peace care if his followers believe that he is co-eternal and consubstantial with the Father or that his mother was a virgin?

Some of the canonized saints were the architects of this deadly sectarian violence. Athanasius of Alexandria (298-373), who was the first to declare to the Christian world that Jesus was equal to God the Father, was a mobster and thug exiled five times by four different emperors for engaging in a host of dirty tricks. Athanasius stealthily orchestrated his election as bishop of Alexandria before the requisite age of thirty by avoiding the approval of fifty-four bishops who were entrusted with finding a successor to the previous bishop, Alexander. Instead, a handful of his friends consecrated him bishop in a private ceremony. Then the brash Athanasius sent off a letter to Constantine announcing his new position, presenting his episcopal elevation as the will of citizens of Alexandria.

Athanasius fashioned a fellow Christian named Arius, who like most of the believers of the time did not share Athanasius's unbiblical premise, into a theological bogeyman. What began as a minor disagreement between two men morphed into a monumental church controversy and challenged the unity of the empire. In response, Constantine called the Council of Nicaea in 325 to resolve it. Arius and the bishops who supported what was until then traditional Christian belief were exiled and their characters assassinated.

Constantine's ongoing contacts with bishops who followed the more traditional beliefs of Arius coupled with Athanasius' violent and vicious attempts to stamp it out changed Constantine's mind. Like his predecessors, Constantine did not wish religion to divide his already fractious empire. In a letter written in 328, Constantine urged Athanasius to re-admit Arius warning, "Since you know my will, grant free admission to all those who wish to enter the church. For if I hear that you have hindered anyone from becoming a member, or have debarred anyone from entrance, I shall immediately send someone to have you deposed at my behest and have you sent into exile."

Athanasius rejected Constantine's attempt at reconciliation and wrote back that there could be no fellowship with anyone who denied the divinity of Christ. Instead, he sent hordes of monks into the churches of his enemies, overturning altars and smashing the communion vessels. When his detractors accused him of "violence and sacrilege," Athanasius replied archly, "No, only violence" (quoted in Rubenstein, 1999).

A modern writer describes the sainted Athanasius:

"In Alexandria itself, he maintained the popular support which he enjoyed from the outset and buttressed his position by organizing an ecclesiastical mafia. If he so desired, he could instigate a riot or prevent the orderly administration of the city. Athanasius possessed a power independent of the emperor which he built up and perpetuated by violence. That was both the strength and weakness of his position. Like a modern gangster, he evoked widespread mistrust, proclaimed total innocence, and usually evaded conviction on specific charges" (Barnes, 1981).

More importantly, Athanasius' contemporaries did not approve of his actions. In 343, a group of bishops charged him with unlawful acts, murder, and the assassination of bishops.

Like many violent, powerful men, Athanasius used floridly outrageous language to malign his fellow Christians. He accused Arius of "rending the robe of Christ" and equated his followers to those who crucified Jesus. Relying upon fear rather than love, Athanasius warned that if his fellow Christians did not accept his Trinitarian theology, pagans would win the battle for God. To the Emperor Constantine who tired of his violent and divisive shenanigans, Athanasius replied, "Be warned, God will judge between you and me!" (quoted in Zarley, 2019)

Athanasius used and abused people to accomplish his ends. When publicly censured for violence, he brought the great cenobite Antony out of the desert to whitewash his unsavory profile and bolster his Trinitarian claims. If the great Antony liked and approved of Athanasius, then surely everyone should like and approve of him as well.

Although Athanasius is credited with being the first to decide upon the books that comprised the New Testament, he also destroyed books that did not support his view, calling upon his followers to "cleanse the church of every defilement" and "reject books filled with "myths, empty and polluted" which would lead to what he called "error" (Pagels, 2005). In response, the desert monks rushed to carefully preserve and bury their beloved books in the hills in a place called Nag Hammadi where they were found sixteen hundred years later.

Modern Christians continue to view Arius as an architect of a dangerous heresy and rejoice in the triumph of the Athanasian position which became Christian doctrine. Few investigate what lies behind the accusations of heresy and the condemnation of a man who stood up for the beliefs held by a majority of fourth century Christians who worshipped in churches harking back to the apostolic age. For orthodox Christians of the period, it was Athanasius and not Arius who was the heretic. Perhaps it is time to rehabilitate Arius.

Church violence continued for decades, reaching another low with Cyril of Alexandria (378-444). For defining Mary as the Theotokos or God Bearer at the Council of Ephesus in 431, Cyril was given the title of Doctor of the Church and canonized a saint. Like Athanasius, however, Cyril was a thug.

Compared to Egyptian pharaohs by Phillip Jenkins (2010), the bishops Cyril and his predecessor and uncle Theophilus followed the directives of Theodosius and attempted to purge their city of undesirable pagans and Jews. Theophilus desecrated pagan burial grounds and paraded pagan relics around the city for Christians to ridicule. He and his rabid followers assaulted the noted pagan temple the Serapeon and forcibly converted it into a Christian church. It remains unknown if Theophilus was responsible for the burning of ancient manuscripts housed there.

After the unexpected death of Theophilus, his nephew Cyril battled with Timothy, a rival claimant for the patriarchal throne. Instead of calming his temperamental flock after his disputed election, Cyril closed the churches of his rivals and confiscated their property. The sainted Cyril then led an assault against the ancient Jewish community in Alexandria. In actions reminiscent of Kristallnacht and Russian pogroms, the rioting Christians broke into and destroyed Jewish shops. Cyril also called for an action that resulted in what we in the twenty-first-century would call "ethnic cleansing" when he demanded the expulsion of the Jewish community that had lived in Alexandria for seven hundred years.

While twenty-first century people might excuse Cyril's behavior as being representative of his time, his contemporaries did not share Cyril's zealotry. Many, some at risk of being labeled heretics and having their sins bound by the powerful bishops, demurred. The moderate Christian governor Orestes, refused to expel the Jewish citizens from their homes. One of the most famous Alexandrines at the time, a prominent woman mathematician named Hypatia, publicly agreed with Orestes' decision.

Hypatia raised Cyril's manly ecclesiastical hackles. How dare she disobey the great Cyril? He whipped his monks into a frenzy by spreading rumors about her. Her considerable gifts were the result of witchcraft. What normal woman studied astronomy and mathematics? She had beguiled Orestes into disagreeing with the sainted Cyril. Completely enamored by Hypatia, Orestes even stopped attending church. The army of monks bided their time, plotting her demise. Descending upon Hypatia while she was driving through the city in her chariot dressed in her philosopher's robe, they dragged her into a temple converted to a Christian church, stripped her naked, and flayed her alive.

If Cyril's actions appear to be horrific and unchristian by modern standards, they were by ancient standards as well. Commenting on Cyril as one who delighted in tumult, excess, and bloodshed, the contemporaneous historian Socrates Scholasticus wrote, "Surely nothing can be farther from the spirit of Christianity than the allowance of massacres, fights, and transactions of that sort." Unlike Athanasius and Cyril, Socrates rejected the use of violence to resolve religious controversies and espoused peace over obedience to doctrine. Although the writings of Socrates Scholasticus were not polemic, he has been described as one who hated Christians.

The Christian emperor Justinian (482—565) sent the Roman army into Syria to exile or murder the Syrian bishops who did not adhere to the theology adopted at the Council of Chalcedon (451). Their churches, monasteries, and convents were either burned to the ground or given to orthodox bishops. It was the followers of Islam who drove out the persecuting Christian Roman army in the seventh century and made the Syriac Orthodox Church a protected people (Amar, 2024).

Hilary, bishop of Poitiers (315–368) whose name means "cheerful," also engaged in the not-so-cheerful practice of hunting out Arians whom he accused without any evidence of rejecting the teaching of the apostles and the scriptures. Obsessed with what he believed was the prevalence of many antichrists disguised as priests and bishops, he was nicknamed the "Hammer of Arians." Considered as the Athanasius of the West, Hilary accused Arians as willfully choosing the antichrist over Jesus Christ.

Like Athanasius and Cyril, Ambrose (340–397) was a pious rogue who progressed from being a new convert to being ordained a deacon, then a priest, and finally a bishop within eight days. When not digging up the bodies of long-dead martyrs to harvest relics, Ambrose, like many church fathers, zealously pursued alleged Arian heretics. It was Ambrose who inspired Theodosius I to promulgate the teachings of the Council of Nicaea as the law of the empire. Like his fellow bishops, Ambrose presented to the emperor the illusion of a unified church as the foundation for a politically unified empire and enthusiastically supported the persecution of non-Christians.

Ambrose was so confident of his episcopal authority that he defied the Arian Empress Justina by refusing to allow her to use a church in his diocese and berated the emperor Theodosius for demanding that Christians reimburse Jews for destroying synagogues, threatening him with excommunication. A braggart in his own family, he insisted that his elder sister and mother acknowledge his position and kneel to kiss his episcopal ring (Brown, 1988).

The Constantinian Church sought to control not only the beliefs of their flocks, but also their bodies. The Christian world has yet to recover fully from Augustine of Hippo's personal sexual proclivities which came to be expressed in the most non-biblical doctrine of original sin. According to Augustine, every evil in the world resulted from Adam's sin that was transmitted through sexual relations: plagues, war, famine, sickness, and finally death. As human beings wallowed in unavoidable and omnipresent sin, only God's elect upon whom the divine would bestow mercy and grace would be saved. Augustine believed he was one of this select group, personally raised up by God from the stain and defilement of sexual relations. Thus, Augustine deformed the sexual act into what Peter Brown called "an abiding, unhealed fissure of the soul permanently tilting a person towards the flesh" (Brown, 1988).

The darkness of his times might have colored Augustine's depressing theology. The city of Rome had lost its imperial luster, decaying into a depopulated backwater after the government moved to Constantinople. A European people called the Visigoths invaded Rome in 410. The Vandals were at the gates of his own city. He saw the North African Donatists and the Pelagians as destroyers of the church unity he was so carefully trying to build. There had to be a reason for the human-created chaos he saw around him. By focusing upon evil rather than good, Augustine arrived at the conclusion that all of humanity was conceived in sin and born in depravity. Despite humanity's unworthiness, God would reserve a special grace for a few special souls who would escape from sin and attain eternal salvation. Augustine reduced God, the Creator of heaven and earth, to a powerful king who played favorites, a divine puppeteer who pulled the strings of favor, like the Fates in Greek mythology.

The church credits Monica, Augustine's Christian mother, with his conversion to Christianity. The story is far more complicated.

Monica was married to an abusive husband who beat her. For centuries, the church lifted her up as a model of womanly humility and fidelity and extolled her for remaining in a violent marriage. Her own son approvingly described her as properly submissive.

After the death of his father, Augustine became his mother's pet project even though she had three other children. She hounded him, following him first to Carthage where she told him that his misbehavior made her feel anew the pangs of childbirth, and then to Rome where Augustine with his partner and son had escaped under the cover of darkness to avoid her constant interference in their lives. The Augustine entourage later embarked for Milan which had become the intellectual center of the empire under Ambrose, a man who is credited for teaching Augustine the rational underpinnings of the Christian faith. The rational Ambrose had no problem, however, miraculously finding and then selling magical charms called relics harvested from long dead martyrs when he needed to raise money to build his basilica or believing that Constantine's mother had found the true cross complete with nails and banner in the dust of Palestine three hundred years after Jesus died.

Like Augustine, Jerome (345-406) also found sex disgusting and women revolting and repulsive. While ignoring the sumptuous robes worn by wealthy churchmen, Jerome fixated upon the dress of women and the bodies underneath, pruriently examining the way they dressed, walked, ate, and spoke. His writings, like that of Augustine, have contributed to the church's long history of oppressing women.

Jerome was awarded the titles of saint and Doctor of the Church for translating both the Hebrew Bible (Old Testament) and the Greek New Testament into Latin, the vernacular of the empire. He was ably assisted by Paula, a Roman widow and member of one of Rome's wealthiest families. Jerome lived on Paula's largesse for most of his life.

Paula (347–404) was a devout Christian and mother of five children who was widowed at age thirty-two. Impressed by stories she had heard of fellow Christians living in splendid isolation from the enchantments of the world in the barren deserts of Palestine, Paula began meeting with a group of like-minded women in Rome. Through their influence, she rejected the accoutrements of her wealthy life. These women were also instrumental in introducing her to Jerome, who was back in Rome after a failed stint as a hermit. Jerome changed the trajectory not only of Paula's life, but also the lives of her children.

After meeting Jerome in 382, Paula never ate a meal with a man or took a bath again, severely restricted her diet, dressed in sackcloth, and slept on the ground. Together, the two made Paula's home a bootcamp for potential hermits. This included a semi-starvation diet for Paula and her daughters. Within three months, Paula's eldest daughter died of starvation. For Jerome, human attachments were suspect, and he criticized Paula for mourning the death of her daughter. To be a true ascetic, he told her, "You would be pleased to get rid of ties." The teenaged Blaesilla was, Jerome wrote, the victor in her struggles with Satan.

The Roman senatorial class blamed Jerome for the young woman's preventable death. Jerome, with Paula and her youngest daughter, Eustochium in tow, left town in a hurry and set sail for Palestine, leaving Paula's two youngest children crying for her on the dock. According to Jerome, Paula overcame her love for her children with her love for God. Neither seemed to realize that Paula could have loved both with equal fervor.

Despite his reputation for personal asceticism, Jerome's letters to young, impressionable girls and women indicate that he blamed women for his inability to control his own sexual urges. His writings expose a voyeur well versed in the female body and feminine dress, "You (women) have a whore's face and you refuse to be ashamed." The British writer E.M. Forster who had a keen nose for sniffing out hypocrisy, labeled Jerome the "detestable father" for his projections of his own untamed sexual desires onto women. In one of his many screeds, Jerome wrote, "The way you dress is an index of your secret desires. Your bodice is purposely ripped apart to show what is beneath, and what is hidden is repulsive. You wear stays to keep your breasts in place and confine your body with a girdle. Sometimes you let your shawl drop to lay bare one of your shoulders" (Quoted in Barr, 1990). Jerome worried constantly about the "virgins" he had created, pressing them into a life where they foreswore sexual relations and children to hasten the second coming.

To Eustochium, Paula's thirteen-year-old second daughter, Jerome wrote a lengthy treatise on the value of virginity, advising her to replace an earthy spouse with Christ. If she succeeded in preserving her "purity," her "spouse," Jesus, would come forward and say, "'Rise, my nearest and dearest, my fair one, my dove...'" He will conduct you to his bedchamber. Ever let Him sport with you. When sleep comes upon you, he will come from behind the partition and put his hand through the opening and will touch your body. You shall rise trembling and say, 'I languish with love.' You will then hear from your Spouse, 'Set me as a seal upon your heart,' and you will cry out, 'Many waters cannot quench love, neither can the floods drown it'" (Jerome, *Letter to Eustochium*).

Jerome's influence over the women in Paula's family reached into the third generation. He warned Paula's daughter not to take her young daughter to the Roman baths lest the little girl see the "revolting" body of a pregnant woman. In fact, he advised, the little girl should not be bathed at all since women should be taught to be disgusted by the sight of their own bodies. Jerome liked his women dirty and thin and pale, even the little ones.

Jerome's horror of women and his belief in their innate inferiority crept into his translation of the Bible. Biblical scholar Jane Barr has pointed out Jerome's deliberate mistranslation of Genesis 3:16. Instead of God saying to women, "I will greatly increase your pangs in childbearing; in pain shall you bring forth children, yet your desire shall be for your husband, and he shall rule over you," Jerome's translation eliminated the suggestion that Eve might desire her husband. Instead, his translation became a dictum for generations of women to come, "You shall be under the power of your husband, and he shall rule over you" (Barr, 1990).

Like the long shelf life of Chrysostom's diatribe against Jews, Jerome's hatred of women had long-term effects on the well-being of women. Subsequent exegetes used Jerome's mistranslation to explain the need to whip women into submission. Seventh-century Bede the Venerable and eighth-century Alcuin added fear into the toxic mix of power asserting that women should be afraid of their husbands. In the twelfth century, St. Victor of Paris gave permission for husbands to physically wound the wives under their rule.

Jerome is not alone in his denigration of women. Despite the well-documented misogynistic screeds made by the doctors of the church, the late John Paul II, who hounded advocates of women's ordination while claiming that he loved and respected women, asserted that they really were good pastors. The quotes of the church fathers, like the actions of John Paul II prove otherwise. By their words and actions, we know that these men committed great sin when they formulated a theology of male supremacy. Jerome might have been a brilliant scholar and adept translator, but he was hardly a saint.

Some of his peers considered him to be a nasty human being.

Of course, there were other Christians who believed something completely different from what became the long anti-woman, anti-sex Roman Catholic invectives. One of those men was Pelagius (354-418). In the face of the same historical forces that beset Rome and powerful men like Augustine, Pelagius remained optimistic. Pelagius had no use for original sin and a darkened will. Unlike his contemporary Augustine, Pelagius did not believe that babies were conceived in sin and born into darkness. Since God gave human beings free will, the Divine knew that human beings would make mistakes. The sin of Adam and Eve affected only them and no one else and the first couple did not visit the specter of death upon their descendants. Like all earthly creatures, they would have died regardless of their sin.

> *"Everything good and everything evil, in respect of which we are either worthy of praise or of blame, is done by us, not born with us. We are not born in our full development, but with a capacity for good and evil; we are begotten as well without virtue as without vice, and before the activity of our own personal will there is nothing in man but what God has stored in him." (Pro lib. Arb., ap Aug. De peccato originali, 14).*

According to Pelagius, Christians did not have to remain mired in the slough of despondency, bemoaning the darkness of ever-present sin and awaiting salvation in the next world. Instead, they could actively work to reform society and improve the lives of their neighbors. Action rather than resignation to the presence of evil enabled human beings to choose to live a good and decent life. Because of God's gift of free will, people could also choose otherwise–of their own volition–and not through a misapplication or withdrawal of God's grace or interference from Satan. Unlike Augustine, Pelagius believed that a fall from grace resulted from a failure of an individual's will rather than an inherent failure of human nature. Most importantly, Pelagius believed that God never commands human beings to do what is beyond their ability:

"We ascribe to the God of knowledge the guilt of twofold ignorance, ignorance of his own creation and of his own commands. As if, forgetting the weakness of men, his own creation, he had laid upon men commands which they were unable to bear. And at the same time, we ascribe to the Just One unrighteousness and cruelty to the Holy One; the first, by complaining that he has commanded the impossible, the second, by imagining that a man will be condemned by him for what he could not help; so that (the blasphemy of it!) God is thought of as seeking our punishment rather than our salvation…No one knows the extent of our strength better than he who gave us that strength…H has not willed to command anything impossible, for he is righteous; and he will not condemn a man for what he could not help, for he is holy" (Letter to Demetrias, xxiii.1110).

For what appears to be a kinder, more charitable, and gentler interpretation of our problematic and often unexplainable human nature, Pelagius was condemned as a heretic. Jerome called him a "corpulent dog (quoted in Miller, 2011).

Pelagianism remains a heresy today.

Like Pelagius, others tried and failed to make the growing Christian less dogmatic and less judgmental. Basilides, dismissed as a Gnostic and a heretic, offered the pursuit of knowledge as the way to finding answers to pain, death, evil, and suffering. Most Gnostics did not see the end of the world as an Armageddon where unbelievers are damned for all time, but rather as a source of enlightenment and harmony. In their interpretation of faith, inquiry superseded unquestioned belief. For this belief orthodox Christians have portrayed Gnostic beliefs as fanciful, incorrect, and unbiblical. However, Gnostic ideas are not any more outrageous than belief in a mortal and deadly sin that God visits upon generations of innocents because of an act committed by an imaginary couple in the misty, distant past or a God who is so touchy that he demands the death of his only child in recompense for human sin.

John Cassian (361-435) also rejected original sin. "What exists in all persons without exceptions, we can only think that it must belong to the very substance of human nature" (quoted in Brown,

1999). The church found Cassian, to be semi-Pelagian for his suggestion that the human will might have something to do with a person's salvation.

Like his contemporary Pelagius, Jovinian (d. 403) did not find asceticism to be superior to marriage. For Jovinian, the gift of universal salvation insured the equality of all believers. Jovinian also debunked the need for a perpetually virgin Mary. Although Jerome dismissed him as the "Epicurus of Christianity," Jovinian followed an early stream of Catholic thought promulgated by Irenaeus (130-202) and Cyprian (210-258) that rejected asceticism and considered marriage a boon. For his efforts, Jovinian was beaten and exiled, and his books were burned.

The authority given to the church in 312 by Constantine resulted in a tragicomedy of errors that relegated Jesus and his gospel to bit players while lifting the pope up as the high priest of Rome. By the end of the fourth century, the bishops of Rome adopted the title and role of Pontifex Maximus, or "supreme high priest," a title once reserved for the emperor. The decretal, a papal letter, took on a dictatorial tone as the Roman bishops created a sideshow called the Petrine Primacy that claimed authority in the name of a poor, illiterate fisherman who never traveled to Rome or bore the name of pope. That primacy gave the pope the ability to speak in the name of God.

Damascus of Rome used the primacy of Peter to his advantage par excellence. On the surface, Damascus (303-384) seems like a perfect saint. His credits are long and illustrious. As bishop of Rome, he presided over the church council that established the books in the New Testament. He changed the language of the church from Greek, in which all the gospels and early liturgies were written, to Latin. His secretary, Jerome, wrote that his boss was "an incomparable person, learned in scripture, a virgin doctor in the virgin church who loved chastity and heard its praises with pleasure." His papacy coincided with the adoption of Christianity as the new state religion.

There is much to add about Damascus.

Damascus rose to the rank of Bishop of Rome after hiring a gang of hoodlums to massacre one hundred and thirty-seven of his opponents inside a basilica. The Roman army had to quell a three-day bloody battle for succession and Damascus was formally charged with homicide. To distract from his bloody and violent deeds, Damascus absolved himself from his sins by designating himself the successor of Peter, the very first bishop of Rome to claim this title (Schenk, 2017).

Damascus devoted eighteen years of his papacy to transforming the Roman catacombs into a pilgrimage site to honor martyrs, an act that added funds to the papal kitty. In the process, he eliminated the tombs of many women saints who remain lost to us (Schenk, 2017).

Leo the Great (400-461) became pope as the power of the Roman Empire listed eastward toward Constantinople. Flexing his muscles as the successor of St. Peter, Leo began to extract obedience from his fellow bishops in the West. While credited with extending charity toward the residents of Rome during a famine, Leo did not extend that charity toward those whose beliefs fell outside the pale of Chalcedon Christianity. He censored churches that allowed Pelagians to receive communion without formally repudiating their errors. Leo pursued another bishop, Hilary of Poitiers, demanding that he make a perilous journey to Rome from France in the middle of a barbarian invasion to answer for an ecclesiastical point of order. The eastern bishops rejected Leo's claim to power. The bishops of Antioch and Alexandria were "papas," that is, popes in their own right. Even Augustine rejected the idea that the Bishop of Rome held the keys to the kingdom. The Bishop of Rome, in fact, remained powerless against Augustine's foes, the Christian Donatists of North Africa who had established an alternative Christian church.

Benedict XVI (1927-2022) claimed that the papacy of Leo was one of the most important in church history. The question is, important to whom? Did Leo's papacy lead to policies that improved the lives of his flock? Or did the papal power he claimed corrupt the office itself, shaping it into a position that men were willing to murder and cheat and conspire to acquire? As the office continued to accumulate authority and prestige it did more to reinforce existing hierarchies than it ever did to usher in the kingdom of God. Few popes, ancient or modern, have been able to disassociate themselves from the power conferred by their office, a power grounded in a bogus primacy dreamed up by Damascus and followed by subsequent popes like Leo into the present. Aided and abetted by sycophants, wealthy donors, and the secular arm of the government, popes throughout the ages have used this power to stifle and punish dissent.

Those who disagreed with the developing ecclesiastical mafia manning the large basilicas throughout the empire regarded themselves as faithful Christians and not heretics. There have always been clerics, bishops, and believers who did not subscribe to what became the position of the dominant party, not because they were demonic, contrary, evil, stubborn or a representative of the anti-Christ, but because, like Pelagius and John Cassian, their understanding of scripture, their pursuit of knowledge, and their devotional practices led them to a different conclusion. Attacking these believers with words or fists, humiliating them, burning their houses of worship and their books, ostracizing them, and persecuting them served no worthwhile purpose.

The Catholic Church has remained a heresy-hunting institution that tolerates no dissenting views. The long tendrils of seminal intolerance reached into the twentieth century and prevented my aunt from marrying my uncle in a self-proclaimed universal church. However, the intolerance extended beyond personal relationships. In a stroke of brazen effrontery to his fellow Christians, John Paul II wrote in *Dominus Jesus* (2000) almost thirty-five years *after* Vatican II that Protestants were fake Christians. The late pope, sainted not long after his death, declared that non-Christian faiths were "gravely deficient." Two years later, the *Boston Globe* would lay bare the grave deficiencies of a church that privileged its prestige and its criminal priests over vulnerable children. Despite the dirty laundry hanging on very public lines, self-described true Catholic believers still perceive toleration and acceptance of other faiths as a sign of weakness, wickedness, and a betrayal of an ancient and unchanging tradition. Unfortunately, that tradition, then, as now, has always included elements of aggression, cruelty, and violence.

For generations, Catholics have glossed over, ignored, and excused the violence the church has committed in their name because the vanquishing of heretics resulted in the victory narrative that they follow today. The heinous crimes committed by corrupt and violent men like Athanasius, Cyril, Damascus, Leo, and Hilary and their followers during the Jesus Wars do not seem to have detracted from their saintly reputations or from what the Roman Church believes is the one and only divine plan. This plan, constructed by circular arguments, seeded with myth and miracles, dusted with accidental and deliberate forgeries and mistranslations, and bolstered by the subjugation of women, the extermination of heretics, and the marginalization of Jews has nothing to do with God.

The intolerance of these powerful men has had consequences. They made spiritual and physical violence the framework and modus operandi of the institutional Roman Church. Even as various popes have belatedly asked for forgiveness for the church's evil heritage of anti-Semitism and their long-term misogyny, they continue, as the native saying goes, "to speak out of both sides of their mouths" as they pursue their latest "heresies," abortion rights and gender politics, proving that the church's ancient moral wound has not healed.

One way to heal this wound would be to demote the church fathers from sainthood. There are better representatives of Jesus's kingdom values. Due to their profound lack of charity, we should regard the doctrine "revealed" by God to churchmen like Ambrose, Athanasius, Augustine, and Cyril with a heavy dose of skepticism. Restraining the Divine within the human construct of a Trinity limits the power of God.

One of the most brilliant things the heresy-hunting Augustine wrote is that no one can define God. When the church fathers approved the doctrine of the Trinity with its endless and complicated processions of substances and ousias they described something other than God.

Because of the violence of their words or actions, Ambrose, Athanasius, Cyril, Damascus, Hilary of Poitiers, Ignatius of Antioch, Irenaeus, Jerome, John Chrysostom, Leo the Great should not be regarded as saints. Monica was an abused wife and not a saint.

Followers of the Way of Jesus
John Cassian, Jovinian, Pelagius

Chapter 5:
MARTYRS

"The blood of martyrs is the seed of the church."

Tertullian (155-220)

Persecution is one of Christianity's most persistent themes. Images of Roman legions marching through city streets and dragging out faithful Christians by the thousands from their homes to be torn apart by hungry animals and gladiators in the colosseum has captured Christian imagination for centuries. The names of martyrs grace the annals of the saints: beautiful young mothers like Felicity and Perpetua (d. 203) who bravely chose their faith over their newborns, Agatha (d. 251) and Lucy (d. 304) who were willing to lose body parts to remain the chaste spouse of Christ; old men like Ignatius of Antioch (d. 140) and Polycarp (d. 155) who relished the opportunity to be sacrificed for Christ; and young boys like Tarcisius (263-275) who were tracked down by the Roman version of the SS and executed for bringing communion to the faithful hiding out in the catacombs. Anonymous authors embellished the stories by adding the deaths of pagan bystanders who were so impressed by the courage of the martyrs that that they acknowledged Jesus on the spot and jumped onto a pyre or threw themselves to the wild beasts.

The truth is very different.

Although many Christians believe that martyrdom was a universal and omnipresent early church experience, many church historians now posit that most Christians were not subjected to dungeon, fire, and sword. The Romans did not arrest thousands of innocent Christians of all ages and stations in life and drag them into court where they were beset by both vile pagan magistrates and howling mobs calling for their blood. Brigades of Christians did not march into the colosseum to die as martyrs. Instead, most persecutions like the one that claimed the lives of Perpetua and Felicity in North Africa and the martyrs in Lyons in 177 were brief and localized. Christians in the western part of the empire were left largely un-scathed. Valerian (d. 264) and Diocletian (d. 312), the two emperors who did target Christians for persecution focused upon eliminating bishops and clergy, leaving rank and file Christians mostly unmo-lested. Even then, the persecution was irregularly implemented and haphazardly enforced. According to Tertullian (155-240), some gov-ernors refused to arrest Christians. Others bragged that they shed no Christian blood. In his 248 rebuttal of the Christian critic Celsus, the theologian Origen wrote, "Only a small number of people, easily counted, have died for the Christian religion" (Origen, 248).

Later Christians vastly overestimated their numbers, their impor-tance, and the threat they posed to Rome. The emperors devoted far more time dealing with the incursions of nomadic tribes than they did with the tiny number of Christian citizens. Thus, the Christians rested outside imperial purview unless their behavior attracted un-wanted attention. As the emperor Trajan wrote in 113 to the im-perial governor Pliny who had asked for guidance in dealing with Christians who were adversely affecting temple attendance in the Roman province of Bithynia,

> *"You observed proper procedure, my dear Pliny, in sifting the cases those who had been denounced to you as Christians. For it is not possible to lay down any general rule to serve as a kind of fixed standard. They are not to be sought out; if they are denounced and proved guilty, they are to be punished, with this reservation, that whoever denies that he is a Christian and really proves it- that is, by worshiping our gods- even though he was under suspicion in the past, shall obtain pardon through repentance. But anonymously posted accusations out to have no place in any prosecution. For this is both a dangerous kind of precedent and out of keeping with the spirit of our age" (Pliny, Letters 10.96-97).*

If Rome did largely ignore their Christian citizens, how did the blood of the martyrs become the seed of the church? Church historians have suggested that it was the forged, repeatedly edited, or mythological stories of the martyrs with their associated miracles that grew the church. Candida Moss wrote that early martyr stories, like tales of the martyred apostles, were "romanticized fiction" (Moss, 2013). Early Christians–like modern ones– enjoyed reading the stories of daring deeds and heroic suffering. Agonizing torture and painful deaths made for good reading.

The story of Ignatius of Antioch (d. 108) dips back into mythological mists and hints more of legend rather than fact. One legend imagines him as one the of the children Jesus blessed in the gospel of Matthew. In a time when there were no popes and communities elected their bishops, Ignatius was believed to have been appointed bishop of Antioch by Peter. During his sojourn in five different cities along his leisurely journey to Rome to meet his eagerly anticipated martyr's death, his captors permitted him to hold court with his adoring Christian fans and granted him enough time to write fifteen lengthy treatises explicating early Christian theology. Roman justice, however, was swift and did not provide an extended grace period to a condemned proselytizer to promote a position that had earned him the death penalty.

The letters of Ignatius were written in the 140's by an anonymous author and described the ecclesiastical structure that existed thirty years after his death. They are notable for the early Christians' morbid fascination with death. His arrest in Antioch is announced with great fanfare as he prepares to "proceed to the glory of God" in Rome where, "inflamed by the blood of God," he will become an "imitator of God" and die a martyr's death. The dying words of a courageous martyr confirmed the growing power of the office of bishop. However, the concept of martyrdom did not exist at the time of Ignatius. (Moss, 2013)

Like Ignatius, Polycarp (d. 155) is believed to been singled out for execution because of his Christian faith. Like the stories of many early Christian martyrs, the story of Polycarp's martyrdom was not written by an eyewitness but by a witness of faith in the late fourth century who embellished an awful death with miraculous details. Condemned to be burned at the stake, the flames refused to burn him, and instead wafted up the aroma of fresh spices to believers with a nose to smell it. Likewise, his burning flesh smelled by baking bread or like gold being refined in a furnace.

There are other unlikely details. The last day of Polycarp's life looks suspiciously like the last days of Jesus. Polycarp prays outside the city, rides into town on a donkey, and is betrayed by an insider. His execution takes place around Passover. In fact, the purported eyewitness wrote that Polycarp's martyrdom was in accordance with the Gospel.

From Ignatius' and Polycarp's eagerly anticipated martyrdom, Christians learned that death, rather than abundant life, was the modus operandi of the new faith. A martyr's death was a direct ticket to heaven. Some zealous Christians lined up for the ride, presenting themselves before Roman magistrates and declaring their faith in expectation of martyrdom. Others deliberately provoked Roman authorities by kicking over sacrificial altars or smashing idols, making themselves martyrs and the magistrates, persecutors. In response to the active pursuit of martyrdom, the Roman magistrate Arrius Antonius suggested that Christians spare him the trouble of a trial and jump off a cliff or hang themselves to fulfill their death wish.

Within this milieu of fabrication and zealotry, Tertullian (d. 220) of North Africa and Eusebius of Caesarea (d. 339) described the Christian faith as the victim of persistent and widespread Roman persecution and the death of martyrs as the seed of the church.

Despite Tertullian's fervent support of martyrdom, he is not believed to have been actively persecuted (Daniel-Hugues and Kotrosits, 2020). Like many colonized people, Tertullian mourned what he perceived as the replacement of his language and cultural values by the invading empire. Pagan Roman baths, theaters, gymnasiums, and arenas supplanted native institutions. Depictions of the emperor constantly reminded the natives that they were subjects of the Roman Empire. Tertullian resented local elites who became representatives of the colonial government and adopted Roman ways. Even Roman gods lorded it over local ones. Like any citizen of a conquered nation, Tertullian wished to shake off the foreigners who he believed were imposing their alien beliefs upon his country. Like the freedom fighters and prophets in Jerusalem, he regarded the mere presence of his Roman overlords as persecution. Tertullian provided Christians with an exaggerated scope of martyrdom and imagined the Romans burning in hell for all eternity as Christians watched in what can only be described as glee.

> *"How vast the spectacle and how wide! What sights shall wake my wonder, what my laughter, my joy and exaltation! As I see kings groaning in the depths of darkness! And magistrates who persecute the name of Jesus liquefying in fiercer flames than they kindled their rage against Christians. Such sights of exaltation!"* (Tertullian, De Spectaculis).

There are other inconvenient truths about martyrs. The florid language and promise of a seat near the throne of God held no allure for many believers when they confronted the stark reality of torture and death or loss of position and income. Church leaders like Cyprian of Carthage skipped town when his time to sacrifice came up. (He later returned and received a martyr's crown). Many Christians did the ancient version of crossing their fingers while they burned incense before the gods of Rome. Others bribed magistrates or had others sacrifice for them. Historian Elaine Pagels wrote that North African Christians were angered by church leaders who urged their family members to embrace martyrdom, regarding them as being complicit in the murder of their loved ones (2000).

Others came to regard martyrdom as human sacrifice. *The Testimony of Truth*, written by an anonymous author in the late second or early third century, in response to the number of people who died during the persecutions of Valerian and Diocletian, challenged the Christian Church's glorification of martyrdom. "If the Father were to desire human sacrifice, he would become vainglorious." For rejecting a God who delighted in the excruciating deaths of his followers, the author was forgotten, and the scroll buried in the Egyptian desert for almost two millennia.

How did Jesus whose expressed reason for his mission was to "heal the broken-hearted, give sight to the blind, and set free the oppressed" (Luke 4:18) become a model for death rather than life?

Christians have always been a touchy bunch who have argued

throughout the centuries that those who were not with them were against them. Their first perceived enemy were the Pharisees and teachers of the Jewish law who flatly rejected Jesus as the Jewish messiah. This bred hard feelings. Writing in the 80's of the first century, the author of Matthew placed words of condemnation into the mouth of Jesus, "Woe to you, teachers of the law and Pharisees, you hypocrites! You are like whitewashed tombs, which look beautiful on the outside but on the inside are full of the bones of the dead and everything unclean" (Matt:23).

The Pharisees, however, were not evil people inspired by Satan to destroy the followers of Jesus. The Pharisees, like the followers of Jesus, were re-thinking the practice of their faith after the Romans destroyed the temple of Jerusalem (where the early Christians still worshipped) in 70 C.E. The Jews who chose not to accept the way of Jesus were not hypocrites but rather faithful believers who continued to find solace in the Torah and the ways of their ancestors. The Pharisees and teachers Jesus mentions with disdain throughout the gospels were arguing and disagreeing with him, not persecuting him. Jesus acknowledged at his trial that he had taught among the people unmolested. It was not until his followers proclaimed him as "the King of the Jews" during Passover that the Roman execution apparatus rolled into motion, for there was no king but Caesar. To claim otherwise was treason.

As mentioned in Chapter Two, Jews and proto-Christians regularly disturbed Rome's rule with their constant in-fighting. This was augmented by the regular uprisings of the Jews against their Roman overlords. When Jewish rebels revolted and evicted the Romans from Jerusalem in 66, Nero sent the future emperor Vespasian to put down the rebellion. Four years and tens of thousands of deaths later, the Roman victory in Palestine was complete. Jerusalem was in ruins and the great temple destroyed. It was never to be rebuilt. The earliest Jewish Christians would have been among the dead.

When John wrote the book of Revelation from the island of Patmos in the year 96, was he reflecting upon the "abomination of desolation" that took place in Jerusalem in 70 where the Romans left no stone piled upon another? Was he writing about persecution and riots, or disagreement? Whatever the inspiration, the book of

Revelation is a blueprint for the destruction of one's enemies, real or perceived. Love had nothing to do with it. John did not direct his readers to turn the other cheek but to fight to the death. Unwilling or incapable of understanding the moral and spiritual universe of those he labeled "agents of Satan," John asserted that future victory for those who believe in Jesus will be secured by an angelic army led by the "Lamb who has been slain." Less than a hundred years after the death of Jesus, Revelation replaced the Prince of Peace with the Four Horsemen of the Apocalypse.

While Ireneus (130-202), Tertullian (155-220), and Eusebius of Caesarea (260-339) claimed that John was writing about a severe persecution of Christians under the emperor Domitian who reigned until 96, modern scholars have dismissed their claims as ancient fake news. No ancient pagan writer reported a persecution by Domitian. In fact, Domitian's imperial lawyer, Pliny, had never encountered one.

Few would dispute the violence inherent in the concept of empire, either ancient or modern. Empires invade and annex land belonging to other nations. They enslave, murder, and tax native people. Control can be maintained only by force. Rebellion, as the Jewish War indicated, is often the chosen portion of a conquered and humiliated people. The response is always more imperial violence. After three major Jewish rebellion in sixty-six years that diverted legions of Roman soldiers to Palestine, the emperor Hadrian (76—138) responded by executing Jewish scholars, burning Hebrew scriptures, and installing Roman gods on the Temple Mount.

Yet the Roman Empire had maintained an uneasy truce within its borders for over two hundred years during the *Pax Romana* (27 B.C.E.—180 C.E.). Unlike many victors, including subsequent Christians, the Romans incorporated conquered gods into their pantheon. While Rome did, indeed, kill people, it did not deliberately destroy gods or religions. While they might have looked down their Roman noses at the quaint and peculiar faiths of Jews and Christians, they did not hunt down Christians and execute them. Instead, the Romans allowed the Jews, and later the Christians to practice their faith unless a religious practice or rebellion threatened Roman rule. Then the apparatus of imperial power rolled in and destroyed enemies of the empire.

Although Christian apologists have liked to portray the Romans as immoral libertarians whose gods mean little to them beyond an occasional nod and a fleeting prayer, the Romans were deeply conservative and did, in fact, honor their gods who were not mere idols but rather the source of Roman power that enabled them to conquer the known world. Like the divine entity in whom Christians and Jews believed, the Roman gods needed to be both respected and continually courted by sacrifices, prayers, and praise lest they turn their divine backs on Rome. Law-abiding Roman citizens could not understand why Christian citizens could not honor both their own God and the gods of Rome when other religious sects were willing to oblige. Refusing to burn incense before the gods was akin to protestors in America kneeling during the national anthem. It was a sign of disrespect. When Christians refused to honor the Roman gods during periods of national celebration or times of distress, they were regarded as unpatriotic atheists and traitors worthy of execution. The perceived lack of respect for the gods of Rome sparked local persecutions like the one in North Africa that killed Perpetua and Felicity.

By the middle of the third century, the gods, it seemed, had turned their faces away from Rome. During the reign of Decius (201-251), the empire was marked by economic instability, corruption, political chaos, Gothic inroads, and a plague that killed five thousand people a day. Decius hoped that reinforcing traditional devotion to the Roman gods would turn away divine wrath and restore the *Pax Romana*, so he issued a decree obliging all citizens to offer sacrifice to the gods. Those who refused to sacrifice were arrested and executed. (Jews were exempted from sacrifice by a two- hundred -year-old imperial decree.) An unknown number of Christians were executed including Fabian, the bishop of Rome who had previously maintained good relations with the government during his tenure. There is, however, no evidence that Decius singled out Christians for persecution in his decree. In fact, he never mentioned Christians. This should not be surprising since there were only two million Christians in the entire empire in the year 250, 2% of the population.

The execution of one's co-religionists, however small the number, remains shocking. Christians felt targeted by the emperor. The fourth- century historian Eusebius blamed Decius' decree on imperial hatred of Christians.

Arrests and executions for treason ended with Decius' death in 251 only to be reinstituted by Valerian (199-264) in 258. Here again, a confluence of natural disasters and foreign invasions inspired Valerian to reinstate compulsory sacrifice to the gods. Unlike Decius, Valerian directed his persecution at Christian clergy and political leaders. Those who refused to sacrifice were martyred: Pope Sixtus II, the deacon Lawrence, Denis in Paris, and Cyprian in Carthage. Valerian's son and successor immediately stopped the persecution.

Rome found other reasons to dislike Christians besides their refusal to sacrifice to the gods. While Judaism was an ancient faith with established beliefs and laws, the Romans regarded Christians as a cult where the converted repudiated their families and gods to follow an executed man named Jesus. The Romans did not like cults, especially those who set themselves up in opposition to polite society.

Most societies do not like cults. Few people are comfortable with their family members joining an unknown group whose leaders demand blind obedience and require believers to renounce parents, spouses, and children. Few want to see their family's wealth turned over to outsiders. Many cults, both ancient and modern are apocalyptic and believe that they are a holy remnant chosen by God to survive a gruesome end designed by a deity who will violently weed out believers at a designated time. Association with their past endangers believers' salvation.

Early Christianity had all the hallmarks of a cult. Those who were baptized left their families and refused to participate in important family and civic duties like honoring the gods, marrying, and having children. Wealthy Christians deposited family fortunes into the coffers of the church. They met in cemeteries, a place that disgusted Romans to honor the Christian dead. The cultish, secretive behavior of the early Christians and their refusal to participate in Roman society alienated their neighbors and some Roman authorities. Problems arose for Christians during times of stress barbarian invasions and plagues. The Romans, like people of many times including our own, looked for a scapegoat. Were the gods angry? Were they punishing Rome for their lack of dedication? Did the Christians cause the gods to turn away their faces? Fear mixed up politics with religion and led to violence. It still does.

Many Christians continue to view themselves as victims of persecution. Indeed, the last two decades have seen a rise in religious intolerance. Muslim extremists in the Middle East have attacked Christians and Christian zealots in the United States have attacked Jews and often vilify Muslims. Equally problematic is the view of some prominent Catholics and evangelicals who perceive disagreement as persecution. Too many people are happy to believe the worst about those they designate as the other.

The late cardinal Francis George of Chicago equated former president Barak Obama's support of abortion rights with religious persecution and the triumph of secularism. In a sweeping affront to the principles of logic, George called secularism "Communism's better scrubbed bedfellow" (McClory, 2012). According to George, the former president's commitment to secularism– even as Mr. Obama and his family regularly attended Sunday services– would lead to an America where his ecclesiastical successors would be jailed as political prisoners and martyred in the public square.

Cardinal Timothy Dolan of New York has written and spoken extensively about the need for Catholics to be able to protect their exercise of religious freedom in America from the onslaught of secularism and the tyranny of the government, as if the Catholic faith were under attack and he and his fellow bishops were constrained from expressing their unpopular viewpoints when they have both the Catholic and secular media as their very willing mouthpieces.

Dolan, like George and too many of his fellow bishops and predecessors cannot accept the fact that people of good will can peacefully disagree on points of morality, theology, and ethics. A move away from patriarchy and hetero centrism is not cancel culture or a violation of anyone's first amendment rights. It does not trample upon religious freedom, nor is it a manifestation of evil secularism. As the Catholic bishops' views become less acceptable and less important to increasing numbers of people, their voices simply begin to fade out as their authority wanes.

Like the modern memorials of crosses, flowers, teddy bears, and balloons that accumulate around the site where innocent victims are killed by gun violence, the graves of martyrs became a place of prayer and remembrance. As these holy places became the site of miraculous cures, the faithful erected chapels that became the site of pilgrimages and a financial bonanza for both the locals and the bishop. So numerous did these shrines and their visitors become that church historian Peter Brown (1981) regarded saints and their shrines rather than the gospel or the Eucharist as the foundation of Christianity.

Ambrose of Milan (340-397) needed funds to cover the building costs of a basilica. The wily bishop conveniently dreamed of the burial place of two local martyrs, Gervasius and Protasius who had died a hundred years earlier. Sure enough, the very next day gravediggers went to the place described by Ambrose in his dream and disinterred two bodies, "men of marvelous stature," according to Ambrose, who, like vampires, were "perfect with much blood" (Ambrose, *Letter 22*). Pilgrims began flocking to the new shrine, paying for relics of the two saints. Ambrose had no problem funding his new basilica.

Ambrose described the bodies of the martyrs as gifts made by God directly to him. "Although this is a gift from God, yet I cannot deny the grace and favor which the Lord Jesus has bestowed on the time of my priesthood. The triumphal sacrifices are to be placed where the propitiatory sacrifice of Christ is commemorated. Upon the altar is He that suffered for all; beneath the altar are they who by his suffering were redeemed" (Ambrose, *Letter 22*).

Some citizens of Milan laughed at Ambrose and his conveniently discovered long-dead martyrs behind his back.

Ambrose uncanny ability to locate long-buried objects not only helped to pay for his new church, but it also helped to canonize the new emperor's mother, Helena who was a divining rod for Christian relics in war-torn Palestine.

In a homily, Ambrose described how the imperial mother traveled to the Holy Land three hundred years and many wars after Jesus' death and miraculously and instantaneously unearthed the cross of Jesus which her son had used as a sign that he would eliminate his fellow claimants to the throne. Helena also found the nails that affixed Jesus to that cross and the cloth banner that read "INRI." She brought the nails home with her and had the implements of Jesus' torture melted into Constantine's helmet and bridle, thus solidifying the myth that brought her son to power.

Helena's trip was marked by one miraculous find after another. She located the humble wooden stable where Jesus had been born in Bethlehem and the exact spot of Jesus' ascension into heaven. She uncovered the bones of the Magi and discovered the thirteen-hundred- year-old bush that God had set afire for Moses. Given unlimited access to the imperial treasury, Helena erected basilicas in Bethlehem, on the Mount of Olives, and on the site where she found the cross. All three sites became the destinations of generations of pilgrims who continue to seek favors from God. For her efforts in locating relics that archeologists can only dream about but rarely find, Helena, the Christian mother of Constantine, was canonized a saint.

The bones of St. Stephen were found in the same astonishing manner. In 415, a priest named Lucius told the bishop of Jerusalem that God informed him of the location of the saint's grave in a dream. "Make haste to open our sepulcher that by our own means God may open to the world the door to his clemency and may take pity on his people in this time of universal tribulation" (quoted in Catholicism.org).

Gravediggers unearthed a goldmine filled with sainted bodies on Lucius' estate. Not only was Stephen miraculously located, so were Nicodemus, a Pharisee mentioned in the gospel of John who took private lessons from Jesus at night, and Gamaliel, a Jewish rabbi who preached tolerance for believers of Jesus in Acts of the Apostles. Visitors to the graves began to report miraculous cures.

Stephen's body was transported in grand style to a church in Jerusalem where his body parts continued to work wonders. Even Augustine in faraway North Africa felt obliged to comment upon this great discovery in his book *City of God*. He sent an envoy to Palestine to secure a piece of Stephen's body that he would use at home to ward off heretics. The North African church later devolved into fighting about whose saint's body parts were holier and more efficacious in working miracles.

Unlike pagans who buried their dead away from the living to prevent disease, Christians regarded the bodies of their sainted dead as a source of holiness and blessing, lucky charms that could ward off evil, sickness, and even death. Thus, not only body parts, but also the clothes, and the possessions of saints were designated as powerful relics that like pagan amulets, could work miraculous cures for believers.

This belief led to the Christian practice of trafficking in dead bodies. The bodies of those judged to be saints were regularly disinterred and divided up into pieces for sale to believing pilgrims and powerful bishops who built up shrines around them. Zealous believers tore off the clothing from the body of Elizabeth of Hungary during her funeral procession. Bystanders mopped up the blood of Thomas Beckett as he lay dying in the aisle of the cathedral at Canterbury. A wealthy woman named Lucilla carried around the thigh bone– the largest bone in the human body–of a martyr and kiss it before receiving communion. Kings and churchmen often stored the bones of the saintly for future use. In 1342, Charles IV of France offered the ribs of his sainted ancestor Louis IX to guests who were attending a royal banquet.

A faith that bemoaned, criticized, and eventually outlawed pagan practices had no problem disinterring the dead, cutting up their bodies into little pieces, and selling their body parts as talismans. Scalawags began digging up dead bodies from cemeteries all over the world and hawking them as bona fide relics of saints and martyrs. Thousands of body parts were sold as pieces of Jesus's foreskin.

Relics and the bodies of saints remain powerful into the twenty-first century. The decomposing body of St. John Newman remains on display in a church in Philadelphia bearing his name. Pilgrims still visit the shrine and ask for his blessing by purchasing a rosary for $43.95 that has touched his body. A church in Maryland owns one of his relics. Families can sign up at church and bring the relic home for the weekend. Relics are also given as gifts on special occasions like ordinations. Relics must lie under the altars of all Catholic churches. When a church is decommissioned, the relics are removed and placed under a different altar.

For those whose bodies have been disinterred and dismembered without their permission, resting in peace is a dark joke. Yet, few Catholics question a practice that desecrates the dead.

There is no doubt that dying for one's faith requires both faith and courage. The late twentieth century witnessed the exemplary lives and heroic deaths of Catholics in Central and South America who followed the example of Jesus to love their neighbor as themselves. Inspired by the liberating spirit of Vatican II, priests, nuns, and lay people in El Salvador worked to fulfill the biblical mandate to free the oppressed from the social, economic, and political power of the predatory descendants of white colonists who had maintained a cozy relationship with the church. Those who insisted upon right relationships were labeled Marxists and hunted down by right-wing militias who massacred entire villages, including pregnant women and children. The church chose not to recognize these brave people as martyrs because it conflated the martyrs' advocacy for the poor with communism or socialism. The United States government made a similar mistake when it labeled the raped and murdered churchwomen of El Salvador as Marxists who by implication deserved to die.

Oscar Romero, who had been appointed as archbishop of El Salvador for his obedience to authority, later disappointed the ruling class by using the gospel to demand justice for the people. Invoking the name of God, Romero asked the militias to put down the weapons they used to massacre peasants. Neither the nominally Catholic government of El Salvador nor the institutional church supported him. Obsessed with the specter of communism, John Paul II believed that the revolt of the peasants over their rapacious overlords was a Marxist plot and wagged a condemnatory finger at the man who preached the gospel. Members of the militia murdered Romero as he stood behind the altar with his arms outstretched in prayer during Mass. Thirty years and two popes later, the man who was shot in the heart for preaching the good news was finally declared a saint.

Nine months after Romero's death, four American churchwomen, Maryknoll sisters Ita Ford (1940–1980) and Maura Clark (1931–1980), Ursuline sister Dorothy Kazel (1939–1980), and laywoman Jean Donovan (1953–1980) were raped and murdered by the militia after refusing to abandon their mission to the poor of El Salvador. A month before her death, Ford reported, "The colonel of the local regiment said to me the other day that the church is indirectly subversive because it is on the side of the weak." (quoted in Huerzo, 2020)

The right-wing government of El Salvador and its faithful supporter, the United States, regarded the martyred women as subversives. Jeanne Kilpatrick, Ronald Reagan's ambassador to the United Nations coldly commented on the brutal rape and murder of her fellow Americans, "The nuns were not just nuns. They were political activists on behalf of the Frente (Salvadorean guerillas)," as if they deserved the horror of their torture and death (Bonner, 2016).

The American government conducted no serious investigation into the rape and murder of four citizens in a foreign country. In 1981, Secretary of State Alexander Haig, who suggested that the women were shot for running through a roadblock, instructed U.S. ambassador to El Salvador Robert White to state publicly that the Salvadorean government was investigating the murders. White refused and was recalled. Haig drummed him out of the State Department (Bonner, 2016).

Nine years later, six Jesuit priests, Ignacio Ellacuria (1930–1989), Ignacio Martin-Baro (1942–1989), Segundo Montes (1933–1989), Juan Ramon Moreno (1933–1989), Joaquin Lopez y Lopez (1918–1989), Armando Lopez (1939–1989) were assassinated in San Salvador for preaching liberation theology. Their housekeeper, Elba Ramos (1947–1989), and her young daughter Celine (1973–1989) were murdered as well.

The Salvadoreans regarded these workers for justice as martyrs even as their church did and has not. They lovingly preserved the martyrs' blood-stained clothes, broken glasses, and torn flip flops behind glass cases or in gruesome but truthful photograph albums with pictures of their dead bodies. These artifacts cry out to observers, "This is what happens to those who follow the gospel!"

When I visited the very humble home of Oscar Romero in 2002, the guide, an elderly nun dressed in a habit, pointed to the tiles surrounding his garden painted with names and dates of miracles accomplished in his name. "The church has not canonized Oscar but we Salvadoreans know he is a saint," she told us.

Perhaps the real miracle is that the church eventually changed its mind. Pope Francis canonized Oscar Romero in 2018. None of the others have received a halo for their faithful witness to the gospel.

Dorothy Stang (1931–2005), a missionary and member of the Congregation of the Sisters of Notre Dame de Namur, was assassinated by a right-wing death squad in Brazil in retaliation for her work with the poor. When the seventy-six-year-old nun was confronted by two young men and asked if she had a weapon, she produced her Bible and began reading the Beatitudes. As she walked away from the militiamen, they shot her in the back. She has not been canonized.

In 1956, a World War II conscientious objector and Catholic scholar named Gordan Zahn discovered the faithful life and death of an Austrian farmer named Franz Jagerstatter (1907–1943). Unlike his fellow villagers, including the parish priest, Jagerstatter was the only person in town who refused to support Nazi rule. When he sought guidance from his bishop after learning that the Nazis were executing his Jewish neighbors, he was advised to go along with the Nazi program. As a conscientious observer, Jagerstatter refused to serve in the German army and was executed for sedition in 1943. Jagerstatter's last words were, "I am completely in union with the Lord." Jagerstatter was beatified in 2007. He is yet to be canonized.

Zahn, along with fellow pacifists Dorothy Day and Thomas Merton, were board members of the Catholic Peace Fellowship founded in 1964 to provide a home for Catholics who did not share their co-religionists' support for the war in Viet Nam. Jagerstatter was a worthy role model for those who espoused the perennially unpopular program of peace. Day commented that Catholics "need such saints (as Jagerstatter) today, to be held up for public veneration." In 1965, Merton used the example of Jagerstatter to ask how the church's mission of protest and prophecy could figure into the pursuit of peace. Jagerstatter's witness extended to people of other faiths, emboldening the unpopular stance of Muhammad Ali and Daniel Ellsberg.

While Jagerstatter's pastor and bishop were advising him to co-operate with the Nazis in Austria, a French Lutheran pastor named Andre Trocme, his wife Magda and their parishioners fearlessly refused to surrender their Jewish neighbors to the invading Germans, saving five thousand human beings from certain slaughter. No member of the village was executed in retaliation.

Irene Sendler (1910–2008) was a Catholic Polish social worker who is credited with smuggling out a large but undetermined number of babies and small children from the Warsaw ghetto during the German occupation of Poland. Sendler, along with a group of like-minded Poles, then placed the smuggled children in Catholic orphanages run by religious sisters. The women risked their own lives every day to save the Jewish children and many of Sendler's fellow workers were killed by the Nazis. Although Sendler was arrested and tortured by the Gestapo, she never divulged the identities or location of the potentially hundreds of children who lived under assumed Christian names for the duration of the war. Sendler wrote the names of the children and their parents on slips of paper and buried them in jars in her yard in order for them to be united after the war. Unfortunately, none of the parents from the ghetto survived.

Sendler received many awards and was nominated for a Nobel Peace Prize. Her name, however, was never submitted for canonization.

While the Trocmes and Sendler were not martyred for their faith, they willingly followed the gospel and risked their lives for their fellow human beings.

Swedish diplomat Raoul Wallenberg (1912, disappeared in 1945) and businessman Oskar Schindler (1908–1974) each saved thousands of Jews from death at great cost to themselves.

Christians whose faith impelled them to save their Jewish sisters and brothers from the Nazis at the cost of their lives and the lives of their families are worthy of canonization. Many of these brave souls are listed in Yad Vashem, a memorial to victims of the Holocaust, as "Righteous Among the Gentiles." The Episcopal Church has set aside a day to honor these faithful people who refused to capitulate to evil. The Catholic Church should do the same.

The martyrs mentioned in the latter part of this chapter began their lives as unknowns. They were mothers, fathers, farmers, scholars, social workers, missionaries, nuns, writers, bishops, deacons, factory owners, diplomats, and residents of villages who lived their lives faithfully and without fanfare— until it mattered. Rather than worrying about their job, their future, their reputation, their business, their farm, or their church, they followed the command of Jesus to love their neighbor as themselves to its conclusion, risking everything. The good of the world, indeed, its very future, depended upon their courageous witness. They are heroes of the Christian faith.

There is a Jewish saying that in all times there are thirty-six special people in the world, and that were it not for all of them, the world would come to an end. The Yad Vashem memorial proves that there are many more than thirty-six good people in the world.

Ambrose was more of a rogue than a saint and Helena, a traveler. We do not know if Nicodemus or Gamaliel ever followed Jesus. Ignatius of Antioch was an anti-Semite and Polycarp was most likely a myth.

We do not want our daughters to emulate the virgin martyrs.

Followers of the Way of Jesus
Maura Clark
Jean Donovan
Ita Ford
Dorothy Kazel
Ignacio Ellacuria
Ignacio Martin-Baro
Segundo Montes
Juan Ramon Moreno
Joaquin Lopez y Lopez
Armando Lopez
Dorothy Stang
Franz Jagerstatter
Irene Sendler
Raoul Wallenberg
Andre and Magda Trocme, and Oskar Schindler who are not martyrs but are surely saints.
The Righteous Among the Gentiles

I have not included Elba and Celine Ramos as saints. Sadly, their lives were sacrificed to protect the identities of the murderers and not necessarily for their faith. We do well, however, to remember them as holy innocents.

Chapter 6:
VIRGINS

"Religion is littered with the corpses of women who were victims of religious men who damaged and killed women in the name of God."

Kayla Oake

"The hymen is the most overrated flap of flesh in the human body."

Cristen Conger

The corner store in my working-class ethnic neighborhood sold magazines that were laid out upon tables in full view of patrons lining up to purchase ice cream cones, candy, and cigarettes. Next to *Time, Life,* and *Modern Bride* were magazines whose covers promised readers a different type of reading enjoyment. Designed to snag the attention of idling male patrons, the covers depicted almost naked women posing in a seductive manner or being mistreated by men. My mother called them "girlie" magazines and told me to avoid them and the men who paged through them in the store. I did not understand what pornography was until years later. Once I did, I realized that the stories of the virgin martyrs were as pornographic as the magazines I saw in our corner store.

The sado-masochistic tales of virgin martyrs are told with sound, fury, and clerical admiration. Their horror is covered with an aura of pedagogy. "Young girls, be like these women!" they shout. "Guard your virginity to your death as did Maria Goretti! God prefers, likes, and rewards virgins! There is little value for women in life without an intact hymen."

Interestingly, no male saint is listed as a "virgin." He may be a doctor of the church, a confessor, or a founder of a religious order.

He may even be a martyr. However, he does not lose bits and pieces of his sexual organs. His hagiographers do not revel in his nakedness. He is not taken to houses of ill repute to be violently raped and his martyrdom is not accompanied by gruesome accounts of humiliation, torture, and dismemberment.

Instead, male saints are more often pictured as men of power wearing liturgical vestments, crowned with miters, and holding staffs, implements of power rather than destruction. The message is clear: Men retain their body parts and their power while women lose everything, including the right to their bodily integrity.

The stories of the virgin martyrs spring from an idea that Jesus desired a harem of virginal brides to surround his throne in heaven even though there is no scriptural basis for this belief. The women in the New Testament, Mary Magdalene, Prisca, Martha, and Mary, Junia, Phoebe, and Chloe followed Jesus because they wanted to be disciples and preach the kingdom of God, not because they wanted to be his wife. Although the church regards Jesus as a lifelong celibate who never married, this is speculative fantasy with no historical or biblical basis. Married or not, Jesus clearly saw the women with whom he shared the last year of his life as a valuable part of his movement. Yet, the concept of virginal brides worked its way into Christian hagiography and produced the ideal of virgin martyrs, women who would rather die than marry because they had pledged their troth to a divine bridegroom.

The virgin martyr stories are devoted to obscene details of torture and humiliation. The government executes innocent young women at the behest of the men who revel in the dismantling of the women they once purportedly loved to distraction. The ancients read these tales of graphic mutilation with the same gusto that modern people watch slasher movies or read pornography with sado-masochistic overtones. "If I can't have her," the men in the stories intimate, "then no one will."

We do not know if the virgin martyrs of the early church–Barbara, Agnes, Cecilia, Agatha, Lucy, Anastasia, Catherine and Dorothy— were real or if they sprang from the tortured minds of sex-obsessed clerics teaching purity tales to impressionable young women. We do know that their stories follow a similar pattern, although they are distinguished from each other by pornographic details. A beautiful, rich, talented, and noble young woman is a dedicated Christian. She decides that she will be the spiritual bride of Jesus rather than of a man. A wealthy man seeks her hand against her expressed wishes. She refuses him. As a result of her impertinence, the Roman authorities–who may include the males in her own family–torture her horribly. Agnes is stripped naked by the authorities and taken to a house of prostitution to be raped. Lucy's eyes are gouged out and Agatha's breasts are torn from her body by pliers. Catherine's bones and flesh are broken and ripped by a wheel studded with spikes. No punishment is too awful or painful for these women. The women are reported to have gloried in their suffering and martyrdom as they saved their virginity for Jesus.

The church honors these women by enshrining their torture. Statuary in churches depicts Agatha's arms tied behind her back as her breasts are gleefully torn off by a man wielding pliers. Lucy is often portrayed extending a plate upon which rests her eyes. Catherine of Egypt's hand rests casually upon the wheel that broke her body into pieces. Those who reflected upon these gruesome stories wrote that the women felt no pain even as detail after gory detail was added to impress the impressionable. The message to women, especially young girls was clear: This is what we expect you to do to preserve your virginity.

The post-Constantinian church continued to exercise control over women's bodies, changing their focus from the gruesome martyrdom of willing virgins to severe asceticism. Like Lucy and Agatha who offered up their body parts for Jesus, women were asked to mortify their flesh through starvation and self-mutilation. Those regarded as church fathers and doctors of the church are portrayed as being celibates themselves despite their perseveration on the bodies of women, especially virgins. John Chrysostom (345– 407) directed women in his pastoral care to "mortify and crucify your bodies and you too will receive the crown of martyrs" for "the bridegroom gave his blood for your dowry."

Many noble women were inspired by this type of preaching and chose to remove themselves from society and live as consecrated virgins, married to Christ. Even then, the churchmen worried obsessively about virginal women who were living apart from the control of men. There are over twenty-five documents written by sexually fixated churchmen dating from the late second century to the sixth that obsess over the consecrated virgins' dress, their prayer life, their diets, their thoughts, their daily lives, and their bodies.

Jerome constantly worried that virgins would repudiate their vows and go rogue as married women. He described Jesus as a jealous husband and forbade the brides of Jesus to attend weddings, go to the market, or visit friends. He also ordered them to stay away from spicy food and wine lest they become consumed by lust and repudiate their vows. Like abusive husbands or lovers who sent their once beloved to their deaths, the churchmen tried to control every aspect of the virgin's life even if it killed her. Such was the case of Paula's daughter, who starved herself to death in her misplaced desire to please God, and, by extension, her mentor, Jerome.

Becoming a consecrated virgin brought a set of rewards to those who either willingly submitted or were forced to undertake the role. The consecrated virgin herself was freed from childbearing and thus prolonged her life. Many of those who rejected marriage and embraced virginity continued to live an elite Roman life, maintaining vast estates with large numbers of servants at their disposal and living as luxuriously as they did prior to their conversion– all without benefit of man (Hunter, 2007).

Others benefitted as well. The growing church was blessed by wealthy virgins who left their fortunes to the church. The families of the consecrated virgins were esteemed for producing such a God-like human being. Entire communities came to believe that their resident consecrated virgin was their intermediary with the Divine. Aided and abetted by churchmen like Athanasius who taught that every church community required a resident virgin whose sexual purity insured their salvation, the friends and neighbors of the virgin became deeply invested in her sex life or its lack thereof. If she fell from grace, so did they.

Slathering their own misplaced and warped virginity over the misogynistic cultural mores of the ancient world, the writings of the church fathers spelled disaster for Christian women unto the generations. Under the guidance of men like Jerome, Ambrose, and

Augustine, an unbroken hymen became a woman's most prized possession. With an intact hymen, a woman shone with a pure radiance. Without it, she was mere dross. Women had to be secreted away in safe houses, veiled, and guarded against what came to be known as defilement. At the same time, women whose hymens had been broken, very often without their permission, were labeled whores and sluts. If children resulted from the rape, they were called bastards. They and their mothers were often ostracized from Christian society.

Here, we turn again to Jerome who wrote to Eustochium, the thirteen-year-old daughter of Paula, "Although God can do all things, he cannot raise up a virgin once she has fallen" (Jerome, *Letter XXII*).

Jerome was not alone. Basil of Caesarea wrote to a virgin who married that she had "flung away the divine union and fled from the chamber of the true king. You have shamefully fallen into this disgraceful and impious corruption" (Letter XLVI).

The heresy-hunting Basil (330–379) who lived amidst the violence of the Jesus wars, found women's virginity to be a more pressing problem than the marauding monks who were murdering their fellow Christians, "You (virgins) have been deceived by the serpent more bitterly than Eve and not only your mind but also your body has been defiled. You have taken the members of Christ and made them members of the harlot. This is an evil that is unmatched."

Basil's fellow heretic-obsessed cleric Ambrose wrote, "He who has persevered in virginity is an angel. He who has lost it is a devil. A fallen virgin is an enemy of God."

It is no wonder that women starved themselves, refused to wash, threw acid on their hands, covered their bodies with veils, or walled themselves off in small rooms.

How did virginity become such a prized possession that women were willing to die for it? How did virginity become conflated with the love and honor of God? How did swearing off sex promote the kingdom values of Jesus?

History provides some answers. For much of the recorded past, most women had no control over their own bodies. Lumped together In Deuteronomy 20:14 with the master of the house's possessions, women were owned by their fathers, brothers, or uncles, and sold to the highest bidder for a pig, a cow, or a kingdom, sometimes at very tender age, often to older men to ensure the production of a male heir. Because of their low status, they were also fair game for rape by any man in the house. The Bible is, in fact, replete with tales of violent rape that Christians and Jews have declared as the Word of God. As an unfortunate result, the Catholic Church and the societies in which it existed became a haven for rape culture. If the great patriarchs and the kings handpicked by God could engage in rape and have it regarded as a boon to society, so could other men.

In her book, *Texts of Terror: Literary-Feminist Readings of Biblical Narratives*, author Phyllis Trible lists these horrifying tales of biblical sexual violence committed against women. The patriarch Abraham used Hagar, the servant of Sarah, as a sex slave. He then sent her, and the son conceived in rape into the desert to die. His grandson Jacob raped Bildah and Zilpha, the servants of his wives. While we do not know the thoughts of Bildah and Zilpha, Hagar raised her voice in despair to God in the arid wilderness as she realized that she would have to watch her son die of thirst before her eyes.

In Samuel 2:13, David's lovely virginal daughter Tamar was lured by her half– brother, Amnon, into his bed chamber where he then raped her. She was ordered by her brother Absalom not to report the incident to anyone, an unfortunate and typical patriarchal response to incest. Because of the patriarchal mores of her time, the completely innocent Tamar remained a "ruined woman" for her entire life, a mere shadow in her father's house.

Rape culture permeated the palace of King David. In a rebellion against his father, Absalom took his father's concubines to the roof of the palace and raped them all in the full sight of "all of Israel" (2 Samuel 16:22).

David's kidnapping and rape of Bathsheba is referred to as "adultery," as if she were a willing participant in a mutually acceptable sexual relationship. The second book of Samuel narrates the story of David and Bathsheba in a mere five verses, leaving little time between royal desire and royal rape: David wakes up one day from a nap and feeling bored, walks on the roof of his palace. A voyeur, he sees a beautiful woman taking a bath and sends his armed palace guards to her house. They escort her to his room, he rapes her, and then sends her home. The baby conceived in rape dies as God's punishment for what is described as a mutual sin. The death of one child to a king who had hundreds of children by a harem of women was probably meaningless to him. To a brand-new mother on the other hand, losing her newborn was most likely a catastrophe.

David's ongoing sexual relationship with Bathsheba, however, did finally produce the Davidic heir Solomon who would move divine history forward by building the great temple of Jerusalem. This child came at the cost of Bathsheba's former life, the life of her first husband, and the life of her first baby. It was hardly a deal made in heaven.

The most horrifying story in all of scripture is the rape of the Levite's concubine in Judges 19. The owner of the concubine pushes her outside the safety of the house where they were staying to be repeatedly gang-raped by the men of the village. At daybreak, when her owner sees her lying unmoving in the doorway, he kicks her and tells her to get up, showing no remorse for a woman who was raped to death. Rather than mourning a woman he had used or giving her a decent burial, he then hacks her body to pieces, as if she had done something wrong.

The faithful are not taught to regard these acts as rapes and crimes against humanity. Instead, they are regarded as being the inevitable, but not necessarily unfortunate consequences of God's plan. In this world view, God needed rapes or caused rapes to happen to move the story Christians call "salvation history" forward. Bathsheba's son, Solomon, had to become king and build the great temple of Jerusalem. This deed overshadows the kidnapping and rape of Solomon's mother. Very few preachers or scriptural scholars have ever considered the effects the glorification of rape had for the women involved in the stories. Thus, rape culture continues to be enshrined in the churches as the word of God.

In the male-defined world of relationships, the women–even a powerless subject of the king like Bathsheba–were regarded as culprits who distracted and led godly men astray. Women were taught that the brutal violation of their bodies was a stamp of their own pollution and a result of their own impurity rather than a crime against their humanity. The millennia-long projection campaign to slough off the crime of men's sexual violence and instead vilify women reached its apex under the guidance of the male doctors and fathers of the church who perseverated and pontificated upon women's bodies with the violence of their own frustrated sexuality. In the allegedly virginal eyes of these men, the only good woman was either a virgin or a dead woman. Motherhood, which involved sexual relations, came in a poor third.

This emphasis upon virginity had nothing to do with Jesus.

When Jesus came preaching the kingdom of God, virginity and asceticism were not his cardinal values. Instead, Jesus proclaimed, "The Spirit of God is upon me, because he has anointed me to bring good news to the poor. He has sent me to proclaim release to the captives and recovery of sight to the blind, to let the oppressed go free, to proclaim the year of God's favor" (Luke 4:18-19). The Beatitudes provided the framework for those who choose his kingdom values, not virginity or asceticism.

In fact, Jesus did not list virginity as a requirement for membership in his kingdom because Judaism, of which he remained a faithful member, had no understanding that sexual purity was necessary to achieve holiness. That requirement inserted itself into early Christianity via mistranslations of the Hebrew Bible and misinterpretations of Greek philosophy.

By the end of the first century C.E., Christianity had attracted more Gentiles and Jews from the Diaspora who were culturally Greek and spoke Greek rather than Aramaic. To make Christianity more palatable and understandable to Gentile converts, the early Christians filled up the tenets of the early faith with Greek philosophy, transforming it into something Jesus and the first disciples would probably neither recognize nor understand. Change, so integral to life on Earth, became suspect. A system of ideal forms encouraged people to seek a perfection that is simply unattainable in the physical world. In this world, Jesus became a perfect, sinless man, completely unlike human men. His purported sinlessness was understood as a deliberate choosing of a virginal state because sexual relations, in their understanding of Greek philosophy, rendered one imperfect, less whole, and therefore, less holy. Sexual desire was declared unnatural and verboten for the spiritually mature. Greek philosophy, however, had nothing to do with the life and teaching of Jesus.

Christians also had adopted and claimed the Hebrew Scriptures as its own. Adopting a body of ancient and established sacred writings established credibility in the Roman Empire. This process necessitated translations from Hebrew/Aramaic to Greek and then to Latin as the two testaments became one volume somewhere in the fifth century.

The Hebrew scriptures were not written down as a unit until after the Babylonian Captivity in the fifth century B.C.E. It was not until around the time of Jesus that these scriptures were translated into Greek, the intellectual language of the ancient world because most Jews in the Diaspora no longer could speak Hebrew. This book is called the Septuagint, since scholars allegedly translated it into Greek in seventy days. To their credit, the translators of the Septuagint were careful to maintain the meanings and ideas of the Hebrew words they translated into Greek (Snaith, 1956). This is not true of subsequent biblical translators.

Because Christianity cut its teeth on Greek culture and Greek philosophy, the scriptures moved away from its Hebrew origins and its basis on the repair of the world and took on a distinctly Greek, otherworldly cast. In his book, *Distinctive Ideas of the Old Testament,* linguist Norman Snaith claimed that the fathers of the church, the architects of the creed and designers of doctrine as well as the translators of scripture were strangers to both the Hebrew language and to the Hebrew traditions that formed Jesus' theological understanding of God. Instead, they were more influenced by the ideas of Aristotle, Plato, and classical Greek than they were by Amos, Micah, and Isaiah or even Jesus himself. Consequently, the Word of God came to be expressed at Christianity's inception through the lens of Greek philosophy. Mistranslations with their ensuing errors were not unusual.

According to Snaith, one of the most unfortunate and monumental mistranslations occurred when the Hebrew word for holiness, "*kadosh*" was translated into the Greek "*hagios,*" which means pure and chaste and "*katharos,*" which means clean (Snaith, 1956). What was lost in the translation from Hebrew to Greek? The meaning of holy, which originally meant concerning all things pertaining to the divine, became a fixation upon ritual sexual purity. All other virtues paled beside adoption of sexual purity. In thrall to Greek philosophy, aspirants to holiness could lose their charitable impulses or even their tempers, but if they lost their virginity, they could never be truly and completely pleasing to God. They became lesser beings. The gaping hole in women's hymens also broke their souls. Spurning their divine spouse became a crime worse than murder.

When sexual purity, rather than Jesus' kingdom values became the visible sign of holiness in Christianity, men and women separated their spiritual life from their physical existence and walked away from the people Jesus loved. They chose to live far away from the purported contamination of their sisters and brothers in fear of defilement by the other, something Jesus never did. The Creator God who commanded human beings to be fruitful and multiply suddenly eschewed sexual relations and supported lifelong chastity as the only way to perfection and holiness.

From scripture, we know that Jesus was not an ascetic and did not starve himself to please his Abba God. Nor did he live apart from his own people high up on a mountain or sequestered in a cave or like John in the desert, but rather among them. He liked to dine out, especially with those who could provide a full table like Simon the Leper or Zaccheus. Scripture suggests that he dined out often enough for some of the more observant Jews to call him a lush. When people were hungry as they sat and listened to him, he didn't tell them to offer their hunger up to God, he fed them. When they were sick or injured, he didn't tell them that suffering on earth would diminish their time repenting for their sins in purgatory, he healed them. In fact, Jesus loved people so much, he cried over them. This was not a man who lived his life with one foot in another more desirable and perfect world. This was a man living within the confines of his Jewish faith where the Hebrew God of justice demanded the repair of the world rather than the establishment of a new one in the next life. That kind of savior did not make sense within the framework of Greek philosophy and so the Jewishness of Jesus was lost.

Thus, the Jesus of the New Testament is very different from the Jesus who was exalted as the King of Kings and Lord of Lords who sits at the right hand of God in Christian theology. The Second Person of the Trinity became an omniscient, unchanging, perfect living god rather than a charismatic man with calloused hands and feet, and a big heart overflowing with God's love for creation.

Jesus, as the ideal Greek God-Man was a perfect man who needed to be born of a perfect woman. That perfect woman was Mary, his mother. What qualities must such a woman have in a Greek Christian world? Traditional female attributes, of course, obedience to men, humility, meekness. She needed to be the kind of woman who said, "Let it be done to me according to your (male) word." The church fathers then lifted Mary out of the human realm by relieving her of the need to have sexual intercourse to procreate. By adding *hagios* and *katharo* to her meekness and abject humility, they made Mary into a caricature of womanhood, a virgin mother, a state no other human woman could emulate. Since all women fell short of the Marian ideal, all were inferior.

Amazingly, one Greek definition of the word virgin or parthenos means "one in herself" or "not attached to any man." The Latin root "vir" means strength, force, and skill. The virgin was not, then, sexually chaste but rather sexually independent like the goddesses Artemis, Athena, and the many derivatives of Astarte. Like Jesus, the great heroes of the ancient world were believed to have been born to sexually independent women: Buddha, Osiris, Genghis Khan, and Augustus Caesar.

Without knowing anything about the real Mary who walked this earth as the mother of Jesus or of her sexual status, the churchmen have taught that Mary's virginity was central to her identity as a person. She is referred to as the Blessed Virgin Mary. To the men of the church, the singular and imagined condition of her hymen rather than her efforts to repair the world signified her consecration and devotion to God. Thus Mary, like women throughout the ages, was defined by her body parts rather than by her achievements.

Churchmen have spent and continue to spend inordinate amounts of time and effort perseverating on Mary's virginity. Pope Martin I (553) taught that Mary was a virgin before, during, after the birth of Jesus although the gospels record that Jesus had siblings including his famous brother, James the Just. Unlike her sisters, Mary experienced no biological disruption in her body when Jesus was conceived or during pregnancy and delivery, eliminating the offending pregnant belly churchmen found so abhorrent. This understanding enabled Ambrose of Milan to write in the fourth century, "Jesus preserved the fence of her chastity and the inviolate seal of her virginity" (Epist. 42, 4PL, XVI). Augustine, author of the doctrine of original sin, heaped a spoonful of sexual perversion on the whole virgin-conception-birth process by writing, "As an infant, he came forth, a spouse from his Bride chamber, that is, the virginal womb, leaving his mother's integrity, inviolate" (*Homilies on St. John's Gospel*, 8, 3-4).

While Mary can be established as the mother of Jesus, her virginity cannot likewise be established despite the ancient pious musings of sexually fixated men raised on Greek philosophy.

Virginity was not initially important to those who followed the Way after Jesus' death since proto-Christianity remained within Judaism, a faith that neither valued nor promoted virginity. In 1 Corinthians: 9:5, Paul rhetorically asked an unnamed audience if he had the right to be accompanied in his mission by a believing wife as did the other apostles including Peter and the brothers of Jesus.

Despite Paul's question, he seemed to espouse a celibate lifestyle. We really do not know if either Paul or Jesus had been married at some point. Both believed in the imminent end of the world when God would intervene and dismantle the evil powers of oppression. As Paul said, why would anyone marry and start a family if it all was going to end very soon? On the other hand, observant Jewish men were married, and celibacy was not an ideal or even something to aspire to. Even the high priests were married. Perhaps the wives of Jesus and Paul died. Perhaps their children had died as well. With the end of the world and transformation possibly a heartbeat away, it would not make sense to marry or remarry and have children.

When the world did not end in the manner Jesus and Paul predicted, many Christians resumed marrying. Priests, bishops, and popes married. The priesthood, in fact, became an inherited office passed down from father to son. The gospel spread through the efforts of married couples like Prisca and Aquila, who settled in major cities throughout the empire. While some of the members of the Corinthian church were insisting upon lifelong virginity after conversion to belief in Jesus, Paul himself was not persuaded. The letter to Timothy written pseudonymously in the name of Paul around 100 C.E. lists the necessary qualities a bishop needs to have; those bishops were married men (1 Timothy: 3-5).

But the Greek ideal of being whole and intact to appease God persisted. By the third century, the church fathers deemed that marriage was a poor substitute for a life of virginity. For some ascetics, not engaging in sexual relations would prevent the birth of any more children, thus hastening the end of the world and the second coming.

Churchmen also had no problem adopting the Aristotelian assertion that women were misbegotten, deformed males incapable of exercising any kind of authority. The fathers of the church happily grandfathered Greek cultural biases into theology and doctrine, thus enshrining prejudice against half of the population of the church as an article of the Christian faith. The mistranslation of Hebrew words like *kodesh* into *hagios* put, to borrow the words of Pope Francis, the "strawberries on the cake" of institutional church misogyny.

However, the unbiblical insistence upon sexual asceticism had the unintended consequence of empowering women. As a consecrated virgin, a woman, not her father, brother, uncle, or cousin, owned her body. Instead of being forced to marry an older man and face the distinct possibility of dying in childbirth, women could be married to Christ. For the first time, Christian women, especially wealthy ones, had a choice about how to live their lives.

As increasing numbers of these sexually independent women converted and opted for the celibate life, their choices were believed to undermine the civic values of Rome, which encouraged marriage and childbearing. Despite the disapprobation of their male relatives, wealthy women did find a way to use their fortunes as they saw fit, often bequeathing vast amounts of property and money to the church, which became extraordinarily rich as a result. Women purchased and then managed huge cemeteries for their families, their fellow Christians, and their retainers. Like the ordained deacon Olympias, they undertook the huge task of feeding the urban poor. Because of their status in society and in the churches they supported, they portrayed themselves in engravings on their tombs as heirs of Jesus, holding scrolls of the gospel. Some are pictured wearing liturgical vestments with outstretched hands in prayer. As Christine Schenk

(2017) wrote in *Crispina and Her Sisters: Women and Authority in Early Christianity*, whatever the churchmen might have thought about the position of women in the early Christian world, the women were thinking something completely different. Wealthy Roman women were writing their own stories in the catacombs and on their gravestones, ignoring the edicts of the churchmen who tried so hard to control them. In the words of Schenk, "Early Christian sarcophagus iconography suggests that many fourth-century Christian women were idealized as learned figures with authority to, at the least, proclaim and teach scripture even as male church leaders struggled to curtail this practice."

The archbishop of Constantinople was so impressed with the worthy deeds and generosity of an independently wealthy Christian woman named Olympias that he ordained her and her three female relatives as deacons. While Olympias was busy feeding the people of God, Pope Damascus was covering up the tributes to women saints and martyrs in the catacombs of Rome. Of his efforts, Schenk wrote (2017),

> *"Damascus's ambitious campaign would eventually transform Rome's founding myth from Romulus and Remus to Peter and Paul. In the process, the church's female martyr-heroines and wealthy woman patrons, would become all but invisible. Even as many influential female Christian martyrs were lost to history, other Christian women would be remembered, primarily because of the men who wrote about them."*

Most Catholics are unfamiliar with important women like Olympias, Crispina, Petronella and all the many "sisters" who appear in Schenk's book. Rather than remembering the powerful women who built up the church of Rome through works of charity and boundless generosity, the churchmen instead bequeathed to the world the names of violated and tortured women who were executed to save their virginity for Jesus who as an observant Jew, would not have understood nor wanted their sacrifice.

Rape culture and the paradoxical insistence upon female virginity have long been hallmarks of the patriarchy. This culture continues to blame women for the sins of men. The patriarchy demands that women dress and act in certain ways to protect themselves from being assaulted by men who have no expectations placed upon them to refrain from sexual activity. It asks that young girls take purity pledges and refrain from sexual relations while refusing to teach them about the workings of their own bodies. It continues to prize virginity as an unmitigated good while demonizing female sexuality.

As a result of the patriarchal enshrining of virginity, all sorts of myths have trickled down to modern society. The first is the most problematic: A woman should be willing to die to "preserve" her "purity." Thus, a virginal body became more important than her life. The second myth is the expectation that a woman will fight to preserve her virginity, even if her violator holds a knife at her throat or the throats of her loved ones. If a woman didn't fight, she wanted to be raped.

The little Italian girl Maria Goretti (1890—1902) has been admiringly called the "Saint Agnes of the Twentieth Century." Maria was canonized in 1950 and is listed as a virgin martyr. Her story is more tragic than heroic and begins in a horrifyingly commonplace way. A twelve-year-old girl is regularly preyed upon by a twenty-year-old boarder in her house who tried to rape her on numerous occasions. Like most abusers, he threatened to kill her if she told anyone. One day he found her alone and tried to rape her again. Enraged by her cries and her desperate attempts to fight off his advances, he stabbed her fourteen times. Some of the wounds went completely through her little body.

Her attempted rape and her murder are quickly slathered over with thick religious overtones. Although no one was present during the attack except for a sleeping baby, Maria is reported to have said as she was reputedly fighting more for her chastity than for her life, "This is a sin. God does not want it." Although she had deep stab wounds in her neck, heart, lungs, and diaphragm which would have caused catastrophic blood loss, she was described as awakening during surgery to forgive her assailant, thus nudging her toward canonization. Despite her murder, the churchmen decided that the unspeakable violence done to her little body was a small price to pay for the preservation of her virginity.

Maria's mother, Assunta, was still alive when her daughter was beatified in 1947. Rather than commiserating with Assunta on the violent death of her daughter, Pius XII said to her, "Blessed mother, happy mother, mother of a Blessed" (*Your Daily Martyr*, 2016). Rather than addressing the sex crimes regularly committed against young girls in Italy and worldwide, Pius said at Maria's canonization in 1950, "Young people, pleasure of the eyes of Jesus, are you determined to resist any attack on your chastity with the help of the grace of God?" In canonizing Maria, the head of the Catholic Church publicly declared that for women and girls, dying for one's virginity was far more important than preserving one's life.

Faced with life in prison, Maria's rapist suddenly acquired religious sensibilities and a vocation to boot. He told a local bishop that Maria had appeared to him in a dream, giving him lilies– the symbol of purity– that burned his hands. When released from prison on the recommendation of the bishop, he became a lay brother and is said to have prayed to Maria, whom he called "his little saint," every day. Thus, the church gave power to a man to define and own his victim both in life and after death.

This story is more horrifying than it is edifying. The child Maria is just like the Agneses, Agathas, Barbaras, Dorothys, Cecilias, and Catherines before her, less a saint and more a poster girl for unaddressed and widely tolerated violence against women and girls that has persisted into the twenty-first century. Whether actual historical persons like Maria or fictional virgin martyrs like those listed above, these women need to be correctly named as victims of violent crime rather than as saints who died to preserve their virginity. It was the churchmen who declared that the murdered women's grievous wounds and untimely deaths were willingly chosen and pleasing to God, thus making them worthy of canonization and emulation.

The wages of male-defined sexual sin for women in some parts of America today is poverty or even death. Like Eve, the women get what they deserve, to bear children in pain and to remain subservient to the men who rule over them.

None of the virgin martyrs should be regarded as saints. They were victims of a perverse theology and male violence. We want our daughters to value their lives more than their hymens.

Chapter 7:
MEDIEVAL SAINTS

"The principal heresy of the Waldensians was and still remains the contempt for ecclesiastical power."

Inquisitor Bernard Gui on the Waldensians

When I was seven, I had a terrible dream. Trauma associated with the dream dropped it permanently into my mental files and it remains vivid to this day. I was dressed in my favorite red shorts and polka dot shirt and lying on the marble altar in my parish church. Above me stood a blonde-haired, Nordic-looking Jesus sporting a Van Dyke beard. He was holding a large knife poised right above my heart and he was going to sacrifice me. I had been a bad girl and Jesus had decided that my punishment was death. I recall writhing in sweat and gasping for breath as I tried to wake myself and escape from the point of the upraised knife wielded by the man who as supposed to be my savior.

How did such a small child dream such a horrible dream? We learned in our very first year of Catholic grade school that God imposed severe consequences upon the tender souls of seven-year-olds who had reached what the church called, "the age of reason." Good behavior led straight to the gates of heaven, guarded by St. Peter who dangled the keys given to him by Jesus. Certain bad behaviors like murder, eating meat on Friday, or missing Mass on Sunday led right to the hammers of Hell where guilty souls burn for all eternity under the evil eye of Satan. Minor sin led to purgatory where those guilty of fighting with one's siblings spent years burning away their sins until the prayers of their relatives or the mercy of God finally kicked in and released them from their agony.

And there were so many sins! My seven-year-old mind recoiled from the thought that taunts on the playground could send me directly to purgatory for thousands of years. Internalizing sin made me anxious and fearful. What if I did not realize I had committed a sin? Would God still punish me? If God drove the hapless Adam and Eve from the Garden of Paradise for eating an apple, punished later generations for their sin and then demanded the death of his only child to appease his wounded divine ego, what would God do to me, a child born into the horror called original sin? In my childish mind, God was a source of terrible anxiety rather than a comfort.

The idea of an angry, vengeful, all-powerful God who intentionally and constantly played "gotcha" developed in the Middle Ages. It was conjured up by popes who recognized the temporal power of the keys to heaven allegedly given to Peter by Jesus. Popes wielded these keys as a weapon rather than as an instrument of love. In a model that eschewed the words of the Prince of Peace to love their neighbor, they lobbed excommunications and anathemas at people who believed differently, burning their books and sometimes their bodies. The second person of the Trinity was an angry judge who subjected the dead to a particular judgment immediately after death. That terrible, swift judgment landed them in a recently discovered otherworldly place called purgatory where the skid marks of life were burned away in an expiatory fire that could last for thousands of years. Although the dead do not return to tell tales about the afterlife, the Second Council of Lyon in 1247 declared the fanciful and unbiblical notion of purgatory to be a real place with real torments from which the poor souls could be released only by the ceaseless prayers of the living which were needed to melt the adamantine heart of a merciless God. Masses and endless prayers for the dead consumed Catholic prayer life and filled the coffers of the local churches. In the 1960s, we were still praying for "the poor souls in purgatory" who needed to make the great leap upward into heaven.

In the twelfth and thirteenth centuries, a series of church councils solidified the power of the priesthood which was less a vocation and more an appointment or an entree into academic life. In some areas, the priesthood was an inherited position handed down from father to son or uncle to nephew. Noble families dominated the papacy and the episcopy of large cities. These families fought, sometimes to the death, for a position that provided them with great wealth and power. Landless younger sons purchased the office of bishop and then used benefices from the church made in good faith by members of the congregation for the souls of their beloved dead to fight wars of plunder that furthered their family's interests. This embroiled Europe in endless internecine battles that repeatedly despoiled lands and annihilated entire settlements. These families also enriched themselves with fees charged for the administration of the sacraments. As the numbers of abbeys, monasteries, and churches grew, the local bishop became the largest landowner and lone source of authority in the area, harshly taxing the peasants in absentia. Eventually, the princes of the church would own enormous amounts of property in Germany, France, and Italy. The pope became the temporal ruler of a large swath of land in Italy called the Papal States compliments of Charlemagne's father, Pepin the Short.

The medieval clergy usurped roles related to marriage and death that once belonged to the community. Churchmen, not elders, now decided who could marry and when and who was worthy of a Christian burial. In 1215, Pope Innocent III convened a council (Lateran IV) attended by four hundred bishops that declared transubstantiation a doctrine of faith, placing the sacred meal entirely in the hands of the ordained. The council also ordered the faithful to confess their sins once a year to untrained and uneducated priests who sometimes charged for their services.

Making transubstantiation a doctrine of faith led to a series of unfortunate events. Rood screens were erected to separate the clergy and the hosts in the chancel from the People of God who sat in the nave. The host was not only transformed into the Body and Blood of Christ, but it also became a living entity that bled if injured. Where once left-over sacramental bread was distributed to feed the poor, a host consecrated through the actions of a priest now needed to be kept under lock and key lest the hands of the laity touch and despoil it. While there was no punishment for committing acts of unfathomable violence against Jews, Muslims, or heretics during Christian led pogroms, desecrating a host brought a sentence of death.

When I made my first communion at age seven in 1959, I was

told not to chew the host which had been specifically designed to melt in your mouth lest my baby teeth harm Jesus. Even today, the gravest sin in the Catholic Church is the desecration of a consecrated host, not mass murder, racism, or sexism. While a consecrated host might reside in a jewel encrusted vessel known as a monstrance, God's children are allowed to live in squalor and misery. Many believers who deeply reverence the real presence of Jesus in a piece of bread cannot seem to find him in the faces of their sisters and brothers in Christ.

In the eighth century, a series of forgeries written by sympathetic allies of the bishop of Rome endowed the church and the pope with the spiritual power to rampage through centuries and civilizations with a force that came to be known as Christendom. These forgeries, called decretals, were written by anonymous pious Christian churchmen in the ninth century to expand papal power, protect the church from interference by secular rulers, and exempt the church from punishment for civil crimes. By placing prevailing ninth century ecclesiastical assumptions and fourth- century quotes from the Latin Vulgate into the mouths of first-century Christian bishops and theologians, the authors sought to make the Roman Pontiff the supreme leader of the Christian church.

Heavy with literary and theological accoutrements more resonant with secular power than the words of a loving God, the decretals reincarnated the Bishop of Rome as the divine-right Roman emperor who ruled over a theocracy established by God himself. Attributed to the papal successors of Peter, the letters describe Rome as the first See of the Christian world established by Christ himself, divinely destined to rule over everyone else. This gave the pope of Rome a plentitude of power. Some of these fake letters were incorporated into canon law, becoming implements of absolute power in the hands of popes like Boniface VIII (1235-1303) who wrote in the papal bull *Unam Sanctum*, "It is absolutely necessary for salvation that every human creature be subject to the Roman Pontiff."

Medieval popes eagerly latched on to a forged letter allegedly written by the putative second pope after Peter, Anacletus "The holy Roman and Apostolic Church...obtained its primacy from the Lord our Savior himself. Therefore, this apostolic see was made the hinge and head of all the churches as ordered by the Lord and ruled by the authority of this See" (Quoted in *The Catholic Layman*, 1853). Few were willing to argue with the words of a successor of Peter.

The letters were declared forgeries in the seventeenth century. Yet, many Roman Christians continue to believe in the exalted position of the Bishop of Rome as the successor of Peter as do the popes and bishops.

Because of the lofty position of the ecclesiasts, the decretals also absolved bishops and the Church from all sin, making them impervious to secular accusations. Based upon the spurious letters, the twelfth-century canon lawyer Gratian decided that the Roman church had the authority to judge all matters.

As a result of the power endowed by the decretels, later canon lawyers and theologians invested the pope and bishops with the power to attack heresy with what the churchmen regarded as righteous persecution. Excommunicated Christians and Jews who did not share church teaching were damned.

Bishops, some of whom were canonized, worked tirelessly to establish their wealth, the wealth of their families, and the temporal power and wealth of the church. As agents of political intrigue, they acted as king–and pope– makers while carefully cultivating an image of sanctity. They supplied mercenaries who fought in royal wars or unending papal crusades against fellow Christians and used excommunication as a weapon of ecclesiastical power against those who stood in their way. They had the coins of their realm stamped with their image and the word Dominus or Lord. In the long history of strife between the clerical and secular rulers, property and power were dressed up in the language of theology.

If the bishops, abbots, and popes had not willingly chosen to accumulate great wealth and to establish themselves as players on the local and international stage, they would not have been involved in endless power plays with rulers who tried to annex their land and considerable wealth. Instead of engaging in endless political intrigues, in petty wars among nobles seeking booty, and in crusades against those who were different, the churchmen could have devoted themselves body and soul to those who needed to be set free from oppression as Jesus had taught. Instead, tens of thousands died in wars and crusades that they led or supported.

A thousand years ago, a substantial number of the faithful began to reject a lazy and immoral clergy even if their official sacerdotal actions did bring them eternal salvation. Christians then like Christians now did not appreciate hypocritical leaders. The people witnessed the blatant misuse of ordination when the sons and nephews of bishops— who had no intention of advancing to the priesthood— were given a tonsure at age seven so that their families could tap into the benefices of the local church. When the discontented pointed out the hypocrisy, they were called heretics.

Sometimes those canonized as saints introduced anti-biblical ideas into Christian theology. Anselm of Canterbury (1033–1109), a brilliant scholar and the author of atonement theology, helped to make suffering the cornerstone of the Christian faith. He was also a wily manipulator who orchestrated his appointment as abbot of a large monastery and then as Archbishop of Canterbury. Like many bishops before and after him, he worked tirelessly to preserve extensive church lands from royal encroachment while dabbling in political intrigue, pitting royal brother against royal brother. When King William II of England was killed in a hunting accident, he supported the future Henry I against Henry's older brother Robert, who was off fighting in the papally endorsed First Crusade. Anselm's dedication to Henry led to the bishop's convenient discovery that Henry's future wife Matilda had not really taken a vow to be a nun which would have disqualified her from marriage thus freeing her to marry the king. After working endlessly to establish the primacy of the See of Canterbury in England, Anselm hurled anathemas from his deathbed at those who did not share his vision. One of his successors, Thomas Becket, requested Anselm's canonization in 1163.

Thomas Becket (1119– 1170) has long been regarded as a martyr for the Christian faith and a symbol of spiritual resistance to royal tyranny. His case is more complicated. Thomas was perceived by his peers as a rogue who ingratiated himself with those in high office to advance his career. He loved luxury and showing off his worldly possessions. A series of fortunate connections, his winsome personality, and his intellect ingratiated him with the Archbishop of Canterbury who sent him abroad to study canon law. The archbishop then appointed him to the position of the archdeacon of Canterbury, a lucrative position with many medieval perks that Thomas used to live the courtly life of a wealthy and powerful noble. At the archbishop's recommendation, Thomas became the chancellor to Henry II of England while retaining the position of archdeacon, largely neglecting the latter and yet loath to let it and its financial largess go when commanded to do so by the king.

When his episcopal benefactor suddenly died, Thomas was consecrated as the new archbishop of Canterbury one day after being ordained a priest, his lavish lifestyle posing no barrier to his appointment. Henry II was infuriated when Thomas resigned his position as chancellor. He had hoped to use Thomas as his royal rubber stamp to control the church.

Biographers claim that Thomas underwent a conversion or transformation after his appointment as archbishop, eagerly participating in the duties of the cathedral, upholding the teaching of the church, and adopting a more austere lifestyle. Apologists have claimed without proof that Thomas was celibate prior to his ordination, dusting him with the mystique of holy sexlessness.

Thomas and the king began to argue immediately over clerical privilege. Clerical criminals were judged by their bishops regardless of the extent of their crimes, often receiving light sentences for egregious offenses like rape and murder. Henry believed that clerics who committed crimes also needed to be judged by lay juries and punished accordingly. He forbade the excommunications of royal officials by bishops, many of which were used to settle political or social scores rather than enforcing a theological point. Thomas disagreed. Sovereigns were subject to the church as they were to God. Their disagreements became more intense, with Henry antagonizing Thomas and Thomas going on sprees of excommunications of fellow bishops and nobles who disagreed with him. In fear of the king, Thomas fled to France, where he lived for six years trying to negotiate via other bishops and the pope for a return to England and the restoration of his property.

After mediators tried to patch up relations between Thomas and the king, Thomas returned to England several weeks before his death and immediately set to work destroying whatever rapprochement might have existed between him and the king. He refused to lift the excommunications of the bishops who supported Henry instead of him and levied new ones upon his opponents. Few of his fellow clerics were amused by the antics of the archbishop, who had come to be disliked for what they regarded as fanaticism.

Henry was infuriated at Thomas's ongoing recalcitrance and asked the ill-fated question as to who was going to relieve him of a cleric who had caused so much trouble for him and for the country. Four knights set out to oblige the king. They burst into the bishop's quarters and threatened him. Thomas ran into the church, clinging to a pillar while the knights berated him as a traitor to the king.

An alleged hidden eyewitness to the violent scene of swords, maces, axes, screamed insults, and intense anger claimed that Thomas said calmly and distinctly enough to be heard in the din, "I am ready to die for my Lord that in my blood the Church may obtain liberty and peace. But in the name of almighty God, I forbid you to hurt my people," before the knights split his skull. Apparently, this eyewitness then had the presence of mind to immediately find quill, ink, and paper to record Thomas' exact last words as the blood of his bishop spilled onto the church floor.

Those who gathered up his blood as he lay dead on the floor later sold it for its miraculous power, ensuring Thomas's sanctity. Numerous tales of miracles led to his canonization in 1173, one of the quickest in history. His tomb soon became a famous pilgrimage site immortalized in *Canterbury Tales*, in which Geoffrey Chaucer (1340s–1400) poked fun at the clerics and his fellow pilgrims making their way to honor "the blissful martyr." Thomas is less a saint than he is a prototype for Lord Acton's nineteenth-century maxim about the corrupting influence of power.

Atonement theology helped to replace the pre-medieval understanding of Jesus the Good Shepherd with a Jesus who demanded recompense for his death. The sacred head surrounded and pierced by thorns, the bloody nail wounds and the gushing wound in his side demanded the punishment of those who caused them. As the medieval Church began to glory in the cross and the grievous wounds of Jesus, they began to persecute the alleged perpetrators of these wounds– the Jews.

The Christian perception of the perfidy of the Jews has always loomed large in the imagination of both churchmen and Christian monarchs. The sainted Louis IX of France (1214–1270), crusader and defender of the faith, forced eminent rabbis to debate equally erudite Christian theologians like St. Albert the Great on the topic of religious truth, an impossible goal and a high presumption, in the Disputation in Paris. The rabbis were forced to argue with one hand tied behind their backs–they could not say anything Louis regarded as being derogatory to the Christian faith. No such constraint was placed upon the Christian theologians. The Christian debaters could use all the ammunition in the arsenal of medieval rhetoric that was at their disposal. Meanwhile, Louis had all copies of the Talmud confiscated. Agents of the government burst into synagogues all over France, ripping the holy books from the hands of faithful Jews. Anyone who resisted was summarily executed. During the debate, Louis became incensed by the disputations of the Jewish rabbis and yelled that instead of discussing faith with a Jew, a good Christian should plunge his sword into him.

Unsurprisingly, the rabbis lost the debate. Twenty-four cartloads of books containing the collective work of generations of Jews were burned near the Cathedral of Notre Dame. It is estimated that the Christians destroyed ten thousand Jewish holy books. Louis of the saintly disposition then signed legislation that banned Jews from France.

The Disputation in Paris in 1242 was followed by the Disputation of Barcelona in 1263 led by the sainted Raymond of Penafort. Like many canonized Christian monks, Raymond of Penafort (1185–1275) was a rabid anti-Semite. He was the author of both *Siete Partidas*, a codification of Spanish law that included virulent anti-Jewish legislation, and the Decretels of Gregory IX that enshrined the values of a persecuting church. Raymond, the inquisitor of Aragon and Castile, also had copies of the Talmud forcibly removed by the government. The books were then vandalized by Christian clerics who had verses that offended them expunged.

Penafort was the confessor to James I, the king of Aragon, who during his crusade to conquer Majorca for Christ, intended to forcibly convert the Muslim residents or kill them.

While Catholic apologists are quick to mention Penafort's charity and sunny disposition, Jewish scholar Norman Roth labeled him a notorious "Jew-hater" who stirred up Spanish animosity against Jews who had lived continuously in Spain for twelve centuries (Roth, 1995).

Raymond is not the only canonized anti-Semite. According to Catholic legend, the mother of Vincent Ferrer (1350–1419) had a dream that her son's name would be famous in all of Europe. Indeed, it was. A charismatic preacher and conspiracy theorist par excellence, Vincent's preaching was in demand all over southern Spain. Unfortunately, his gospel message was diluted with large doses of virulent and hateful anti-Semitism. Jews, he thundered, were mortal enemies of Christ, solidly on the side of Satan. Their malice, stubbornness, and pride had no limit. Believers should be willing to defend their faith as vassals defend their lords–to the death. After listening to Vincent rant and rave about the evil nature of Jews, Christians would leave church and rush into Jewish neighborhoods to burn homes and bash in heads. A proponent of medieval conspiracy theories, Ferrer feared that Christian women were being contaminated by Jewish men who surreptitiously crept into Christian home and impregnated them, thus mixing the sacred with the profane. He set loose a violent Christian rampage by preaching this fever dream without fact. The Jesus of his preaching was neither kind nor gentle. In one of his sermons, he described the resurrected Jesus wounding the damned with a knife on Judgment Day. Perhaps Vincent is the source of my dream of the murderous Jesus.

Juan of Capistrano (1386–1456) was a fanatic persecutor of Jews and heretics and a firm advocate of papal supremacy. His deeds belie his sanctity. Admiringly labeled the "Scourge of Jews," he believed it was an act of love to preach against Judaism. Traveling to parts of southern Germany that had previously granted special privileges to Jews, Capistrano's anti-Semitic preaching led to riots and the expulsion of Jews who had lived in peace with their Christian neighbors for centuries. In the city of Breslau in what is now southwestern Poland, he orchestrated a round-up of Jews after accusing them of desecrating a host. He then tortured innocent citizens into confessing their role in a fabricated sacrilege. As a result, forty Jews were burned at the stake. The swallows in the city named for him in California obscure the true nature of this hater of humanity.

While churchmen like Raymond of Penafort, Vincent Ferrer, and Juan Capistrano were busy inveigling against Jews, many ordinary citizens continued to regard Jews as neighbors, friends, and business associates. Roger II of Sicily employed Jews and Muslims in his court. Many Christian rulers engaged educated Jews as governmental officials and teachers of their children. Preachers meanwhile condemned the tolerance of those who dared to speak with "enemies of our Lord God Jesus Christ" and rulers who refused to enforce the specific clothing Jews were supposed to wear to mark them as Jesus's assassins.

The clergy's accumulation of great wealth, their endless battle for territory and power, and their violent preaching did not go unnoticed by the populace. People rarely accept and ignore blatant hypocrisy in their faith leaders. By the eleventh century, many believers called for a return to the apostolic piety and poverty that their current clergy were sorely lacking. This discontent spawned the rise of unlicensed itinerant preachers who did practice apostolic poverty and followed the Way of Jesus. The Humiliati or the Poor Men of Lyon, the Waldensians, Joachimites, Beguines, Apostolic Brethren, Fraticelli, and the Lollards are among many groups that existed within and alongside the Roman version of Christianity. Many of the faithful found the humility, poverty, and teachings of the itinerant preachers to be a viable alternative to a clergy they viewed as corrupt.

The wealthy of every age are usually spared from personal encounters with abject poverty. The servants or slaves who prepare and serve their food, wash their clothes, and clean their homes are one-dimensional moveable parts who appear and disappear at will. Their circle of family, friends, neighbors, and business acquaintances does not include the poor. Like the Buddha, a young Francis of Assisi (1181–1226) was confronted by a different side of life when a beggar asked him for alms while Francis was selling expensive cloth in a marketplace for his wealthy merchant father. A shocked Francis gave the money from the transaction to the beggar, incurring the wrath of his father and the ridicule of his friends.

Francis went on to abjure his life of wealth and comfort. While we do not know if Francis encountered itinerant members of the groups mentioned above, he adopted their playbook. Like the Waldensians, Francis dedicated his life to apostolic poverty. The tonsure he received from a visit to Pope Innocent III protected Francis and his new group of like-minded men from accusations of heresy when they began preaching many of the same ideas that the Waldensians preached.

Aside from his embrace of poverty, there is much else in Francis that is admirable. Francis feared the effects of power within the order he founded and eschewed titles of leadership. Perhaps his relationship with his own father led him to reject the authority of a paterfamilias within the order. Instead, he wrote to one of his mentees, saying, "I am speaking, my son, in this way, as a mother would." Francis is the first representative of the traditional church to refer to the world as "Sister Earth."

While Clare of Assisi is usually portrayed as a pupil of Francis, a Franciscan groupie or wanna be, or even a constant companion to Francis on a joint journey to heaven, she was none of these. She was the founder of the Poor Clare order and a correspondent with four popes. While Francis's preaching about the value and necessity of poverty moved Clare to enclose herself in a monastery at age eighteen and gather a group of like-minded women around her to live in extreme poverty like she believed Jesus did, her actual contact with Francis was limited to several days.

Francis and Clare worked independently. He did not mention either Clare or her order of nuns in any of his writings. Clare used Francis to protect the rule she designed for the Poor Clare order from the interference of popes who wanted to control her.

Francis, in fact, shared the opinion of many monks and priests that there was nothing more dangerous to a man in religious life than a woman. When he was asked to preach to the Poor Clare sisters in their chapel, he entered the room without looking at them, drew a line of ashes to separate himself from his sisters in Christ, poured the rest of the ashes on his head, intoned the Miserere, "Have mercy on me, God, in your kindness. In your compassion blot out my offense. O wash me more and more from my guilt and cleanse me from my sin. My offenses truly I know them; my sin is always before me.

Against you, you alone, have I sinned; what is evil in your sight I have done," and then left (Dalarun, 2005).

Francis is often portrayed as a pacifist. Instead, he was a zealot who believed that all people on earth needed to believe in Christ or face damnation. Francis never condemned the crusades or war. His much-touted trip to Egypt during the Fifth Crusade was not a mission to broker peace between the warring sides but rather an attempt at martyrdom as he announced to the Sultan that the Muslim ruler must convert or be damned. Apologists credit Francis with transforming the sultan from a wild beast to a gentle man. Meanwhile, Christian crusaders ate the dead bodies of their Muslim foes in front of the townspeople of Ma'arra in modern day Syria to force the prompt surrender of the town. Yet, it was the Muslims who were considered barbaric.

Some of the followers of Francis inherited and augmented his boundless passion for unconditional conversion to Christianity and became fanatic preachers of the crusades and operatives of the Inquisition. Almost three centuries later, they carried their mission-ary zeal to the Americas where Indigenous people were presented with the same message that Francis delivered to the sultan– convert or be damned.

Regarded as saints during their lifetimes, Francis and Clare were quickly canonized after their deaths by popes eager for the populace to embrace the lives of charismatic people who strengthened a faith they insisted was constantly assaulted by heretics, Jews, and Muslims. Clare, for instance, was canonized two years after her death. Her rapid canonization is partly based upon a legend that she repelled Muslim mercenaries hired by the Holy Roman Emperor, Ferdinand II, with a monstrance containing the Blessed Sacrament.

While the Franciscans and Poor Clares operated with the approv-al of Rome, there were many medieval outliers who did not. Walter Map (1130—1210), a secular English cleric educated in Paris and serving in the court of Henry II of England feared the attraction of wandering preachers.

"These people have no settled abodes. They go about two by two barefoot, clad in woolen, owning nothing but having all things in

> *common like the apostles, nakedly following a naked Christ. They*
> *are now beginning, in a very humble guise, because they cannot*
> *get their foot in. But if we let them in, we shall be turned out"*
> *(Kreider, 1984).*

Prejudices that move human beings to create and then fear "the other" evolve into more sinister forms of behavior. Map was not alone in his fears or his condemnations. Medieval churchmen who were being educated at the earliest universities in Europe founded specifically to combat heresy became fixated upon sin and punishment, the ubiquity of the devil, the wrath of God, and the evil influence of those the church regarded as different. Men like Bernard of Clairvaux, Dominic Guzman, and the popes Innocent III and Gregory IX overestimated the number, the power, and the organization of the Waldensians, Humiliati, Hussites, Poor Men of Lyon, and the Beguines rendering them specters of evil and instruments of the devil who needed to be destroyed.

Contrary to the overactive imaginations of the churchmen, like the modern Antifa, none of these groups was organized or related to one another. Nor did the itinerant preachers and their followers arise from a perverse sense of disobedience and dislike of the Christian faith. Instead, they were staunch believers who tried to reform what the church had empirically proven to be true: the accumulation of wealth, land, and titles was incompatible with the teaching of Jesus who had directed his followers to give away their possessions to the poor. The faithful of many different countries viewed the royal, wealthy church with dismay and disgust.

Through the voices of ecclesiastically approved preachers, the church heartily condemned the inroads of these groups using the intemperate language used by zealots. Those who lived as poor and humble servants according to the Way of Jesus were demonized and labeled heretics, agents of Satan and the antichrist. They were accused of bewitching ignorant folks with their criticism of Holy Mother Church, or they were sexual deviants who had sexual relations with the devil. Bernard of Clairvaux and his fellow Cistercians labeled those who disagreed with the church as a menace to all who were faithful. They were heretics who deserved to die.

The rise in the power of the clergy led to a rise in accusations of heresy. By 1178, the church had reached a point in its development where it had acquired the mechanisms of government and the educated staff it needed to enforce Roman Catholicism as the only true faith. By the early thirteenth century, the church had established an effective apparatus to seek out and destroy their fellow human beings who had a different idea about God. The Inquisition harnessed all levels of society to eliminate those who were regarded as perfidious heretics.

Innocent III prepared the soil for the Inquisition by sending specially trained preachers to spread the fantastical lie among the faithful that huge numbers of heretics lay in wait to capture their souls and send them to eternal damnation in hell. Where previous generations of bishops and popes dismissed these stories, Innocent embraced them, embellished them, and created an alternative reality of fear and horror into which Catholics had to buy lest they lose their possessions, their status in society, or their lives. Thus, the fabric of Europe was altered for the next five hundred years as fire became the punishment of choice for heretics and witches. Empowered by the pope, the Dominicans, founded by Dominic Guzman (1170-1221), formed the advance guard in the increasingly violent war against heretics.

To the surprise of Guzman, the itinerant preachers he encountered were theologically educated and could engage in substantive debate with the papal minion. He also found that the preachers were men of integrity, greatly admired by the people of the area, who referred to them as "good men," a fact that made them dangerous to Dominic for whom anyone outside the pale of the institution was suspect. Dominic engaged them in public debate, hoping that both they and their admirers would be moved by Dominic's arguments to obey the church.

Innocent III perceived the failure of Dominic and Bernard's Cistercian order to quickly transform southern France into a bastion of orthodox Catholicism as a menace to a divinely approved unity. Like all institutional messaging machines, the medieval one operated on misinformation and outright lies. Innocent III reached back six hundred years to reclaim an ancient epithet and deride the people who lived in southern France as "impious Manichaeans who call themselves Cathars" and unleashed what is known as the Albigensian Crusade against the Christians of southern France. To compel belief where persuasion failed, Innocent decided upon a crusade on a magnitude greater than those sent to the Holy Land against Muslims. Upon the promise of indulgences and booty, a Christian army larger than any mustered to fight the Muslims assembled to seek out and destroy their fellow Christians in June of 1209.

The hypocrisy was not lost on the people who had been taught to believe that Muslims were their real enemy. Common Christian lay people criticized a crusade fought against fellow Christians despite real fear of this Inquisition which tolerated no criticism. Some brave and outspoken residents of southern France called the pope "a new Judas" for taxing them to fight papal wars against sisters and brothers in Christ. As Christian crusaders besieged the city of Toulouse in 1229, a resident tailor named Guillem Figueira wrote,

> *"Deceitful Rome, avarice ensnares you so that you shear the wool of your sheep too much. O Rome, you will never have a truce with me because you are false and perfidious with the Greeks (the crusaders attacked Constantinople in 1204) and the Latins. Rome, you do little harm to the Saracens, but you massacre Greeks and Latins. In hell fire and ruin, you have your seat"* (quoted in Moore, 2012).

The medieval war machine, assisted by the pope and the Dominicans initiated a twenty-year reign of terror in which tens of thousands of people perished. Led at first by Guy of Clermont with his sidekick, the archbishop of Bordeaux, the army rampaged through the countryside, burning towns and people at will. In July of 1209 the army besieged and then sacked, plundered, and burned the city of Beziers with "great joy" according to the eyewitness, Peter of Les Vaux de Cerney (Moore). With great satisfaction, the papal legate informed the pope that twenty thousand people were executed without regard to rank, sex, or age, including those who sought sanctuary in the churches. Estates and farms were laid waste for generations. The fateful words "Kill them all, the Lord will know his own" emerged from this scene of epic carnage (Moore). Drunk with the spilling of blood, the crusaders decided to slaughter the residents of any castle that refused to surrender to them. Leadership of the crusade later fell to Simon de Montfort, a close friend of Dominic Guzman, who had baptized the leader's daughter and officiated at his son's wedding.

Catholic hagiographers are quick to cover up any suspicions about Dominic's complicity in the Albigensian Crusade with tales of his intense devotion to God and his extreme asceticism, both of which contributed to his purported ability to levitate at will during prayer. While it might be difficult to outright accuse Dominic of violence during the Albigensian Crusade, he, like other churchmen, believed in using the violence of the state to kill heretics when persuasion failed. His presence with de Montfort during key battles indicates an acceptance of the horrors perpetrated by de Montfort. Dominic was in Carcassone with de Montfort after its defeat while heretics were being tried. In the spring of 1211, Dominic travelled with de Montfort and the bishops of Lisieux and Bayeux and their armies to lay siege to Lavaux. There, de Montfort hanged the leader of the garrison along with eighty knights. He also threw the Lady Girauda de Laurac into a well for treating heretics in her realm with respect. In 1213, Dominic inspired the crusaders to take the city of Muret, which resulted in the death of the king of Aragon. De Montfort attributed his military success to the prayers of Dominic Guzman. Despite the hagiography, the saintly, ascetic, levitating Dominic seems to have a great deal of blood on his hands.

In all, those engaged in the Albigensian crusade against their fellow Christians laid siege to forty-five cities and towns and waged four field battles between 1209 and 1218. These battles destabilized the area for generations and enabled the King of France to annex a previously independent area.

When Simon de Montfort was killed by a falling rock that crushed his skull during the battle of Toulouse, the bishop immediately wanted to canonize him a saint and declare him a martyr for his devotion to the church. In an unsparing diatribe, an anonymous speaker expressed his disgust with any bishop who would elect to canonize the man who despoiled a country:

"And the epitaph relates to me who can read it that he (Simon de Montfort) is a saint and a martyr, and that he is destined to rise on the last day to inherit and enjoy the marvelous bliss of heaven and wear the crown and sit in the kingdom of heaven. And I heard it may be so: if by killing men, by shedding blood, by destroying souls, by consent to murders, by following evil counsels, by starting conflagrations, by destroying barons, by bringing nobility to shame, by seizing lands, by advancing the wicked, by kindling evil, by extinguishing good, by killing women and destroying children, one can gain Jesus Christ in this world, on should wear a crown and shine in heaven" (Throop, 1938).

This brief passage highlights the problems associated with a rapid declaration of popular figures as saints and martyrs.

Dominic's herculean efforts to combat heresy were directed and supported by Innocent III, Honorius III, and Gregory IX, the latter of whom was the nephew of Innocent III and friend of Raymond, Dominic, and Francis, and advisor to Clare of Assisi. A man regarded as a bulwark of moral integrity with ferocious devotion to the faith, Gregory established the Inquisition in 1133 as one of the first acts of his papacy. He precipitously canonized Elizabeth of Hungary, Anthony of Padua, Francis of Assisi, and Dominic shortly after their deaths. He also appointed the earliest members of the Dominican order as inquisitors, empowering them to deprive the priests suspected of heretical beliefs of "benefices forever." He directed the Dominican inquisitors to proceed against all heretics without appeal, calling in the aid of the king if necessary.

Under the jurisdiction of fanatics like Gregory, the alleged heretics were thrown into a nightmare from which many would never emerge. In a preview of twentieth-century totalitarian regimes, the accused had no right to counsel. They were denied the right to know the names of their accusers, or the nature of the charges made against them. Nor were they allowed to ask. Those who refused to confess were tortured. Confession brought no reprieve. After receiving absolution for sins they had no idea they had committed, the now shriven heretics were burned without mercy. The thorough Dominicans tortured other members of the heretic's families, including children, to root out even the hint of heresy.

The Dominicans were prosecutor, judge, and jury. Boys over fourteen and girls over the age of twelve were called to make accusations of heresy against the members of their community. If no heretics were forthcoming, the entire village became suspect.

Despite the real threat of the Inquisition, some people reacted furiously to clerical violence. Following the receipt of a sentence in Bologna, a man called out, "It would be good to go to the house of the friars, set it on fire, and burn the inquisitors" (Hardstaff, 2018). Once the Albigensian Crusade ended, those who survived the wars drove out the inquisitors from Toulouse, Carcassonne, and Albi. Many people came to despise both the Inquisition and its agents, including Dominic, who once had to be protected by the troops of Louis IX while visiting a monastery in France. The people referred to the order with the less than friendly moniker "God's watchdogs," and Dominic is frequently pictured in iconography with a dog. Some villages and cities expelled or murdered the hated inquisitors. At the University of Paris, members of the inquisitorial Dominican order were shunned by their fellow students for belonging to a sect that placed itself outside the laws that governed everyone else.

While the irrational forces of religious fundamentalism descended upon both sleepy hamlets and vibrant cities, monks like Thomas Aquinas (1225–1274), who had recently encountered the philosophical works of Aristotle and Plato through his teacher Albert the Great (1200–1280), laid out a manual and rationale for church domination using the ancients as his inspiration. Thomas baptized Aristotle's religiously neutral unmoved mover the Christian God, something a skeptical Aristotle could have hardly imagined. Thomas firmly believed in the dual but unequal governing authorities of church and state, with the latter clearly subordinated to the former, which to Thomas was an absolute and incontestable force. Thomas used the teachings of Aristotle to establish a hierarchy of human beings that later supported the Christian understanding of slavery and the church's ongoing misogyny. It was God who rendered some human beings subservient to others. To criticize the intentions attributed to the Divine by churchmen was a sin.

Thomas's magnus opus *Summa Theologica* is less a synthesizing of ideas than an appropriation of Greek philosophy by Catholicism. Regardless of the many useful merits of Greek philosophy, a follower of Jesus might wonder why so many churchmen felt the need to reorient Christianity along what are clearly secular pagan lines of thought. These lines lay along an axis quite different from Jesus' very Jewish kingdom values, which were based upon the Torah and the words of the prophets, that Jesus, as a good Jew, had written upon his heart. Churchmen like Thomas subsumed the message of Jesus to repair the world under newly proclaimed medieval doctrine of transubstantiation which endowed clerics with magical powers to confect Christ.

While there is no actual link between Thomas Aquinas, the Crusades, and the Inquisition, he was one of the earliest Dominicans, an order that managed and oversaw the Inquisition established by Gregory IX in 1233. Aquinas would have been aware of Dominican practices that uncovered, tried, and condemned heretics to death in cities all over Western Europe. He wrote, "With regard to heretics two points must be observed: one, on their own side; the other, on the side of the church. On their own side there is the sin, whereby they deserve not only to be separated from the church by excommunication, but also to be severed from the world by death. For it is a much graver matter to corrupt the faith which quickens the soul, than to forge money, which supports temporal life. Wherefore if forgers of money and other evil doers are forthwith condemned to death by the secular authority, much more reason is there for heretics, as soon as they are convicted of heresy, to be not only excommunicated but even put to death." In his treatment of his fellow human beings, Aquinas was hardly saintly even while waxing eloquently on the Aristotelian exposition of virtue.

For a long time, the theology of Thomas Aquinas was indistinguishable from Catholic theology. In 1914, Pius X declared that the teachings of the church could not be understood without the underpinnings of pagan Greek philosophy, claiming that the scholastic theology of Thomas was the basis of sacred studies. About Thomas, Pius wrote in *Doctoris Angelici* or "angelic doctor, "No true Catholic has ever ventured to call into question the opinion of the angelic doctor."

The methodology of the inquisitors seeped into the private lives of believers. The young widow Elizabeth of Hungary (1207—1231) had the misfortune of being assigned future inquisitor Conrad of Marburg as her confessor. Married at fourteen and widowed at twenty, the impressionable and grief-stricken young mother of three small children fell under the punishing influence of her spiritual advisor, who proceeded to control her food intake, her actions, and her family. He forced her to send her children away so he could "break her will and direct her whole desire to God." Conrad honed his budding inquisitorial skills on Elizabeth and her maids, frequently forcing the young women to strip down to their undergarments so he could personally whip them. During an infrequent visit to see the baby Conrad forced her to abandon, Conrad had another friar whip her and her maid with a heavy rod while he watched from the doorway chanting "Lord have pity on me." Elizabeth died at age twenty-four from starvation and Conrad's prurient brutality. The inquisitor pope Gregory IX canonized her physical, mental, and spiritual destruction by naming her a saint four years after her untimely death.

Hagiographers were quick to cover up Elizabeth's untimely death in a series of miracles and tales of extraordinary charitable giving, throwing up smokescreens to protect Conrad from blame and project it on her husband whom she had loved. When her husband roughly tore open her cloak to expose the riches that she was giving to the poor, he found roses and not gold. She was said to have put a leper between her and her husband in their marriage bed despite the fact that she was happily married and had three children.

With the death of Elizabeth, Conrad was now free to direct his sadistic energies against those he deemed to be heretics. The mantra of Conrad and his two assistants testify to the extent of his brutality: "We like to burn one hundred innocent people among whom there is one guilty person" (Annals of Worms, 24,402). Their unholy pursuit of the innocent ended when Conrad accused a wealthy and popular count of heresy. He and his two henchmen were quickly and conveniently dispatched.

The role of the preaching orders like the Cistercians, the Dominicans, and the Franciscans in stirring up hatred against those they labeled as heretics and later, witches, should not be minimized.

The Franciscan St. Anthony of Padua (1195–1231), who is portrayed as tenderly holding the infant Jesus, was renowned for his preaching against the Cathars. His nickname is the "Hammer of Heretics." The scholar St. Albert the Great (1200–1280) preached a crusade called by Urban IV. While Dominic, Francis, Albert, Thomas, and Anthony cannot be accused of ordering or directing massacres, their xenophobic views led many of their followers to violence. Members of the Dominican order, founded specifically to combat heresy, became the willing instruments of church-sponsored bloodshed, manning the inquisition tribunals that led to the death of thousands. Although scripture warns repeatedly of the poisonous effects of fear, fear of the other allowed the evil spirit of intolerance to eject love from the very heart of the Catholic Church. Preaching violence against those designated as enemies in the twelfth century is like preaching violence in the twenty-first: it often leads to unintended consequences.

While the deeply held beliefs of the preaching orders were inspiring believers to murder their fellow human beings, the deeply held beliefs of others were painting a different picture of what the church could be. As with every age, the story of the Middle Ages is complex. It is so much more than the pope and his minions of crusading and inquisitor bishops, abbots, and friars. While canonized saints like Louis IX of France were marching off to war to kill Muslims and ripping off the lips of those who blasphemed, others who have not been canonized were preaching a much different gospel.

Meister Eckhart (1260–1338) was a Dominican monk, a theologian, a professor, and a mystic who believed that believers could be one with their Creator through contemplative prayer. It is Eckhart who is known for the prayer, "if the only prayer you ever say is thank you, it is enough." While his contemporaries taught that God was a wholly other stern judge who issued those who questioned a quick ticket to hell, Eckhart described a compassionate deity who held frail human beings in the divine arms. Unlike his fellow clerics who were raging through southern France killing heretics, Eckhart taught that God perfects rather than destroys. While his fellow theologians believed that God a static entity who existed in a perfect realm, Eckhart said that God, who Eckhart described as "delicious" was continually re-creating the universe in the present.

Almost everything Eckhart taught and believed fell outside traditional church theology. He saw God in everyone and everything. The omnipresence of God paled in comparison to doctrine. "Is this not a holy trinity: the firmament, the Earth, and our bodies? And is it not an act of worship to hold a child or tip a cup? Is communion not seeking your lover's soul before accepting anything offered by a priest?"

Eckhart also debunked the value of asceticism. "Asceticism is not of great importance. There is a better way to treat your passions than to heap on them practices which so often reveal a great ego and create more rather than less self-consciousness. And that is to put on a bridle of love. The person who has done this will travel much farther than all those who practice mortification put together." Spirituality, he believed, could not be learned by fleeing from the world and from people or living in solitary splendor without the people that God so loved. Why not accept the pleasure associated with life?

Eckhart's portrait of a generous, loving God endeared him to many people of his age who saw God as a lover rather than as a strict taskmaster. His popularity got him into trouble with the archbishop of Cologne who charged him with heresy, the only medieval theologian to be so charged. He had the good fortune to die before he had to face the Inquisition.

While popes blessed Thomas Acquinas with the title "angelic doctor," the mystic, poet, musician, playwright, scientist, healer, and visionary abbess Hildegard of Bingen (1098–1179) barely made it into the annals of sainthood. Like other great medieval abbesses, Hildegard's considerable gifts flourished in the medieval center of learning– the monastery. When universities supplanted monasteries as educational establishments, women lost their opportunity for higher education. By 1231, the University of Paris banned women students. Other universities followed suit.

Hildegard believed that the Earth was filled with a cosmic force of good that enfolded it in greenness and life rather than the realm of Satan. In this world, all natural things were sacred: animals, trees, plants, and grass. In her words, "All living creatures are sparks from the radiation of God's brilliance emerging from God like the rays of the sun," and "the truly holy person welcomes all that is earthly."

Hildegard described the unity of all living things with God. "Humanity, take a good look at yourself. Inside, you've got heaven and earth and all of creation. You are a world; everything is hidden in you."

In her final theological work, *The Book of Divine Works* (1174), Hildegarde portrayed the personification of divine love as a strong woman wearing a gold band around her head announcing, "I am the supreme and fiery force who sets all living sparks. I have ordered the cosmos rightly. But I am also the fiery life and divine essence: I blaze above the beauty of the fields, I shine in the waters, I burn with the sun, the moon, and the stars."

In a time of rigid gender roles, Hildegard regularly corresponded with abbots, statespeople, and popes. Four hundred of her letters survive. She also went on preaching tours, delivering homilies to both clerics and members of the laity.

Hildegarde was and is a woman for all seasons. In addition to writing and preaching, she also healed petitioners through holistic medicine. Her contemporaries recognized her holiness and genius. Adherents offered her name for canonization four times. Unlike the swift canonization of two of her correspondents, Bernard of Clairvaux and Thomas Becket, Hildegard was not officially canonized until 2012. Even then, her canonization was a left-handed compliment made by Benedict XVI, who labeled it an equivalent canonization since she had been regarded as a saint for centuries.

There were, of course, many other women who should also have been canonized. Their names and deeds have been lost to us. Unfortunately, women who stepped outside of the boundaries set by the churchmen were usually regarded as heretics instead of saints. Such was the case of both Milita of Monte-Meato and Julieta of Florence, who were described as daughters of iniquity rather than as holy women.

> *"Milita, like another Martha, feigned anxiety about the state of repair of the cathedral roof, while Julieta, like Mary, pretended to embrace the contemplative life. Many of the ladies of our city and their relations began to respect them as very holy women. So, as*

beloved enemies or highly virulent germs these snakes in the grass drew many men and women into the labyrinth of their heresy under the pretext of piety" (Moore, 2012).

Some of my contemporaries who have lived through the Viet Nam war, race riots, ethnic cleansing, two invasions of Iraq and one of Afghanistan, the Russian invasion of Ukraine, and the senseless violence in Gaza and Israel have often commented to me that the medieval era was a violent time when "everyone" acted violently. They claimed that twenty-first century people should not apply modern standards of behavior to the past despite the fact that Christians have always had the gospel of Jesus as their gold standard and that there were always others like Meister Eckhart and Hildegarde who did not act with violence or prejudice. They often console themselves with the idea that history progresses in a linear manner from a time of less civilization to more civilization, with the twenty-first century American society being the highest level of society the world has ever seen. Seen in a rosy glow of materialistic progress, we are, indeed, an advanced society while the thirteenth century was still in learning mode.

Published in 2021, the book *The Dawn of Everything,* by David Graeber and David Wengrow proposed that humans do not progress in a linear fashion from more violent, less civilized to more civilized, less violent societies. Instead, the authors have indicated that some of the world's earliest cities were not ruled by warriors seeking to expand their territory and wealth. Instead, their citizens lived in egalitarian peace without violent, capricious, and rapacious rulers taxing and repressing them or religious zealots trying to impose unity.

Thus, the violence of the Middle Ages was neither endemic nor all-pervasive any more than it is in the twenty-first century. Many of the residents of southern France were loath to participate in a religious crusade against their neighbors. Lords and ladies employed those deemed heretics in their courts and as tutors to their children. When the bishop of Toulouse demanded to know why a local knight was protecting the enemies of the church, the knight replied, "We have been brought upside-by-side with them. Our closest kinsmen are among them. Every day we see them living worthy and honorable lives in our midst" (Moore, 2012). Unlike the crusading clerics, the non-ordained recognized the bonds of love that joined them together with the church-designated heretics.

In 2018, I visited Marburg, Germany, the home of Conrad the Inquisitor and Elizabeth of Hungary. Thousand-year-old churches within the city testified to the concept of the fortress church. Huge rood screens separated the clergy from the people. Whatever sacred rites the priests engaged in, they performed behind the screen with its one small opening at the top where the priest proclaimed the gospel in Latin, a language the people could not understand. There were also no pews, so the people were left to muddle around in the nave, talking or praying and essentially ignoring what was going on behind the screen. It is no wonder that when the priest reappeared from behind the screen with the host and announced, "Hoc est corpus meum," (This is my body) some people jokingly referred to what the twentieth century would later declare the summit of Catholic worship as "Hocus pocus."

Because of the violence they inspired against their neighbors, Albert the Great, Anselm of Canterbury, Anthony of Padua, Thomas Acquinas, Thomas Beckett, Vincent Ferrer, Dominic Guzman, Louis IX, Raymond of Penafort should not be regarded as saints.

I do not find the founders of religious orders to be particularly worthy of canonization based upon the money and effort their orders make to have them canonized, especially when their behavior leads much to be desired. I leave it to the readers to make up their own minds.

Followers of the Way of Jesus
Hildegarde of Bingen
Meister Eckhart

Chapter 8:
REVOLT

"A civilization which leaves so large a number of its
participants unsatisfied and drives them to revolt neither has
nor deserves the prospect of a lasting existence."

Sigmund Freud

There were five ethnic parishes in my working-class neighborhood in Philadelphia—all within a one-mile radius. Each was founded in the late 1800s or early 1900s to serve the influx of immigrants into what was then a vibrant manufacturing area flush with jobs and opportunities. While the parishes and their schools were segregated according to ethnicity, people of all ethnic backgrounds lived together as neighbors on the area's many small streets. Living in close proximity to one another often led to love. People who might have been mortal enemies in Europe married each other in their new country.

Somewhere in the streets of the neighborhood, my working-class Irish American maternal grandmother met my bootlegger Polish immigrant grandfather. They were married in 1924 against the expressed wishes of both sets of parents who clearly found their respective child's prospective mate and their families less than satisfactory. Six years later, the nuns at the Irish parish to which my grandmother and her family of origin belonged refused to enroll my aunt, who bore a Polish surname, in the parish school. Nana, a scrappy woman who was not in awe of religious authority, marched over to the rectory, demanded to see the pastor, and insisted that my aunt be enrolled because she was half Irish. I am not sure if the pastor feared my tough grandma or if he saw the wisdom of her argument, but he allowed my aunt with the Polish surname to attend first grade in the

Irish parish.

Falling in love outside of one's faith brought another set of problems. During the same 1920s era that brought my maternal grandparents together, a family friend named Agnes met a young Protestant man and wanted to marry him. Her family was aghast that she would even consider marrying outside of her faith and insisted that she break the engagement. A dutiful Irish daughter, Agnes put aside her fiancé and settled upon an approved Irish Catholic man named Lyons who drank and beat her and their son. While the Protestant man became a prosperous shopkeeper who made a decent life for his family, Agnes found herself penniless when the drunkard who beat both her and her son left the marriage. The family that was so concerned about the state of her soul had little concern for the life of Agnes and her child. She had made her bed, they said, and now she needed to lie in it. Agnes and her son lived in heatless rooms and begged for food during the Depression with little to no help from her pious family.

Agnes's son dropped out of school at age fourteen to support them. When World War II broke out, he enlisted in the army despite the fact that could have gotten a deferment because he was the sole support of his mother. He told Agnes that if he died, she could live on his veteran benefits.

Unfortunately, Sergeant Frank Lyons did, indeed, die on July 7, 1944, somewhere among the hedgerows in Normandy a month after he landed in France on D Day. His mother decided to have him buried "where he fell," she said. When I was around thirteen, I promised Agnes with all the fervor of my outraged youth that when I grew up, I would put a flower on Frank's grave. In October of 2019, I stood in the carefully tended green grass by her beloved son's grave that looked out over the deep blue of the English Channel over which he had sailed on the fateful June night seventy-five years earlier. I had finally fulfilled my promise to Agnes.

Despite the dreadful events in her life, Agnes was a role model for forgiveness, patience, understanding, and wisdom—a quintessential Christian. She never complained, nor was she ever bitter. Agnes taught me about the virtue of patience. Her life also served as a pointed example of the toxic effects of prejudice. How could a violent Irish Catholic drunk be more acceptable to her family than a decent and loving Protestant? The answer to this question harked back to the Protestant Reformation.

Catholics call the Reformation the Protestant Revolt as if those who insisted that institution remedy their concerns were mindless rebels rather than reformers. European serfs are often portrayed as humble folk with little to no agency who were steamrolled by their betters into abject submission. Contrary to that popular understanding, peasants did not blindly accept all pronouncements from the pulpits of their priests, bishops, and the pope. In fact, they regularly poked fun at those who understood themselves to be a stand-in for God. Medieval jingles like "No penny, no Pater Noster" and "As soon as the coffer rings, the soul from purgatory is sprung" reflected their exasperation with the greed of the clergy.

When clerical power removed their voices from participating in the liturgy and put the Eucharist behind a rood screen, personal piety such as honoring saints and relics and devotion to Mary rather than public worship became their religion. Church attendance was so lax that Innocent III (1161–1216) had to order all believers to confess their sins and receive Communion at least once a year under penalty of mortal sin. Common folk sought guidance from women hermits who had shut themselves up in small cells adjacent to local churches. Self-flagellates marched through villages repenting for their sins, eschewing the services of clergy. Confraternities of lay people extended charity to the poor, founded hospitals, or comforted prisoners enroute to execution. Itinerant preachers condemned church wealth.

After the crusades, two calamities befell the late Middle Ages. Five generations of kings tore apart France and England during the Hundred Year's War (1337–1453), and the Black Death (1346–1352) killed 30 to 60 percent of the world's population. The people observed that the church and their own personal prayers for deliverance were powerless to contain these disasters. Faith declined.

The decrease in the number of workers caused wages to rise and freed the serfs from the estates of their lords. Wages in England increased by forty percent between 1340 and 1360. As wages outpaced prices, the standard of living improved. The seeds of the middle class were born in the aftermath of the calamitous plague. The moveable press invented in 1436 revolutionized knowledge as the printed word became available to more people, thus increasing literacy. War, plague, a revolutionary invention, and religious dissatisfaction rather than deliberate disobedience moved Europe toward religious revolt and reformation.

The Reformation succeeded where the previous attempts at transformation had failed. The invention of the printing press should not be underestimated. This invention caused the church to lose its monopoly on the interpretation of scripture as increasing numbers of people read the Bible and noted the discrepancy between the words of Jesus and the actions of the institution and behavior of the clergy.

A variety of saints emerged from these tumultuous times.

John Wycliff (1320–1384) and Joan of Arc (1412–1431) stand at different ends of the catastrophe known as the Hundred Years' War. John, a heretic, and Joan, a saint, held very different opinions about the morality of an armed conflict aimed at destroying one's fellow human beings. Unlike Joan, who proudly rode into battle to reclaim territory for her king, Wycliff believed that rulers who resort to war lacked grace. While both John and Joan lived in a world of intense factions, Wycliff rejected violence, regarding it as a lack of both charity and justice. He was regarded as a heretic in his own time, and he remains one in ours. Joan, on the other hand, stands in a long line of canonized saints who accepted and engaged in violence against their fellow human beings.

Like John Wycliff, there were always those who preached against the waging of war as they followed the directives of the Prince of Peace. Wycliff and his followers, the Lollards, whom Catholics described as idlers and hypocrites, believed that all actions should be governed by Jesus' law of love. Joan's followers, on the other hand, pillaged cities and burned down people's homes.

Joan was a fearless and confident young woman who firmly believed that God had chosen her personally to save France from the English. To her, the visitation of Saints Catherine, Margaret, and Michael confirmed the holiness and righteousness of her intent. Thus, it was allegedly God, and not patriotism, that led her to shed the blood of her fellow Christians.

While the generals were laughing themselves silly over the military aspirations of a peasant girl, Joan managed to have herself dressed in men's armor and installed at the head of an army where she led hardened men into battle that resulted in a string of victories, earning her the title "Maid of Orleans." The laughing of the French generals eventually turned to admiration. Joan the Maid was a better soldier and strategist than they were. She succeeded in having the dauphin crowned king and stood beside him at his coronation dressed in full armor, exuding an invincibility that women were not supposed to have. Her victories and the crowning of the dauphin would come at great personal cost. The French generals were not happy with her attitude, her dress, and her military prowess, all of which they attributed to entities other than the saints in heaven.

Like the French, the English were astonished by Joan's military and leadership abilities. They also thought she was possessed by Satan and were determined to put an end to her escapades. With the help of the French Burgundians, they captured Joan and concocted a nonsensical charge of witchcraft. Her trial before English bishops was, like all the trials of the church inquisitors, a sham. Joan, the inspirational battle hero who saved France, was denied a warrior's death in battle. Instead, she was unceremoniously burned at the stake as a witch on the orders of the British bishops.

The French's embarrassment at her military success must have been acute because Joan had no cult following after her death. No clerics demanded her instant canonization. In fact, she was never glorified as a holy woman and had no miracles attributed to her until five hundred years after her death. Despite the fact that Joan served the state and not the church, Pope Benedict XV canonized Joan in 1920 in the papal bull, *Divina disponente*, calling her "a most brilliant shining light of the church triumphant" (Benedict XV, 1920).

Joan of Arc is truly an amazing historical character whose exploits in battle and deep patriotism should be honored by her fellow French and by all who admire military valor. She is a paragon of courage and patriotism. Although Joan is a hero and a patriot, she is not a saint. Warfare should not be canonized. Those who lead armies into battle are members of an army, not shining lights of the church or representatives of the Prince of Peace. In reply to one of her supporters at her trial who asked, "Do you see the hand of God in all of this?" the answer should have been "no." God does not play favorites and would not support the French over the English in a bloody, territorial war that lasted a hundred years and killed tens of thousands of people. It is human beings who claim the power of God and claim to speak in the name of the divine who are the architects of war. God has nothing to do with it.

John Wycliff was not just a pacifist. Unfortunately, he had many other ideas that the church declared an anathema. Like many reformers, Wycliff rejected the greed of the clergy. He condemned the adoration of saints as idolatrous and declared that there was no scriptural basis for fasting, oaths, pilgrimages, and prayers for the dead, a major clerical fundraising enterprise. He also rejected the recently declared doctrine of transubstantiation. For Wycliff, the priesthood was common to all believers and conferred no special spiritual or social privilege. He condemned the excesses of cathedrals and vast sums spent upon art and attracted the disapprobation of his fellow clerics by insisting that the church had no right to interfere with the government of England.

During his life, English nobles protected him from the Inquisition. Wycliff, the apostle of peace, died in 1384 and rested undisturbed in his grave for thirty-one years until the long and vengeful arm of the church finally caught up with him. In a fit of pique, the Council of Constance (1414–1418) declared him a heretic, dug up and burned his body, and dumped his ashes into the Thames.

This post-mortem auto da fe stemmed from the council's treatment of the Bohemian priest Jan Hus (1372–1415), who had adopted views very similar to Wycliff's. Hus was a Czech priest and university professor who addressed the selling of indulgences for clerical profit and publicly shared Wycliff's opinion that both the clergy and the laity had equal status in the church. Like Wycliff, Hus eschewed violence and advised the pope and the bishops to pray for their enemies and bless them rather than taking up arms against them. Like many learned theologians of the time, Hus repudiated the newly promulgated doctrine of transubstantiation, a mystery that even modern people have trouble understanding. Hus was excommunicated and forbidden to preach or teach, directives his conscience impelled him to ignore.

Although Hus was guaranteed safe passage to the Council of Constance to explain his positions, the vested and mitered churchmen arrested him and demanded that he recant. Hus responded, "I would not for a chapel of gold retreat from the truth."

After being held prisoner in various Dominican and Franciscan monasteries by the bishops, Hus was given a fraudulent trial where he was forbidden to present witnesses for his defense. Hus had one humble request— that his prosecutors use scripture to prove where he was wrong. In reply, the churchmen turned Hus over to the secular authorities for execution declaring that God's church could do nothing more with him. As Hus knelt to pray before he was set afire, he asked God to bless the men who issued his writ of execution. Like Wycliff, Hus is regarded as a heretic.

Although Jesus is called the "Prince of Peace," pacifism was and remains an anomaly in the Christian faith. Churchmen have been more likely to bless rather than condemn war and many saints engaged in mental and moral gymnastics to strong-arm God into sanctioning wars against unbelievers. Consequently, true Christian pacifist saints have been rare.

Like John Wycliff and Jan Hus, Erasmus of Rotterdam (1466–1536), was a prophet of peace whose work was never recognized by the church. Unlike his fellow churchmen whose feet rushed to shed the innocent blood of heretics and unbelievers, Erasmus tried mightily to foster goodwill and defuse potential conflicts. He repudiated the commonly trod pathways of desolation and destruction, insisting that even in a just war, terrible and unacceptable things happen to ordinary people on both sides of the battle: the land of the peasants is plundered causing mass starvation, children are left orphans, parents are left in lifelong desolation by the deaths of their children, and the elderly are left without any means of support.

In *The Complaint of Peace*, Erasmus wrote, "If there is any human activity which should be approached with caution, or rather be avoided by all possible means, resisted, and shunned, that act is war. There is nothing more wicked, more disastrous, more destructive, more hateful, and more unworthy of a Christian."

Erasmus believed that religious belief should not be coerced, not by the Catholic Church nor by the developing Protestant sects. He criticized the imperial policy of Spain which forcibly converted native peoples under threat of death in the newly discovered Americas and shared his concerns with the son of Christopher Columbus. In a 1526 spoof that poked fun at the church's insistence on following human-made laws like not eating meat on Friday while ignoring the command of love in the gospels, Erasmus pointed out what should have been obvious. The invading Europeans would gain far more by seeking fellowship with the Indigenous people of the Americas than they would ever gain by extortion and enslavement. Erasmus could not stop the armor-clad feet of soldiers from marching across Europe and into the jungles of Central and South America. For the Christian colonists, it was easier to believe the worst about those designated the enemy and kill or enslave them.

His writings fell afoul of the church. Unlike orthodox believers, Erasmus believed that people had the freedom to choose their own salvation. As the printing press flooded Europe with copies of the Bible, Erasmus claimed that the authority to interpret scripture was based upon a consensus of believers and not upon the opinion of the clergy. It should be read, he insisted, with peace rather than dogma in mind. Observing the superstitious practices of the day, he said that external acts of piety and attendance at church ceremonies were not an exercise in genuine religion. God, he wrote, has little need of lighted candles, litanies to the saints, or the repetition of prayer, all of which he declared were more superstitious than substantive. Religion, in fact, was simple. "If we acknowledge Christ as our authority, and if he is love, if he taught nothing and handed down nothing but love and peace, well, let us declare him, not by wearing his name and badge, but in our deeds and love" (quoted in Dallimayr, 2006).

Uber Catholics denounced Erasmus, calling him a traitor to the gospel and an influencer of Martin Luther with whom he agreed on many of the latter's ninety-five theses. Erasmus wrote to the Dutch pope Adrian VI encouraging reconciliation with Luther and his followers. Do not threaten people with mortal sin for not following church rules. Let the laity drink from the chalice. Allow priests to marry.

The churchmen refused to walk in the pathways of peace or find peace in the scripture they acknowledged as the word of God. Instead, their way to God was littered with the dead bodies of unbelievers and dissenters. When Erasmus pointed out that the churchmen had turned back justice and caused truth to go into a freefall, his work was placed in the *Index of Forbidden Books*.

The man who followed the example of the Prince of Peace and encouraged believers to actively practice the ways of peace until war became the anomaly was never canonized a saint. The modern world might look very different if the church had canonized the irenic theology of John Wycliff, Jan Hus, and Erasmus instead of condemning them.

The peaceful path of Erasmus differed sharply from that of his friend and colleague, Thomas More (1478–1535), who lost his head for refusing to acknowledge Henry VIII as the head of the Church of England.

More is portrayed as a martyr to conscience and is honored as both a man of integrity and a saint. He was canonized in 1935, during a time when the powerful states of Russia and Germany threatened the sovereign powers of Europe. The world had watched in horror as the "Godless" power of Communism dismantled the Orthodox Church and punished believers in Russia. More and his unbreakable conscience were perceived as a form of resistance against an intolerant government, a role model for the primacy of conscience and religious freedom—hence his canonization four hundred years after his death. His book *Utopia* is regarded as a testimony to religious freedom.

However, More as Lord Chancellor of England, was the representative of the all- powerful state. When the pope bestowed the title of Defender of the Faith upon Henry VIII prior to his marriage to Anne Boleyn, there was no room for religious dissenters in Catholic England and More willingly enforced English law against prisoners of conscience. This included the torture and execution of heretics. More found these practices lawful and necessary because the "scabbed heretics" needed to be excised from the "clean flock" (Miles, 1965). When a man was burned to death under his aegis, More commented, "There was never a wretch...better worthy to be burned" (Miles).

Although More declared himself to be fair and just, his justice did not extend to the heretics whom he believed had no right to confront their accusers. Nor would he acknowledge the possibility that accusations of heresy could be made out of personal malice. Trials, whatever their outcome, were necessary to prevent the spread of heresy. More was perfectly willing to sacrifice the life of an innocent person unjustly accused of heresy because he believed it impossible to make a law where no innocent person could ever be harmed.

It is rare to see the negative side of the great intellectual and Catholic apologist Thomas More, for whom high schools, colleges, and societies are named. Yet More, like so many of the canonized, eagerly participated in acts that deprived his fellow English citizens of their livelihood and their lives because of a difference in belief. At least four people were burned to death under his administration as Lord Chancellor of England. He was instrumental in having copies of William Tyndale's forbidden English translation of the New Testament burned. *Utopia* was just a stop along the line of his thought, one he obviously repudiated when he sent prisoners of conscience to their deaths.

Apologists claim that More was a man of his time and therefore unable to extricate himself from behaving in a cruel and inhumane manner. There were those, however, who recognized the danger of engaging in the persecution of one's fellow human beings. They refused to use the intemperate and vituperative language that More regularly employed in his diatribes against heretics, whom he confessed to his friend Erasmus that he hated. It is surely a wonder that More and Erasmus were friends. Unlike More, Erasmus refused to engage in ad hominem attacks against those with whom he disagreed.

When More's friend John Colet, the Dean of St. Paul's, was asked to advise his fellow bishops on how to treat the Lollards (followers of Wycliff), he responded that the only heresy they needed to worry about was in themselves. When More's fellow solicitor Christopher St. Germaine remarked that he didn't know a single heretic in the land who required punishment, More fiercely challenged him with scathing essays repeatedly debunking him and his stance.

More called William Tyndale (1494–1530), a theologian who translated the Bible into English, a crime punishable by death, a "beast" and "the captain of our English heretics" who "like all heretics, must be destroyed." (Quoted in Miles, 1965) Tyndale, like More, was executed for following his conscience. Tyndale was not rewarded with a saint's halo for having an equally unbreakable conscience.

Watching the conflagration called the Inquisition grip Europe, Tyndale, who had a wit as great as More's, wrote that the clergy "love you so well that they would rather burn you than have fellowship with Christ" (Pineas, 1963). About More's insistence on the existence of purgatory, Tyndale claimed that the clergy were not content with ruling over the living and so they created purgatory to rule over the dead. While More defended the veneration of relics, Tyndale accused More of worshiping the cardinal's hat.

In the play "A Man for All Seasons," playwright Robert Bolt portrays the English bishops and their flocks as traitors to the faith and willing dupes of a clearly insane Henry VIII. Only Thomas More, it seemed, had the backbone to stand up for his principles and defend his faith. However, even as he languished in prison, More continued to write diatribes against those he regarded as heretics, insisting that they needed to be punished. In the end, More was a hypocrite, a funny and erudite one, but a hypocrite nevertheless. In More's universe, the only worthy conscience was his own.

While some have heard of Erasmus, few today recognize the names of Colet, St. Germaine, or Tyndale. Instead, it is More, the persecutor and heretic hater whose name and deeds have been recognized and admired by later generations of Catholics as they too reject any law that they claim violates their conscience. Like More, they deny the same freedom of conscience to others.

The people who disagreed with More and lost their heads were not evil. If More had followed the script in the parable of the Prodigal Son, he would have understood that there was no limit to the love of God and refused to send people to their deaths. Then he would have been a true hero, a man of integrity, a martyr for the faith as taught by Jesus, where charity and love always prevail and a loving God forgives all sin. If he had taken Paul to heart, he would have realized that only God can judge. Instead, he repudiated the word of God and resorted to the violence of the state to enforce a secular law that clearly violated the conscience of dissenters. More was smart and he was brave, but he was hardly a staunch supporter of conscience or a saint.

A man of sterling character, Bishop John Fisher (1469–1535) of England agreed with the reformers' low estimation of the clergy. After visiting Rome, he found his fellow clergymen offering themselves up to luxury and lust rather than to prayer and fasting. Yet he insisted that the pope who emerged from and led this mess was the successor to St. Peter and the representative of Jesus on Earth.

Like More, Fisher is regarded as a prisoner of conscience who was martyred for refusing to acknowledge Henry VIII as head of the Church of England. However, Fisher participated in activities that would be regarded as traitorous even by people in the twenty-first century. He betrayed his country by negotiating with an agent of a foreign nation to invade his country and depose its reigning monarch. While Fisher might have been a good Catholic, he was a traitor and not a martyr or a saint.

The machinations against the English crown by Catholics would continue during the reign of Henry's daughter, Elizabeth I (1533–1603).

The papal party in Rome refused to entertain the idea that monarchs and their citizens could freely choose not to follow the tenets of the Roman faith. Twelve years after Elizabeth had ascended to the throne, the fanatic St. Pius V (1504–1572), wrote that God (himself) has chosen the Roman pontiff to be the sole ruler over people and kingdoms. More importantly, the spectacle of a woman as the head of Church of England raised his manly, clerical hackles. Pius excommunicated Elizabeth and released her subjects from allegiance to her, claiming that she had "seized the crown and monstrously usurped the place of supreme head of the church in all England." Pius declared that his excommunication "deprived her of her pretend title" (Coffey, 2020). Pius regarded Elizabeth's cousin, the Catholic Mary Stuart, Queen of Scotland (1542-1587) as the legitimate ruler of England. Three successive popes agreed with him. They encouraged Elizabeth's assassination by sponsoring armed rebellions led by English Catholics in 1571, 1583, and 1586, and a foreign invasion in 1588 to accomplish the goal of reinstating Roman Catholicism in England.

Mary Stuart is often portrayed as a sympathetic figure who was unjustly denied the rightful throne of England by evil Protestants, including her cousin Elizabeth. It was Mary, the legitimate great-granddaughter of Henry VII who should have been the queen many Catholics believed. The reality is, of course, vastly more complicated. A wily politician, Mary had laid claim to the English throne in her marriage contract with the future king of France. Under this contract, if she were to predecease her French husband, he would inherit the throne of England. During her marriages to Francis II of France and later her Scottish Stuart cousin, Henry, Mary never repudiated her claim to the English throne, much to Elizabeth's chagrin. When Mary sought Elizabeth's protection after Protestants removed her from the throne of Scotland, the wary Elizabeth kept her confined in a series of castles for nineteen years. Mary was beheaded for treason only after she approved of the papal plan to have the Spain invade England in 1588 and assassinate her cousin Elizabeth.

The extravagant amount of money and lives and goodwill squandered on a fool's errand to depose Elizabeth splintered the English church and English society. It drove the English farther away from the Roman fold and changed Elizabeth's policy of uneasy tolerance toward Catholics to one of arrest and execution of some Catholics as traitors to the realm. Popes Pius V, Gregory XIII and Sixtus V contributed to the growing animosity by extending Elizabeth's excommunication to English citizens who refused to repudiate her sovereignty. This placed English Catholics in the precarious position of having to choose loyalty either to the pope or to their queen. The writ of excommunication was not without ramifications for future generations of both Catholics and Protestants, the later who feared, with some justification, that Catholics were more loyal to the pope than they were to their country. This untenable situation eventually led to the torture and deaths of one hundred and eighty-nine Catholics for treason. The Catholic Church regards these unfortunates as saints and martyrs for the faith without acknowledging the three hundred Protestant souls who lost their lives for their religious faith during the reign of Elizabeth's predecessor, the Catholic Mary I.

Catholic machinations against the English throne continued into the reign of Elizabeth's successor, James I, the son of Mary Stuart. In 1605, Catholic conspirators planned to blow up the House of Lords and assassinate the Protestant James in what is known as the Gunpowder Plot.

Despite Catholic opposition to Elizabeth I, she was neither an iconoclast nor a religious reformer. Contrary to the more radical members of her Parliament, she did not advocate the removal of traditional Catholic trappings from what become Anglican churches. Unlike the stark simplicity of reform churches, Anglican churches often look comfortably Catholic complete with stained glass windows, shrines devoted to Mary and the saints, votive candles, and incense. Priests and bishops wear the same type of vestments that Catholic priests wear. There also remains a striking similarity between the Anglican and Roman Catholic liturgies, sometimes to the point that the differences are unrecognizable. The barrier that has divided the two denominations for the last six centuries has been the power and status of the pope. Upon the conscience of this morally compromised office should lie the deaths of both the Catholic and Protestant martyrs.

For reasons of her own, Elizabeth had enough personal power not to use her body as a bartering tool, much to the chagrin of her contemporaries and even of some modern historians, who have written that she contributed to her country's unrest by refusing to marry and produce an heir. Elizabeth I had too much respect for herself and the inviolability of her own body, which she used at her own will and not at the will of a male relative. While Elizabeth might or might not have been the "Virgin Queen," her sexual life belonged to her and not to the male members of her family or to the church.

The church did, however, chose to own and control the bodies of women who gathered together in convents and lived in religious orders.

Why did the Catholic Church canonize Catherine of Siena (1347–1380) and Teresa of Avila (1515–1582), perennial favorites of both men and women? Why were they given the august title Doctor of the Church? Clearly both women were intelligent. Both stood up to contemporary ecclesiastical and secular powers and named the evil that existed in the church. There were, however, other women who were equally as intelligent, wrote equally compelling books, and also stood up to the powers of the time. One such woman was Marguerite Porete, who wrote a book entitled *The Mirror of the Simple Soul* in the 1290s. Unlike Catherine and Teresa, Marguerite was burned at the stake by the Inquisition. Why?

Marguerite Porete was one of very few medieval women authors. She had the temerity to write about God in old French and not in Latin, the language God seemed to require when human beings spoke about the Divine. In 1310, the Inquisition declared her book heretical for saying the God is love.

Marguerite was not cowed by the powers of the Inquisition. Not only did she refuse to recant, but she also refused to take an oath that was necessary to begin the proceedings against her. Exasperated by her obduracy, the inquisitor described her with the worst epithet he could muster—a fake woman!

The woman who dared to live in community caring for the downtrodden and who wrote that God is love was burned at the stake. The people of Paris were moved by her serenity as she approached her funeral pyre.

For their part, Catherine and Teresa's warped sense of divine love spurred them to engage in severe and life-long self-mortification practices to make themselves pleasing to the all-male godhead. Teresa's circle of friends described her ongoing self-torture with admiration claiming that the love of God compelled her to martyr her body. Catherine starved herself to death at age 33. Today, we would label both women anorexic and masochists, qualities that are distinctively not admirable. Nor were they necessarily at the time. Marguerite Porete wrote that there was no value in gratuitous suffering for God. She paid for her opinion with her life.

Many twenty-first century women admire those like Catherine, Teresa, and other medieval mystics although these women could see their path to God only through pain and suffering expressed in the language of rape and personal annihilation. Their language teems with terms of sexual violence. Teresa described an angel causing exquisite internal pain by plunging a fire-tipped golden dart deep into her body. Catherine so wanted to suffer like Jesus that she claimed to have received the stigmata, wounds that only she, however, could see. She also believed that she was married to Jesus, who gave her a wedding ring composed of his foreskin.

The works of many women mystics are filled with descriptions of God and Jesus as assaulting their persons and piercing them with pain until their souls are annihilated. The only way they could feel the love of God was through pain. The language labeled as "mystical" includes phrases of agonizing things done to them by the male deity; they are "crushed by grace," "scourged by shame," "slapped with powerlessness." Like the canonized virgin martyrs in the early church who were burned, beheaded, broken, and blinded, the canonization of women like Catherine and Teresa has enshrined violence against women, making it holy and acceptable, worthy of emulation, even necessary to attain union with the divine. Holy women walled themselves off in tiny cells attached to churches, minimizing their wants, needs, and even their persons in order to please God. The best way to be was not to be. Those regarded as the holiest women were those who annihilated their very selves for God and, by extension, for the churchmen.

Teresa lived during a time when some twenty percent of well-to-do European women were forced into convents by fathers and elder brothers who declined to spend the family fortune on dowries for their unmarried female relatives (Hsia, 1988). These women lived not only in forced celibacy and childlessness, but they were also cloistered to protect their purity from, as Charles Borromeo worried, evil men. The vast majority of these women did not have a vocation. Their enforced cloister needed to be made bearable by comforts from home: food, servants, books, furniture, and visits from female friends. Reformers like Teresa repudiated these feminine "frivolities" and sought to further enclose and isolate her sisters, making them even more invisible to the world.

Both Catherine and Teresa were brilliant writers and theologians. Perhaps they were, indeed, holy, although their words and behavior indicate what twenty-first century people might regard as severe mental illness. Engaging in starvation and self-inflicted pain to earn the love of a male God is not behavior women should follow. Why would God, who is love, expect, and demand pain in return for love? The transformation of ego and self-interest into love is not the same as the annihilation of the self that God gifted to us. For it is in that self that God is expressed as love.

Teresa was regarded as a saint while she was still alive. When she died away from her residence, the convents began to fight over her remains, since relics would bring in a tidy sum to whoever actually entombed whatever was left of her. Her body was repeatedly disinterred, harvested for relics for clerics and nobles, and reburied. The body she tortured for God during life was repeatedly violated in death by churchmen anxious to make a profit.

There were other women who declined to render their fellow women religious invisible and whose spiritual direction did not include the infliction of physical pain. Angela Merici (1474–1540) founded the first teaching religious order of women, the Ursulines, in 1535. The group consisted of both married and unmarried women who lived according to simple rules written down by Merici. Unlike the Carmelites, who engaged in personal religious practices away from the perceived corruption of the world, the Ursulines wore no habit and lived, like Jesus, among the People of God, founding orphanages and schools for girls. Merici had the foresight or the experience to warn her sisters in her will about the unsavory behavior of some male confessors and religious. Angela was canonized as a saint in 1807.

There are, as always, better ways of honoring and modeling the love of the divine than physical punishment. Julian of Norwich (1343–1416), author of *Revelations of Divine Love*, was a female contemporary of Catherine. Unlike Catherine's vision of God as an abusive lover, Julian envisioned God as a loving Mother who forgave all sins. Julian, like Meister Eckhart and all great mystics, saw no difference between human beings and God. "We ought to rejoice that God dwells in our soul and our soul in God, so that between God and our soul there is nothing, but as though it were all God."

Although Julian accepted the church's belief in hell and purgatory, she believed in goodness rather than in punishment. Unlike many of her contemporaries, Julian did not heap blame upon Jews for the death of Jesus. In a prevailing worldview that saw heretics and Jews as agents of destruction and God as a vengeful warrior demanding purity of belief, Julian saw God as a mother giving birth to a good world where all "things shall be well."

Julian has neither been canonized nor awarded the title Doctor of the Church.

Catherine of Siena, Joan of Arc, Teresa of Avila, and Thomas More should not be regarded as saints because of the violence they perpetrated either against themselves or upon others.

John Fisher might have lived a saintly life, but he was not a martyr for the faith. He was a traitor to his country.

Followers of the Way of Jesus
Angela Merici
Erasmus
Jan Hus
Agnes Lyons
Julian of Norwich
Marguerite Porete
William Tyndale
John Wycliff

Both the Catholic and Protestants who were tortured and executed for their faith were, indeed, victims of conscience and should be honored with the title of martyr.

Chapter 9:
RETRENCHMENT

"The saints have never hesitated to break idols, destroy their temples, or legislate against pagan or heretical practices. The Church-without ever forcing anyone to believe or be baptized-has always recognized its right and duty to protect the faith of her children and to impede, whenever possible, the public exercise of false cults."

Society of St. Pius X (2012).

My Girl Scout leader was the epitome of tolerance. As a Catholic born in 1920s Glasgow which heartily despised its Catholic residents, Lillian McNamee personally experienced bitter religious persecution. She immigrated to New York before World War II and worked as a nanny in a wealthy home. There she met her future husband, Barney, the chauffeur of the estate, who was born in Belfast. He too had experienced religious persecution. The two married after the war and moved to Philadelphia.

Philadelphia in the 1960s was a city defined by race, class, and religion. While the elite attended fancy, pricey private schools both religious and secular, the white middle-and working-class Catholics attended local parish Catholic schools which were at that time tuition free. All of these schools were segregated. White Protestants, Jews, and Black people attended mostly segregated public schools. Racial relations were tense. Black families who moved into white areas were frequently burned out of their homes by their church-going white Catholic neighbors. White people fled en masse from neighborhoods when Black folks moved in. Although I attended church every Sunday throughout this time, I do not recall hearing one priest in our parish addressing the racist behavior playing out in real time in our neighborhoods and on television.

Because of her painful experience in Scotland, Mrs. McNamee rejected both racial and religious intolerance. Since all of our friends, families, and neighbors were Catholics, she frequently sought out experiences that would help to open up our very insular up-bringing. She took us swimming at a nearby YWCA, the Young Women's Christian Association. Our pastor, a man who always wore black vestments in constant mourning for the death of Jesus, demanded to know what a Catholic Girl Scout leader was doing bringing innocent girls into the YWCA, a place he regarded as a hotbed of Protestantism and a near occasion of serious sin. The visits to the YWCA stopped.

While our parish sponsored our troop, Protestant churches and synagogues sponsored troops as well. I suppose the pastor did not know that we all met up each summer at day camp where our religious and racial differences did not matter. All we wanted to do was have fun. It was at day camp that I first met Jewish and Protestant girls and got to know them as friends rather than as avowed enemies of the Catholic Church. Little by little, my parochial world opened up to allow different religious points of view.

The Catholic world was opening up as well. The 1965 encyclical *Dignitatus Humanae*, promulgated by Paul VI, maintained that while the Catholic Church was the one true faith, religious freedom is based upon the dignity of human beings. The declaration effectively broke the chains that secured the hearts and minds of Catholics to reflexive obedience to the pope and church doctrine. Catholics were finally able to think without guilt. The faithful began to question without fear of public condemnation or excommunication until John Paul II (1920—2005) began his long campaign of spiritual violence against those labeled cafeteria Catholics.

Dignitatus Humanae, however, came four hundred years too late for the Catholic Church. Had the church recognized the dignity of human beings in the early sixteenth century on the cusp of the Enlightenment, they might have maintained an uneasy unity and tens of thousands of people would not have perished in bitter religious wars. Unfortunately, the men who ruled as pope during that period refused to address their critics and chose instead to nest comfortably in the lap of empire and wealth. As a result, the Christian world fractured, and another set of Jesus wars decimated the Body of Christ.

The church's answer to the splintering of Christianity called the Reformation was the Council of Trent, whose first session was held in 1545, twenty-eight years after Luther nailed his ultimatum to the church door and eleven years after Henry VIII declared himself head of the Church of England. Although the council is often hailed as a testament to the reestablishment of orthodox Catholicism, the pope would never regain the power he had once wielded over Western Europe as powerful developing nation states and secular rulers now vied for supremacy.

Why would the popes wait so long to convene a council, giving the Reformation time to establish an alternate church and letting its new tenets sink into the hearts and minds of the formerly Catholic? The popes postponed the council because they worried more about challenges to their power than they did about the reformers who were dismantling the church before their eyes. All efforts at reform were officially rejected if they encroached upon papal power (Hsia, 1999)

When the council finally opened, a grand total of twenty-nine Italian bishops were in attendance. Although more bishops showed up at subsequent sessions, the ecclesiastical turnout at what is regarded as the crowning glory of Roman Catholicism in Europe never approached the five hundred and twenty bishops who attended the Council of Chalcedon in 451 C.E. No bishops from Poland, Hungary, or Switzerland attended. Germany, the origin of the Protestant revolt, sent no bishops even though the Catholic Holy Roman Emperor Charles V (1500–1558) hoped that the council would restore unity to his fractured kingdom. From start to finish the council was wracked by political ambition both within and without. Nations and bishops jockeyed for position, playing one side against the other. As always, there were Catholics who tried and failed to reach a compromise with the dissenters in order to spare Europe from more warfare.

Rome bristled with arguments against the heretics, their hearts hardened against dissent that challenged their power. Rather than engaging in any sort of reasoned discussion with members who had legitimate concerns, attendees at Trent ignored them and instead fixated upon the old Catholic standbys— original sin, and the sacraments. Much to the chagrin of the reformers and some of the bishops, the council also elevated the magisterium or the church's teaching authority as equal to scripture and tradition. Affirming the doctrine of transubstantiation, a doctrine that was first proclaimed in the twelfth century to solidify and extend clerical power, caused the definitive break between the warring factions of Christendom. By 1552, Ferdinand (1503–1564), who succeeded his brother Charles V (1500–1558) as Holy Roman Emperor, recognized Lutheranism as a legal religious faith in the Holy Roman Empire

The church was, however, in great need of reform. Although ordination was widespread, there were no seminaries until the latter part of the sixteenth century and few priests were educated or owned books. The hierarchy exercised no control over priests and there was no such thing as a background check to determine if the priest had a vocation or possessed virtue and character. The priesthood remained a coveted position since ordination protected priests from secular law and taxation.

The bishops also spent a considerable amount of council time protecting their wealth and status. Although most parish priests were poor, appointment to the curia or papal court depended upon wealth and connections and had little or nothing to do with holiness or even with God. Those members of wealthy or noble families who eventually became bishops and cardinals received the tonsure as young as seven. Charles Borromeo, the nephew of Pius IV, received it at age twelve. This simple haircut entitled its recipient to receive life-long benefices from parish churches or abbeys even if he never sought ordination, enriching both himself and his family.

In addition, nepotism and simony were accepted and expected practices within the hierarchy. Through the appointment of nephews to church office, the ecclesiasts' families insinuated themselves comfortably into the wealth of the church. Thus, appointment to a bishopric in a large city or to the Roman Curia was a bonanza for the tonsured, who shared what was often fabulous wealth with their family. Cardinals eagerly contended for the papal office, often to the point of violence. Once in position, they secured the money in their family coffers by appointing their nephews or the nephews of benefactors or friends to favorable positions. Borromeo was elevated to the office of cardinal by his uncle Pius IV at age twenty-one without being ordained a priest. While this papal act did not seem to cause a stir in ecclesiastical politics, Pius's subsequent elevation of a fourteen-year-old and an eighteen-year-old during a session of Trent led the Spanish ambassador and the Holy Roman Emperor Ferdinand to despair of any type of reform.

The accumulation of vast wealth by a small number of families with prominent ecclesiasts rendered reform moot. One family, the Borghese, exemplified the ongoing and blatant graft in the Italian church. Between 1605 and 1620, papal nephews acquired one hundred and fifty-eight offices and titles through purchase and gifts. With church money, the family purchased vast amounts of land around Rome and acquired a large number of books from the Vatican library. Their money and power rather than God influenced both secular and church politics.

Since the papacy remained one of the West's most coveted positions, the papal court remained in constant turmoil, especially when a pope died. Consequently, the power of the papacy was often challenged, as it was during the Conciliar movement in the fifteenth century, when some cardinals tried to make the power of councils superior to the power of popes. By the fifteenth and sixteen centuries, the political milieu within the College of Cardinals changed. When reformers from within challenged papal power, the popes packed the College of Cardinals with loyal family and friends whose wealth depended upon securing ongoing papal favor. Who would choose to find fault with the family's cash cow and disagree with the pope? Consequently, between 1415 and 1586, the number of cardinals rose from twenty-four to seventy.

Great wealth is attached to great sin. From a position acquired through stealth and wealth, greed and ambition, subterfuge and violence, the popes continued to regard themselves as the Vicars of Christ. With the phantom keys of Peter held securely in their dirty hands, popes alone defined the holy. They gave an imprimatur to the rapacious colonizers and ignorant missionaries who claimed the

Americas for European countries, augmenting the wealth of ecclesiastical and well as secular powerful families. Any pope or bishop who ruled within this paradigm cannot be regarded as a saint.

Pius V (1504–1572) is one of these misbegotten saints. Like Dominic Guzman, Pius never met an inquisition he did not like. When he was named Inquisitor General, he enjoyed watching interrogators question and then torture their terrified and often innocent victims. Charles Borromeo, who also liked to persecute heretics, admired him for his holiness and zeal and presented him as a papal candidate.

Pius's obsession for unity in the Papal States, of which he was both the political as well as spiritual leader, led him to banish Jews from all ecclesiastical domains (except for Rome and Ancona) lest they corrupt the faithful with their heretical beliefs. The man who liked to watch heretics tortured excommunicated Elizabeth of England for heresy. He retained the Society of Crusaders to protect the power of the Inquisition, which would soon extend into European colonies in the Americas and to India.

Pius strenuously opposed the Huguenots in France, removing French bishops he perceived as fraternizing with the enemy Protestants. Between three and ten thousand French Protestants were massacred on the eve of St. Bartholomew's Day in 1572 as Catholic nobles stirred up anti-Protestant sentiment against their non-Roman Catholic neighbors.

Pius is credited with implementing the reforms of the Council of Trent: standardizing the Roman rite of the Mass, instituting seminary training for priests, and reforming religious life. However, the framework of the papacy and the Italian curia negated the chance for any true church reform. The curia depended upon church wealth for their personal use, making them immune to reform. The office of Supreme Pontiff infused most men who would be pope with delusions of grandeur. The tonsure of little boys, the distribution of funds, the titles, and the nepotism continued.

When the still-Catholic Augustinian monk Martin Luther visited Rome in 1510, like the sainted John Fisher, he saw what other presumably faithful Catholic visitors saw and heard: worldly ecclesiasts living in splendor and immorality while disregarding the poor, selling indulgences for clerical profit, and engaging in nepotism and simony. While Fisher returned to England and was martyred for supporting the office of the reprobates he saw in Rome, Luther took them to task demanding to know why the pope with all his riches decided to build the grand basilica of St. Peter's with the money of the poor. Luther's question, one that deserved an answer, earned him a writ of excommunication and the title of "outlaw." The sainted men and women who pledged their undying loyalty to the pope and followed him without question, comment, or criticism while observing the excesses of pontiffs' violence, greed, wars, and executions need to have their canonization examined.

The interplay of the Reformation and the Council of Trent did change the church. In reaction to the Protestants who taught their faith to their children via catechisms, Charles Borromeo developed a Catholic catechism based upon the Protestant question and answer format. ("Who made you?" "God made me." "Why did God make me?") Like the reformers who had advocated for an educated clergy for centuries, the Council of Trent promoted the establishment of seminaries. While the Catholic Mass was still centered upon the Eucharist, priests, like their Protestant counterparts, now preached homilies. For the first time, priests were trained in the practice of hearing confessions.

Church architecture changed as well. Instead of people milling around in the nave as priests mumbled prayers in a foreign language behind a rood screen that blocked the assembly's view of the altar, churches now had pews where people sat down and listened to homilies.

Besides Pius V, there are other saints of the Catholic Reformation, all of whom were notable for trying to restore the church to its former glory. The Catholic Church regards Charles Borromeo (1538–1584) as the architect of the post- Tridentine church. For this, the church rewarded him with a saint's halo. On paper, Charles resembles a quintessential holy man. Like More and other sainted men before him, however, he did his best to strong-arm the faithful into religious submission.

A Catholic website mentioned that Charles was a "rare good fruit of nepotism." I am uncertain if his flock in Milan would share in this modern assessment. Uncle Pius IV made his untried and inexperienced nephew a cardinal at age twenty-two and the archbishop of Milan at twenty-eight.

Even in a world where children grew up quickly, governing a large and wealthy diocese at that tender age went right to Charles' head. When he arrived in Milan, a cosmopolitan city situated near trade routes that led into Protestant Germany, as a fresh young man of twenty-eight, one of the first things he did was divide the naves of churches into separate sections for women and men. He threatened to excommunicate all Catholics who participated in carnivals. Meanwhile, he led a procession of one thousand self-flagellants begging God to remove the plague, which he believed was spread by the incursion of "foreigners" who brought both disease and strange ideas, infecting his diocese. The governor found him arrogant and disrespectful, and canons from one of the churches in the diocese denied him entry due to what they believed was his unwarranted power mongering. When he tried to disband a group of Humiliati labeled by later Catholic sources as "dirty" and "immoral," a member of the group tried to assassinate him.

Empowered by his uncle, Charles was full of energy and ideas on how to combat and eliminate heretics, who he described as wolves in sheep's clothing angling to devour the faithful. He used the now refined skills of the diocesan bureaucracy to keep lists of heretical words, texts, and men. Like all tyrants before and after him, he banned books and urged pastors to inspect women for irregularities of faith.

Unlike Jesus, who advised his followers not to let their hearts be troubled, Borromeo opened his heart to the siren call of fear. In a Europe beset with waves of endemic disease, Borromeo, like More, described heresy as an infection that needed to be stamped out like the plague. The clerical definition of "heresy" as a contaminant of the faithful lasted until Vatican II issued a decree approving religious toleration in the early 1960s. The deeply held beliefs of More, Pius, and Borromeo created a xenophobic mindset in the Catholic Church that ruined the life of our family friend—and many others who had the misfortune of falling in love with people of the wrong faith—four hundred years later.

Charles was just one of many powerful men who recognized the importance of the newly invented printing press. He directed parishes to issue printed tickets of "good health" to those who made their confession. Each shriven person would then present the ticket to a priest before receiving communion. No ticket, no Body of Christ. The sick and the suffering also had to present their ticket of confessional purity in order to receive the services of the doctor. If a doctor dared to care for a non-confessed patient, Charles would excommunicate him. (Midura, 2021).

Charles' xenophobic policies included having all foreigners report to the metropolitan church to register their names and their itineraries. He once wrote to the king complaining about visiting German merchants, whose tendency to eat meat on Friday without permission was corrupting members of his diocese. (Midura).

While the Mennonites and the Society of Friends rededicated themselves to the Prince of Peace and refused to fight in wars, architects of the fortress church like Charles erected battlements that walled off believers from those now defined as "the other." Catholics and Protestants became official enemies instead of brothers and sisters in Christ. The bastion of faith protected by the church militant on Earth and the jealous warrior God in heaven actively repudiated all other faiths. The presence of heretics contributed to conspiracy-theory advocates like More and Borromeo. Myths of Catholic persecution and conspiracy theories have remained in place well into the twenty-first century.

Charles' policies necessitated an army of enforcers and spies, as do all inquisitions run by tyrants. The people in his diocese eventually lived in what can be described as a sixteenth-century police state where citizens and visitors needed to monitor their behavior lest they get reported to the Inquisition.

The sixteenth century also witnessed the beginning of a murderous campaign against women accused as witches. The church's belief that women were defective men, misbegotten and deficient as proclaimed by Thomas Aquinas had come home to roost in the minds of those who saw themselves as *imageo Christi*. Between 1517 and 1650, tens of thousands of women were murdered by both Catholics and Protestants as agents of Satan and heirs of Hell. These unfortunate women were accused, horribly tortured, tried, convicted, and executed by men. Male priests who perceived women as agents of insatiable lust were their judge and jury as well as companions on the route to the pyre or the gallows, praying loudly for their salvation, holding a crucifix up to their burning lips, and then calmly watching them die in agony.

Historians throughout the centuries have blamed the victims for their own persecution and death. The women were old or weird. They were midwives who might have engaged in birth control, abortion, or infanticide. They conjured spells and sold charms that cured people, just like relics and prayers to the saints did. There were just too many unmarried women around the towns who had time on their hands and, like juvenile delinquents, engaged in crime. Few historians place the blame where it should lie–at the feet of both the Catholic and Protestant clergy–whose low opinion of women enabled them to murder tens of thousands of innocents in over a century–long orgy of violence.

Charles Borromeo was on the cusp of witch-burnings and shared his fellow churchmen's low opinion of women. He and his entourage traveled to the cantons of Switzerland on what was described as a pastoral visit. There, the good saint had one hundred and fifty people arrested for witchcraft. Eleven women and one man were burned to death at the stake.

The Catholic seminary in Philadelphia is named for Charles Borromeo. This honor glosses over his role in the unjustified executions of twelve people and overlooks the numerous church leaders who did not engage in church-sanctioned torture and murder.

Charles might have saved the imperial church for another four hundred years by establishing seminaries and authoring a catechism, but he was a zealot and hardly a saint.

As the post-Reformation world changed the religious landscape for all Christians, the Catholic world had to shore up its losses and take measures to prevent further departures from its fold. Traveling preachers made the rounds of cities and villages preaching damnation and hellfire for those who strayed. Jesuits founded colleges to instruct young men in the faith, raising up generations of militant Catholic public servants and missionary priests. Upwardly mobile men had to produce certificates of confession and conformity to Catholic doctrine. There was now a catechism to be taught to children, including girls, to be trained in the faith so that they would not depart from it when exposed to Protestants and the ways of the world. The church became even more combative in its effort to impose discipline and regularity upon every aspect of Christian life. The church now required armies of men and women to both instruct and police the faithful.

While Borromeo and Teresa of Avila preferred to keep women in religious life enclosed, women in the sixteenth century who lived through the Reformation and its aftermath were exposed to the fervent need for religious education outside the stifling walls of the convent. It was they who carved out their role amid the constraints of the patriarchal society. Spurred on by orders like the Jesuits who were creating a literate and devout populace in reaction to Protestantism, these women developed their own ideas about ministry. Just as women mystics required priests to validate their visions, the founders of non-cloistered religious orders of nuns needed a male confessor-advisor to lend credence to their ideas.

In 1610, Jane Frances de Chantal (1572–1641) and Francis de Sales (1567–1622) founded the Visitation order, the first non-cloistered religious order for women. The founders shared a trauma bond. Jane, the mother of four young children, was widowed at age twenty-eight. Francis had turned to religious life after a paralyzing fear for his salvation caused him to fall into a deep despair that made him physically ill. Jane and Francis used their respective life experiences to establish an order that did not rely upon asceticism and physical self-punishment as a way to God. Their way to God was through education of the young.

Francis's recovery from despair made him gentle toward himself and others, including Jane, who replaced her earlier rigid spiritual advisor with Francis. The pair founded convents all over France, work Jane continued after the death of her companion in ministry. The two fast friends were buried together in the same cemetery.

Mary Ward (1585–1645), a contemporary of Jane and Francis, was not fortunate enough to find a priest mentor to help her found a religious order. The Jesuits initially supported her work and then roundly rejected her after she tried to base the rules for her new order on theirs, an act that caused detractors to disparagingly refer to her and her followers as "Jesuitesses." Although Mary felt called to religious life after a childhood filled with trauma (her home was burned down by Protestant zealots and her three uncles executed for their role in the Catholic Guy Fawkes plot to blow up Parliament), she was not attracted to an enclosed, contemplative life. Instead, she hoped to walk in the world as Jesus did, curing, teaching, and preaching. In 1606, she founded a religious order called the Congregation of Jesus. She established schools to educate girls insisting that there was no difference between men and women in their ability to accomplish great things. The men, even the Jesuits upon whom she based the rules for her order, strenuously disagreed.

With the fellow members of her order dismissed as "galloping girls" and "wandering nuns," Mary's independence from men led to accusations of heresy, temporary imprisonment in a convent by the Inquisition, and the suppression of her schools for girls.

When Mary died at age sixty from overwork, her friends secretly buried her lest her body be desecrated by her detractors. She was so admired for her work with the poor that Anglicans attended her funeral. She was later rehabilitated and declared venerable by Benedict XVI in 2009.

Unlike Mary Ward, who had no cheering gallery nudging her toward canonization, Jane Frances de Chantal and Francis de Sales were canonized in 1767 and 1665 respectively through the tireless efforts of the Visitation order which spent a fortune orchestrating the necessary church theater with the required miracles that led to the comparatively swift canonization of its founders.

There is no doubt that de Chantal and de Sales led exemplary lives in stark contrast to many of their fellow Catholics. On the other hand, there were large numbers of Catholics who lived just and holy lives just as they did but who were not canonized because they had no wealth or connections.

Did de Chantel and de Sales live lives of heroic holiness, or did they elect to live up to their baptismal promises and simply do what was required of them? De Sales was declared a Doctor of the Church and is regarded as the father of spiritual direction. Clearly a man of insight who had greatly suffered from despair, de Sales urged his directees to do everything in love and find God in carrying out the duties of each day, wise but hardly saintly or even original words. Both de Chantal and de Sales were dedicated workers, like other members of religious orders and like countless numbers of parents who brought their children up to be devout Catholics. Would they have been canonized without the fanfare provided by their supporters, who produced pious biographies and religious medals, and donated an extraordinary amount of money to further the cause of canonization?

The canonization of Ignatius Loyola (1491–1556), the founder of the Jesuit order, is another example of canonization by connivance. Like de Chantal and de Sales, Ignatius was not renowned for miracle-working either during or immediately after his life. Instead, he was known for his service to the church. His followers, however, wanted to put the Jesuits on equal footing with the Dominicans, whose founder, Dominic, had been canonized. The Jesuits created a figure worthy of canonization to solidify their historic role in the church.

Ignatius had no miracles under his saintly cincture until the first Jesuit cardinal visited Ignatius's tomb. Suddenly, it began to blossom with miracles, forming a cult of honor. Woodcuts and engravings crowned him with the halo of holiness. Jean Paul Rubens painted a gigantic picture over the high altar of a church with Ignatius shining in the light of the divine while casting out demons from among his fellow Jesuits. As a result, Ignatius was beatified in 1609 and canonized in 1622, sixty-six years after his death.

Phillip Neri (1506–1552) was canonized the same day in 1622 as Ignatius and another Jesuit, Francis Xavier. Neri, like de Sales, was also a kind man who eschewed atonement and ascetic practices as ways to God. Instead, he served the sick and poor of Rome, mainly as a layman who did not seek ordination until meeting Ignatius Loyola. After his ordination, he founded an order of secular priests who were dedicated to preaching and prayer. Without the miracles ascribed to him by his followers, would Philip have been enrolled in the list of saints?

Rosa of Lima (1586–1617), the first Catholic saint of the

Americas, was abused by her parents and forbidden to enter a convent. Like many abused children, Rosa developed a negative self-image. She chose to live alone in a tent infested with insects, wearing a chain around her waist, starving and beating herself until blood ran onto the floor in order to punish herself and please a jealous God. Describing her self-inflicted wounds as caresses from Jesus, Rosa, like her role models Catherine and Teresa, believed that Jesus was a jealous boyfriend who expected Rosa to punish herself for momentarily forgetting him while taking a brief respite from self-flagellation to read and eat. Her story is the stuff of sado-masochistic pornography. As the thirty-one-year-old lay dying, her Dominican biographer gloried in her protracted suffering.

The faithful who had observed the abuse she inflicted upon her body reveled in its dismantling and demanded her canonization. They, like her, had absorbed the Catholic loathing of the female body, an object that needed to be covered, controlled, shut away, starved, beaten, and allowed to die a slow and agonizing death for the glory of God. As the old saying goes, God apparently did not give Rosa anything she could not bear even though it killed her. Like Teresa of Avila, Rosa had a multitude of male spiritual directors: eight Dominicans and four Jesuits, all of whom helped move along her canonization after her premature death. Unlike Francis de Sales, none of these men chose to stop her self-destruction.

Rosa of Lima was clearly not a saint. She was severely mentally ill, as abused children and girls who are taught to feel badly about their bodies sometimes are. Twenty-first century teens who starve and cut themselves receive psychiatric care rather than encouragement to continue their destructive habits to prove their spiritual strength and physical mettle. Although they would not have had the language to label Rosa's behavior as illness, Meister Eckhart, Julian of Norwich, Marguerite Porete, Erasmus, Jane de Chantal, and Francis de Sales would not have equated Rosa's self-destructive practices with holiness. Jane de Chantal, Angela Merici, and Mary Ward, who urged the women in their communities to find suitable and caring spiritual advisors, would have counseled Rosa about the choice of men in her life.

Generations of Christians have bought into the fable of redemptive suffering. This type of needless and unjustified suffering is different from the pain and suffering that arises from the exigencies of being a human being living in an imperfect world. Those who follow Jesus should mitigate rather encourage suffering, as Jesus did when he fed the hungry and healed the sick.

Young boys aspiring to martyrdom via asceticism and self-punishment were also encouraged and supported by their superiors and confessors.

The Polish boy saint Stanislaus Kostka (1550–1568) was beatified a mere thirty-seven years after his untimely death. As a pious schoolboy, the young Stanislaus often passed out from the severity of his religious devotions. While unconscious, he once had a vision of two angels bringing him communion. While his tutor did not see this vision, he was somehow able to confirm the unconscious Stanislaus's account of this visitation, putting the young man's feet on the pathway to notoriety that culminated in his canonization.

Not only was Kostka ill, but he was also so badly abused by his older brother that he left home without permission to enter the Jesuit novitiate. After traveling hundreds of miles on foot, Stanislaus arrived in Rome frail and sick. For his ten remaining months of life, his body was ravaged by fevers so high that he would apply cold compresses to his chest.

The master of novices wrote that the sick young man was a "model and mirror" of religious perfection and approved Kostka's ongoing penitential activities in spite of his debilitating pain. At some point the young man—but apparently not the adults in charge—realized he was dying and wrote a letter to the Blessed Mother asking her to "call him to the skies" on the feast of the Assumption. Mary seemed to have answered his prayer. The young man died of illness and harsh ascetic practices on her feast day.

Kostka's family is often vilified by his hagiographers for refusing to honor what is, according to the church historical record, a strong vocation to the priesthood. Did his family know that the young teen suffered from a chronic illness? Did they believe—with justification—that joining a religious order would exacerbate that illness? Why would the church canonize a sickly young man who clearly suffered from febrile seizures that produced hallucinations?

Another sickly, ascetic young man named Aloysius Gonzaga (1568–1591) was fortunate enough to have two doctors of the church as friends and confessors, a fact that hastened his canonization. Although the young Gonzaga suffered from a chronic and serious kidney condition that caused debilitating headaches and skin rashes, the Jesuits accepted him as a novice. His religious superiors were aware of his ongoing poor health since he was frequently confined to bed. They were also aware of the severity of his penitential practices because they directed him to moderate them. Interestingly, they also directed him to be friendlier toward his fellow novices. When one is deeply involved with self-abuse, one has little energy left over for one's peers and the building up of community.

Gonzaga, like Kostka and unlike the adults in the order, knew he was dying. During a febrile hallucination, Gonzaga predicted that he would die on the Octave of Corpus Christi. After receiving the last rites from St. Robert Bellarmine, the young man passed away on the date he mentioned in his vision at age twenty-three.

Hagiographers link his ascetic, self-abusing practices to his vow of sexual purity. In trying to destroy the normal sexual urges of young adulthood, Aloysius destroyed himself. The populace is described by his confessors as wanting him immediately canonized for his work with plague victims—work done by many other non-canonized faithful Christians. However, like Stanislaus and Rosa of Lima, Aloysius is not a saint but rather a poster boy for self-abuse in the name of God.

Like Charles Borromeo, Robert Bellarmine (1542–1621), was a prominent spokesperson for the Catholic cause and the post-Tridentine church. Like Charles Borromeo and Thomas More, he was fond of seeing people and the issues they represented in stark black-and-white contrast. Where some of those who attended Trent tried to accommodate critics, Bellarmine stood firm with his list of anathemas against dissenters. According to Bellarmine, the pope, not Jesus, was the foundation of the church.

Bellarmine was the Professor of Controversy at the Roman College (now the Gregorian Pontifical University) and wrote a tome in three parts refuting Protestant thought that included over seven thousand citations against them. This included engaging in ad hominem attacks against fellow Catholics like Erasmus whom he regarded as a forerunner of Luther.

He was one of ten cardinals who sat on the Inquisition, and the only one who received a saint's halo. This group condemned Giordano Bruno (1548–1600) to death, proclaiming, "We declare you, the aforementioned Father Giordano Bruno, to be an impenitent, pertinacious, and obstinate heretic… We now expel you from our holy and immaculate Church, of whose mercy you have now rendered yourself unworthy" (Quoted in Rowland, 2008).

What were the crimes of this pertinacious and obstinate heretic? Bruno was a panentheist who saw God in all things. Just as God had no limit, neither did the universe that Bruno believed God had created. Not only did he believe, like Copernicus, that the Earth revolved around the sun, but he also posited the existence of many suns in other parts of an infinite universe with their own contingent of revolving planets. Bruno's scientific writings refuted what Robert Bellarmine had determined were the unchanging and irrefutable scriptural views of the church, which made the Earth and the Catholic Church the center of the entire universe. For Bellarmine, rewriting the story of the heavens would irreparably alter religious belief.

Bellarmine was not totally wrong in thinking beliefs would change if the heavens were opened up to speculation. While twenty-first-century Catholic conservatives famously point to the ordination of women in mainline Protestant churches and the Vatican II–inspired liturgical changes as the cause of the decline in church attendance and belief in God, few consider the effect photographs taken of the Earth from space had on those who believed that God, the angels, and the saints lived up in the skies beyond the clouds. The NASA photographs "Earthrise" (1968) and "Blue Marble" (1972) show the bright blue beautiful earth floating along in its orbit in a velvety black sky devoid of anything that could be construed as the court of heaven or the throne of God. After seeing that photo, few could picture God peering down in judgment from what they saw with their very eyes was an uninhabited heaven. Bruno, Copernicus, Nicholas of Cusa, and Galileo set the stage for the dismantling of heaven and, by extension, hell.

Bruno's theological views were more unwelcome than his scientific ones. Like the ancient philosopher Lucretius, Bruno posited an atomic theory, writing that all things were comprised of elements he called seeds. God was not separated from human beings far away in heaven, but rather in every seed. Thus, all things were infused with the Divine. The omnipresence of God eliminated original sin and the virgin birth and negated the need for a messiah. Discarding the beloved Catholic theological belief in hierarchy, Bruno asserted that all things were equal. His views earned him the title of heretic.

More troubling to the pious than his theological and scientific views, however, was Bruno's savage wit. Like contemporary social critics George Carlin and Bill Maher, Bruno lacerated the prominent religious figures of the time with the unvarnished truth, skewering episcopal egos.

In a play entitled "The Torch Bearer by Bruno Nolan, Graduate of No Academy, Called the Nuisance," Bruno castigated the church, writing, "You will see, in mixed confusion, snatches of cutpurses, wiles of cheats, enterprises of rogues, also delicious repulsiveness, bitter sweets, foolish decisions, mistaken faith and crippled hope, cheating charities, judges noble in their own voices of craft and not of mercy so that he who believes most is most foolish—and everywhere the love of gold."

No tyrant appreciates the taunts of those they regard as lesser beings. In a fit of ecclesiastical pique, the eminent Cardinal Bellarmine went after Bruno with the long arm of the Inquisition, much like Donald Trump went after "Saturday Night Live" for its weekly roasts of him, but with deadly results. The sainted Bellarmine, appointed as an Inquisitor by Clement VIII and hero of the Tridentine church, had Bruno tried for his ideas. Condemned as a heretic, the secular government had Bruno stripped naked and burned alive, after having his tongue tied to prevent "wicked words" from escaping his lips as he died.

Four hundred years after the Church executed Bruno, the Vatican Secretary of State, Angelo Sodano, stated that his prosecutors were justified in trying Bruno for heresy (Gagliotti, 2000). According to Soldano, however, Bellarmine and his fellow inquisitors did everything they could to save Bruno's life, except of course, to actually save it by choosing not to execute him.

The Vatican Archives contain a summary of the legal proceedings against Giordano Bruno. Sixteen years after Bruno's trial for heresy, Bellarmine questioned Galileo about the relationship between science and faith in the very same room. Fortunately, Galileo got off with a warning.

One wonders if Bellarmine felt sorrier about Bruno's fate than Soldano did four hundred years later.

Chapter 10:
THE PRICE OF MISSIONARY WORK

"Here (pointing to the Spanish Catholics' gold) is the God the Spaniards worship. For these they fight and kill; for these they persecute us and that is why we have to throw them into the sea (.)... They tell us, these tyrants, that they adore a God of peace and equality, and yet they usurp our land and make us their slaves. They speak to us of an immortal soul and of their eternal rewards and punishments, and yet they rob our belongs, seduce our women, violate our daughters. Incapable of matching us in valor, these cowards cover themselves with iron that our weapons cannot break."

Taino Chief Hateuy (d. 1512).

"It was a happiness for these colored people (slaves) to have all the means necessary to work out their salvation, and I do not doubt that those who emigrated with us from Maryland (to Missouri leaving their families behind) blessed God for his wonderful providence over them, though we sometimes heard their earnest desire to be free in a free country, it was difficult not to say almost impossible to convince them of their happiness."

Felix Verreydt, S. J. (Quoted by Kelly Schmidt, "The Pervasive Institution: Slavery and Its Legacy in U.S. Catholicism, 2022).

Back in the 1960s, our Catholic grade school would take up a collection supporting missionary work during Lent called "Pagan Babies." Raised on a steady diet of Catholic exceptionalism and triumphalism, we were imbued with a sense of responsibility to save the benighted foreign children whose knees did not know they should bend upon hearing the holy name of Jesus. So, we offered up our hard-earned pennies and nickels for the rescue of those we were taught to regard as unfortunate. The sisters then endowed twelve-year-olds with the power to rename other people's babies through the long-distance agency of a missionary priest. Our personal pagan baby, now baptized with a brand-new Christian name that erased the name their parents gave them, would not languish in limbo for all eternity.

We pre-Vatican II children stood in a very long and ancient line of zealous Christians who were taught that Christianity— most particularly, the Roman Catholic variety— is the one, true religious faith. Our goal was to save a world filled with crude and uncultured heathens and claim them for Christ. These benighted, ignorant folks steeped in, as Paul wrote, the worship of nature, were believed to be actively or unknowingly but always achingly searching for the Christian God and the Catholic Church that was headed by Christ's representative on Earth, the pope.

Benedict XVI apparently subscribed to this belief, oblivious to the evils of colonialism and the accompanying horror of the slave trade. In a 2010 speech in Lisbon, he remarked that the Portuguese explorers and missionaries were led to the far reaches of the world by a "sense of global responsibility" and their dreams of "the Christian ideals of universality and fraternity," neither of which existed in the fifteenth century. In no way, the erudite Benedict claimed, did the evangelization of Indigenous people throughout the world involve an alienation of their own culture or the imposition of a foreign one (Chakravarti, 2020).

The Native American children who lost their language, their culture, their parents, and sometimes their lives on reservations and in the mission schools in Canada and the United States would tell a far different tale. So would the Africans kidnapped from their homeland by colonizer Christians who then violently erased their names, customs, language, and religious faiths through involuntary baptisms and centuries of enslavement. The damage of the colonizers continues to haunt the Americas through the poisonous fruit of racism that is still practiced by some of the heirs of those colonizers.

The reality of Christian missionary work has always been different from Benedict's rosy and comforting, but blinkered view. From the church's point of view, missionary activity has been an overwhelming success. From sunrise to sunset, millions of knees do bend every day at the name of Jesus. For the fifty- four million native people who died in the Americas between 1492 and 1600 and the millions of abducted Africans and their descendants, however, colonizer Christianity was and remains an unmitigated disaster.

The amount of damage inflicted by Christians on native peoples and cultures on their march to convert the world has been spectacular. They destroyed pagan temples and statues and burned pagan books in Europe, India, and the Americas. According to British scholar Eberhard Sauer, "There can be no doubt on the basis of written and archeological evidence that the Christianization of the Roman Empire and early medieval Europe involved the destruction of works of art on a scale never seen before in human history" (2009).

In the beginning, the destruction of pagan temples and images was a boon for the growth Christianity. According to Augustine:

"Gaudentius and Jovius, commissioners of the emperor Honorius destroyed on March 19 the temples of false gods in the most famous and important city in Africa, Carthage, and smashed their idols. Who would not see how much the worship of the name of Christ has grown from then to our present time over nearly thirty years?" (City of God 18)

Like his justification for war, Augustine justified force used in the name of God:

"I have yielded to the facts…My own city… which had been wholly Donatist…was converted to Catholic unity by the fear of imperial laws. This has been beneficial. Some people now say: 'This (orthodox Christianity) is what we wanted all along,' but thanks be to god who has given us an opportunity to act at once and has cut off all our little delays and postponements!" (Epistle 93)

In his *Life of Saint Martin of Tours*, Sulpicius Severus (363-425) wrote that the persuasion of the great saint was not sufficient to convert the locals. Martin had to first destroy the pagan shrines and replace them with either churches or monasteries in order to convert the populace (13,9).

When the temples and the priesthood that supported them

were destroyed, pagan teachers also found themselves unemployed. Pagan books were either destroyed or no longer copied because the Christian worldview would no longer accept the pagan wisdom of the ages. The works of ancients like Lucretius, who first proposed the atomic theory several decades before the birth of Christ, were lost for a thousand years. Ancient scriptures falling outside the canon that came to compose the New Testament were buried away in caves to protect them from book-burning zealots. It was the Muslim Arabs who preserved the writings of Plato and Aristotle.

By attaching violence to mission, it took only a couple of generations post-Constantine for the ancient pagan cultures to be replaced by the Christian one, making it seem as if the pagans in antiquity were ripe for conversion and just waiting to be saved. For a millennium and a half, the destruction of Indigenous life and culture by Christians was regarded as the will of God and a bona fide good that allowed the world to progress along the triumphal axis that historians call Western civilization.

Those whose religious lives were being destroyed, however, were not silent. Just as modern people regarded the Taliban's destruction of fifteen-hundred-year-old sandstone statues of Buddha with horror and dismay, so did the non-Christian Romans regard the mindless destruction of ancient temples and statues.

The pagan orator Libanius described the marauding monks who were destroying the world he knew and loved: "This black-robed tribe hasten to attack temples with sticks and stones and bars of iron. Then utter desolation follows, with the stripping of roofs, demolition of walls, the tearing down of statues, and the overthrowing of altars. The priests must either keep quiet or die. After demolishing one, they scurry to another, and to a third, and trophy is piled on trophy in contravention of the law. In estate after estate, shrine after shrine has been wiped out by their (the monks') insolence, greed, and deliberate lack of self-control. Shrines, great and small alike, in which the weary used to find repose, have all been demolished" (Libanius, *Oration XXX. 8-10, 386*). The monks, apparently, were not above murdering those they named "enemies." Libanius wrote, "I forebear to mention the numbers they have murdered in their rioting in utter disregard of the name they share." (*Orations 30*) Christians would share in Libanius's despair if their own beloved churches were so wantonly destroyed.

These acts of Christian destruction and desecration occurred all over the empire after the very Christian emperor Theodosius I banned the practice of any faith except for Christianity. Like the persecution of Christians by some Romans, it was the zealotry of the locals that determined the extent of the destruction. In addition, not everyone shared the view of the fanatics. Neither Basil of Caesarea (330–379) nor Gregory of Nazianzus (329–390) supported forced conversions.

However, the Christian faith that developed after Theodosius I at the behest of Ambrose of Milan was, despite the words of Basil and Gregory, one based upon the destruction and elimination of pagans by a joint church-state machine. Theodosius went on to bar citizens "polluted by heresy" or who practiced the "crime of pagan rites" from the imperial household, the army, and the civil service in his imperial decrees. The entire Roman Empire must now be Christian whether they liked it or not.

As missionary activity became a joint church-state venture after 313 C.E., the emperors in Constantinople used politics and economics to make offers to pagan princes that they could ill afford to refuse. The emperor arranged an ancient gentleman's agreement by sending out missionaries trained as diplomats to persuade the princes to convert. The patriarch of Constantinople would then pile on with letters promising economic prosperity in the name of God upon conversion. Since Greek culture usually preceded the arrival of the missionaries, the Eastern pagan princes often accepted the Christian faith due to the widespread belief in Greek cultural superiority. Perhaps they had also heard stories of non-believers knocked down from their horses and blinded or struck dead by the apostles. The miraculous story of an executed carpenter rising from the dead to establish a universal church that replaced the Roman Empire might have also given them a nudge. In addition to baptism of desire and baptism of fire, there is a long history of baptism of convenience and baptism of fear when Indigenous people were confronted by Christian missionaries and the prodigious military might of the Byzantine Empire.

In the Western empire, missionary activity was fraught with more danger. Without the direct support of the emperor in place, the missionaries had to seek out the favor of the local prince in order to convert their citizens. Missionaries like Augustine of Canterbury (active in the late sixth century) used the protection of the local king, Aethelbert, who was married to a Christian, Bertha, to accomplish his goals. With Aethelbert's help and Bertha's influence, Augustine was able to engage in bogus mass conversions and baptize thousands of people into the church on Christmas Day, 597.

Portraying themselves as superior men with a superior religion against whom the pagan gods were powerless, the missionaries Boniface, (675–759), Columba, (521–597), and Gall (550–646) likewise used the power of the local prince to further their mission. A converted prince resulted in the automatic conversion of the populace whose beliefs were deemed barbaric, unworthy, and inferior by the missionaries. The conversion of the local strongman brought great rewards to the missionaries in the form of land grants upon which the first monasteries were built. Monks taught the new faith to the children of the prince and the nobles. Once the children were de-paganized, so eventually was society. Thus, the Christian faith post-Constantine was often forcibly imposed from the top down rather than from the bottom up. It took more than a shamrock and a bunch of gullible peasants for St. Patrick to convert the Irish.

Clovis (466–511), king of the Franks, was baptized on Christmas Day, 508 by the pope after a long military career of conquest that included the murder and the execution of rivals. His expedient conversion combined with military prowess enabled him to unite the Frankish tribes under his rule. His wife, Clothilde, is credited with his conversion. For her efforts she was rewarded with a halo.

The modus operandi of conversion remained unchanged in the tenth century. When Harald aspired to the throne of Denmark, he requested military help from Rome. There was a quid pro quo. Harald and his army needed to convert to Christianity, an offer the king accepted with alacrity. The archbishop of Rheims baptized the king and four hundred of his warriors and Harald ascended the throne.

Olaf (c. 960–1000) is credited with the Christianization of

Norway. A sea raider who preyed upon coastal communities in Europe, Olaf was baptized as a means to concentrate political power in the hands of the king. He punished soldiers with death who refused to convert to Christianity.

These types of mass conversions were never problem-free and often did not readily "stick." Controlling the conquered and quasi-converted masses has always been a problem to colonizers, as most people do not take kindly to foreign invasions. They often fought for years to overthrow their conquerors, who cut down sacred trees, desecrated temples, banned local faith practices, and closed down worship sites. Like Mother Macabee and her seven sons who resisted the forced imposition of Greek manners and customs in Israel, the local people in western Europe often had little respect for the foreign Christian missionaries or their faith and had little interest in being Romanized and Christianized. Unlike the Maccabees who are honored for resisting colonization by the Greeks to the point of martyrdom, the pagan rebels who resisted conversion were regarded as insurgents and barbarians. Some Indigenous people went so far as to murder respected missionaries like Boniface, a man who used war and alliances with the Frankish kings as a means of conversion. While Christians regard Boniface as a saint and martyr, the locals saw him as an agent of destruction.

In icons, Boniface is portrayed dressed in bishop robes holding a crucifix in his left hand with an axe casually draped over his right shoulder. Why was an educated, saintly man holding an axe? Boniface was believed to be in the process of deliberately cutting down a sacred and beloved tree that the German people called a "Jove" or "Thor" tree in order to prove Christian superiority. A sudden gust of wind deemed an act of God facilitated Boniface's desecration of a holy object and obligingly blew the tree down. The locals are described by Christian apologists as being overcome with the realization that their gods had no power against the Christian God and immediately converted. In an in-your-face gesture, Boniface then used the wood from the sacred tree to build a church. Christian legend sanitized this act of sacrilege by crediting Boniface with the origin of the Christmas tree.

In the sixth century, the Irish missionaries Columba and Gall found an abandoned church near Lake Constance in present day Switzerland that the residents had re-purposed and outfitted with the gilded images of their gods. Locals regarded these images as the ancient protectors of the surrounding areas like Christians regarded saints as protectors of cities and countries. Gall summoned the people, told them to convert and believe in Jesus, and then smashed their beloved images to smithereens and threw them into the lake. His companion Columba then declared the temple a church and blessed it with holy water. Unlike Boniface, Columba and Gall ran away from the rage of the local people and lived another day to destroy more sacred sites.

The wanton destruction of things deemed sacred by native populations continued throughout the centuries and into the present. In 2006, Kenyan Nobel Peace Prize winner Wangari Maathai claimed that some Christian missionaries were very keen on chopping down immense fig trees that native Kenyans regarded as holy. The people revered the fig trees because their enormous roots broke through rocks and tapped the water that lay beneath the surface, dotting the dry countryside with springs. The trees also stabilized the hillsides, preventing landslides. Dismissing the reverence of the trees as nature worship and idolatry, Christian missionaries cut them down, depriving people not only of their religious faith, but also of their water source.

Far too often, however, it was people who were destroyed by religious zealotry. Charles the Great, known better as Charlemagne (748–814)—who is not canonized—is often described as a man of devout religious faith. He is also credited with reviving art and science after a period of several centuries Christian would later describe as the "Dark Ages." Despite his deep Christian faith, Charlemagne was a man of violence who waged an intermittent thirty-year war against the Saxons. Like many conquered people, the Saxons refused to accept the Christian God and rejected the imposition of Christian culture. Both had to be imposed by force and violence. In a time where all religion was political and all politics religious, Charlemagne had 4,500 Saxon knights beheaded in one day at Verden in 782. The goal of the campaign is recorded in the *Royal Frankish Annals* (775). The Franks would "persist in this war until (the Saxons) are either defeated or forced to accept the Christian religion or be entirely exterminated (Quoted in Williams, 2015).

In a society that believed that all things, including the destruction of culture and the murder of dissenters, worked for the glory of God, later apologists regarded this appalling act of Charlemagne as a display of piety. In a world where death, however heinous, led to eternal life for the baptized, and hell, for Christians enemies, there were few voices that disagreed. One was the French writer Voltaire (1694–1778), who called Charlemagne's massacre a centerpiece of barbarism. Polite academics and history books do not mention the violence that accompanied the establishment of the Holy Roman Empire under Charlemagne.

Unlike Voltaire, few historians, philosophers, theologians, or Christians have questioned the motif of the church as the army of God marching to the ends of the to forcibly impose a celestial/terrestrial unity of church and state. Within the construct of the Church Militant (the Body of Christ on Earth), all things: war, genocide, poverty, and rape worked for the glory of God. According to the beliefs of the missionaries and the ones who sent them, acknowledging Christ brought eternal salvation. Salvation in the afterlife was far more important than life, limb, body integrity, ecology, and culture on Earth. While historians often write about the invasion of Europe by the barbarians, few feel the need to discuss the effects the Christian invasion had upon Europe and the rest of the world. What might the world look like had the army of God not conquered a good part of the world?

Too often Christian missionaries assumed that the local people they wanted to convert had a deep void in their lives that they needed to fill with the Christian God. This God is not only was superior to other gods; He was the only God. Throughout the centuries, the zealous have assumed that the pagans were ripe for conversion; their faiths were lacking a personal god, their idols, useless, their deeply held religious beliefs lacking in substance, their spirituality, vacuous. Native names honoring nature or ancestors needed to be replaced by the names of Christian saints. Only by repudiating their past and adopting Christian ways of speech, dress, and belief could the native people get to heaven and see the one true God.

The missionaries who condemned idol worshippers and described pagan attachment to their holy objects like trees as fetishes, never have recognized the idolatry of their own beliefs and their own culture's fetishes. Twenty-first-century Christians continue to honor the body parts of dead saints called relics, sanctified pieces of cloth called scapulars, and medals devoted to Mary to ward off evil, bless believers, and slice off time in purgatory. Missionaries who destroyed the ancient artifacts beloved by Indigenous people carried these talismans around in processions to honor Mary and the saints.

All cultures, of course, have both blessings and curses. Deeply entrenched patriarchal societies have engaged in physically harmful practices such as female circumcision, purdah, and foot binding to insure female inferiority and submission. Murder, pillaging, holy wars, and the destruction of rival religious artifacts remain a practice of many societies. Such practices are worthy of condemnation. Barbaric and less than savory Catholic practices are likewise in need of examination and rejection. When the missionaries engaged in practices that were not dissimilar from those of the people they hoped to convert—worshipping the Mother Goddess, kneeling and praying before graven images of entities who were not God, using talismans to ward off evil, and performing miracles—it was perfectly acceptable. When Indigenous people engaged in similar practices, it needed to be stamped out, by force, if necessary.

Of course, converts in conquered areas did not remain passive in the face of coercion and often added their own adaptations to their new faith. As Catholic churches put relics of the dead under their altars, Central American Indigenous people put the bones of their ancestors in the foundations of the churches built by Spanish missionaries. The mother goddess so zealously and obsessively excised from ancient Hebrew worship was reintroduced by Christians in the form of the virgin mother of Jesus because the masculine Trinity and the all-male clergy left no room for the maternal aspect of God. Converts were not always attracted by an all-male Trinity.

This worship of the female aspect of God still inspires the faithful, including the men of the church. Pope John Paul II was so enamored of Mary that his motto was "Totus Tuus," meaning, "all yours," i.e., Mary's. This is an odd thing for a grown man to say about a woman he regarded as his mother, even if she is a spiritual figure. Mary, the virgin mother, is, according to John Paul II, "the friend, companion, guide, and confidant of priests." She represents "the union between mothers and sons," a relationship most mothers and sons in healthy relationships would find gross and unimaginable. It is also odd that an adult man would offer himself totally—body, mind, and spirit— to a woman he regarded as his mother. Only in discredited pagan temples do devotees have intimate relations with their gods.

Five hundred years after the Holy Roman Emperor slew 4,500 human beings for refusing conversion, Spanish missionaries arrived on the shores of what has been incorrectly called "the New World." That world was, in fact, quite old and quite lovely. It contained one of the largest and most beautiful cities in the world, Tenochtitlan, a city five times the size of London of that day, filled with aqueducts, causeways, and floating gardens. The city was so beautiful that colonizer Bernal del Castillo commented that he had never seen or dreamed something could be so enchanting. This eyewitness account stands in stark contrast to that of former Pennsylvania senator and presidential candidate Rick Santorum, who claimed that when the conquistadores and missionaries arrived in America, "There was nothing there" (Jimenez, 2021).

Santorum stands in a long line of Christians who have believed over the centuries that the absence of European Christians in the Americas, Asia, and Africa meant that entire continents were nothing but vacant *Monopoly*™ properties ready to be acquired, occupied, and developed by Christian Europeans. This nonsensical, and unchristian belief was first presented to fifteenth-century Christians and their nation states by Pope Alexander VI in 1493, one year after Columbus landed in Hispaniola. The bull, the "Division of the Undiscovered World between Spain and Portugal" issued under the Latin name, *Inter Caetera*, stated that any land not inhabited by "Christians" could be stolen from native people and claimed in the name of the rulers of Spain and Portugal to be "exploited" by Christian rulers. This mandate to steal, enslave, and murder included the directive to "extol the Catholic faith everywhere" so that "barbarous nations could be overthrown and brought to the faith."

One of Alexander's predecessors, Nicholas V, baptized slavery in his 1452 bull, *Dum Diversas* which gave permission to European Catholic monarchs to permanently subjugate and enslave "Saracens and pagans and any other unbelievers."

> *"We, weighing all and singular the premises with due meditation, and noting that since we had formerly by other letters of ours granted among other things free and ample faculty t the aforesaid King Alfonso-to invade, search out, capture, vanquish, and subdue all Saracens and pagans whatsoever, and other enemies of Christ wheresoever placed, and the kingdoms, dukedoms, principalities, dominions, possessions, and all moveable and immovable goods whatsoever held and possessed by them and to reduce their persons to perpetual slavery, and to apply and appropriate to himself and his successors the kingdoms, dukedoms, countries, principalities, dominions, possessions and goods, and to convert them to his and their use and profit-by having secured the said faculty, the said King Alfonso, or, by his authority, the aforesaid infante, justly and lawfully has acquired and possessed, and doth possess these islands, lands, harbors, and seas, and they do of right belong and pertain to the said King Alfonso and his successors."*

Three years later, he followed up this bull with another entitled *Romanus Pontifex* that put the seal of Peter and, by extension, Christ, upon both the theft of land owned by non-believers as well as their enslavement. Signed by the hand that wore the ring of the fisherman, these papal bulls were harbingers of horror to the people of the Americas.

Thus, for Spain, the islands of Hispaniola, Jamaica, and Cuba, nestled in the turquoise Caribbean Sea, and the lands of Mexico and South America were not considered to be possible trading partners and potential allies but rather places and people to conquer, exploit, and enslave. The representatives of Christian European countries who had been quite happy to invade each other in their home countries gleefully invaded, conquered, and exploited the lands in the Americas. The carte blanche given to them by Nicholas V and Alexander VI blessed the usurpation of foreign lands and the exploitation of their people in the name of God.

Christopher Columbus (1450-1524) commented upon the hospitable and generous nature of the Caribbean Arawaks. Their easy-going nature, he wrote in a 1493 letter to Ferdinand and Isabella, would make them fine slaves rather than valuable allies and trading partners.

"They ... brought us parrots and balls of cotton and spears and many other things, which they exchanged for glass beads and hawks' bells. They willingly traded everything they owned... They were well-built, with good bodies and handsome features.... They do not bear arms, and do not know them, for I showed them a sword, they took it by the edge and cut themselves out of ignorance. They have no iron. Their spears are made of cane... They would make fine servants.... With fifty men we could subjugate them all and make them do whatever we want.

As soon as I arrived in the Indies, on the first Island which I found, I took some of the natives by force in order that they might learn and might give me information of whatever there is in these parts" (Columbus, 1492).

The Castilian jurist, Juan Lopez de Palacios Rubios, nicknamed "El Doctor" for his expertise in canon law, provided the Catholic Spanish monarchs Ferdinand and Isabella with the religious and legal justification for invading, colonizing, and forcibly converting the Americas. Rubios is the author of the 1513 travesty called the "Requierimento" or requirement. Read by conquistadores bristling with swords to uncomprehending native people or on empty beaches or even from the deck of a ship as it approached land, it apprised native people of their future— do what we tell you to do or be killed or enslaved. This tidy little document absolved the Spanish ahead of time of the serious sins they were about to commit against their American sisters and brothers. The Indigenous people were, after all, forewarned.

The English translation of the Spanish *El Requierimento* (Requirement) of 1513 reads:

"On the part of the King, Don Fernando, and of Doña Juana, his daughter, Queen of Castille and León, subduers of the barbarous nations, we their servants notify and make known to you, as best we

can, that the Lord our God, living and eternal, created the heaven and the earth, and one man and one woman, of whom you and we, and all the men of the world, were and are all descendants, and all those who come after us. Of all these nations God our Lord gave charge to one man, called St. Peter, that he should be lord and superior of all the men in the world, that all should obey him, and that he should be the head of the whole human race, wherever men should live, and under whatever law, sect, or belief they should be; and he gave him the world for his kingdom and jurisdiction. One of these pontiffs, who succeeded St. Peter as lord of the world in the dignity and seat which I have before mentioned, made donation of these isles and Terra Firma to the aforesaid King and Queen and to their successors, our lords, with all that there are in these territories, Wherefore, as best we can, we ask and require you that you consider what we have said to you, and you take the time that shall be necessary to understand and deliberate upon it, and that you acknowledge the Church as the ruler and superior of the whole world, But if you do not do this, and maliciously make delay in it, I certify to you that, with the help of God, we shall powerfully enter into your country, and shall make war against you in all ways and manners that we can, and shall subject you to the yoke and obedience of the Church and of their highnesses; we shall take you, and your wives, and your children, and shall make slaves of them, and as such shall sell and dispose of them as their highnesses may command; and we shall take away your goods, and shall do you all the mischief and damage that we can, as to vassals who do not obey, and refuse to receive their lord, and resist and contradict him: and we protest that the deaths and losses which shall accrue from this are your fault, and not that of their highnesses, or ours, nor of these cavaliers who come with us" (nih.gov/nativevoicestimeline).

Using the practices that worked so well for Augustine of Canterbury, Boniface, Columba, and Gall in Europe, the missionaries allowed the Spanish and Portuguese armies to pave their way. The people of the New World and Asia were claimed for Spain and for Christ almost simultaneously. A foreign invasion by armed forces of God determined to suppress indigenous economic, cultural, social, and religious systems is hardly the stuff of good news. While there were some efforts made by both Spain and the Vatican to curb the worst excesses of the conquistadores, they were either ignored or repealed. Many members of the ruling class, including large numbers of bishops, reaped great wealth from the exploitation of the West Indies and the enslavement and extermination of its inhabitants. Consequently, there were few critics. Those who did support the native people were often silenced or imprisoned. As a result of the idolatry of their ancestors, few Christians recognize the idol of mammon that sits comfortably upon the altars of Christian churches, co-equal with Jesus Christ.

Columbus forced the Native people to work in the mines. Da Gama tortured and executed his prisoners. Instead of Christian charity, Christian invaders used massacre, mutilation, enslavement, and torture to bring the Indigenous people under European control.

The behavior and beliefs of some of the missionaries was far from stellar and sometimes rivaled that of the bloodthirsty conquistadores. While missionaries sported a patina of gentleness and patience, the love they purported to bear for the potential converts was more often a need to "save" those believed to be inferior from their own culture and religious practices. This endowed them with an undeserved sense of superiority.

Francis Xavier (1506–1552), the Apostle to the (East) Indies, wrote to Ignatius Loyola that the poor character of native populations made them unsuitable subjects for conversion. Junipera Serra beat and imprisoned the Indians who tried to flee from his missions in California. Peter Claver whipped the enslaved Africans he purported to love for dancing and singing. Some missionaries regarded their prospective converts as passive children who needed to be parented and then bludgeoned into the Christian way of life. Others saw them as potential agents of their martyrdom, an end many of them actively courted and welcomed as they trashed native religious practices, stirring up native anger and inciting the people to bestow upon them a martyr's death thus assuring their canonization. There was no understanding on the part of most missionaries that the native people had not sought out conversion and had a right to reject their advances.

Both John Paul II and Francis I have both apologized to the original inhabitants of the Americas for the catastrophe that was visited upon them by the European missionaries. John Paul II apologized in 1992 on a visit to the Dominican Republic for the pain and suffering of the Indigenous people. In July of 2015 Francis fleshed out the depth and scope of what he called grave sins committed against the Indigenous people of the Americas: "I say this to you with regret: many grave sins were committed against the native peoples of the Americas in the name of God. Here, I want to be quite clear, as was John Paul II; I humbly ask forgiveness for the offenses of the Church herself, but also for the crimes against native people during the so-called conquest of America" (Catholic News Agency, 2015). Two months later, against the expressed wishes of the Native Americans to whom he had just apologized, Francis canonized Junipero Serra.

Although Junipero Serra (1713–1784) had a comfortable teaching position in Spain, he was fascinated with tales of martyrs. Hoping to add his name to that illustrious registry, he left his position and set sail on an arduous journey to Mexico. Obsessed with personal sin, Serra whipped himself with chains and hit himself in the chest with heavy stones each night in repentance for sin. It was not surprising, therefore, that he would whip the Indians in the missions he founded in California for what he regarded as infractions.

Unlike many other missionaries, Serra did protect the mission Indians from encroachment by Spanish soldiers, traveling from California back to Mexico City to insist that the baptized Indigenous people were children of God. However, those who forcibly impose an alien faith, and then beat, shackle, imprison, and even kill those who run away from his violent ministrations are hardly saints.

Serra was preceded much earlier by Bartolome Las Casas, a very early eyewitness to what is called the "Great Dying" in the Americas. The author of *A Short Account of the Destruction of the Indies*, Las Casas (1484–1566) emigrated with his father, a friend of Columbus, in 1502, to Hispaniola, where he fully embraced the dream of extracting wealth from what he considered to be a brand-new world awaiting the arrival of the European Christians. He was a willing participant in slave raids and owned an encomienda, a precursor to plantations where Indigenous people were forced to labor with little food or access to native medicines. Las Casas, like many of his clerical confreres, combined his priestly duties with those of being a slave master.

The overwhelming death rate of the native people caused Las Casas to reconsider their servitude. Black Africans, he suggested, might provide a stronger and healthier workforce. In the end, Las Casas distanced himself from the enslavement of either peoples. He traveled to Europe and preached to anyone who cared to listen to him that the Indians were human beings with the same rights as the colonizing Spaniards. While he did try to put a kind face upon the barbarism of the conquistadores, he did not repudiate colonization.

Of the Great Dying, Las Casas wrote, "Who of those born in future generations would believe this? I, myself who am writing this and saw it and know most about it can hardly believe such was possible" (Las Casas, 1552). Las Casas' book, however, was by his decree not published during his lifetime. When it was published forty years later, the people of the Americas had already entered into a decline from which they would not recover.

Las Casas estimated that there had been four million people on the island of Hispaniola in 1492. Most historians have postulated the number to be closer to between 300,000 and 500,000 people. The census of 1508 recorded a population of only 66,000 indigenous people, and by 1570, a mere 22,000 native people remained. While apologists often claim that missionaries, like the conquistadores were people of their time and acted accordingly, there were people like Las Casas and others who saw the horror unfolding before their eyes and raised their voices in protest.

Dominican Francisco Vitoria (1483–1546) loudly criticized the colonization of the Americas. A student of Erasmus, Vitoria wrote that the Indigenous people of the Americas had dominion over both their private and public matters just as Christians did. They were the rightful owners of their own land, which should not be arbitrarily taken away from them by Europeans. Nor should they be forcibly converted. Their chiefs, and not the conquistadores, had legitimate authority over them. Mammon, however, had a far louder voice.

In 1510 the Spanish Dominican Antonio De Montesinos, appalled by the massive death and destruction of the native people, informed the colonists, including the son of Columbus, that they were agents of murder rather than the good Christians they believed themselves to be. He and his fellow Dominicans refused to give communion to or absolve the colonists, demanding to know in a homily preached in a thatched church on the island of Hispaniola in 1511:

> *"Tell me by what right of justice do you hold these Indians in such a criminal and horrible servitude? On what authority do you wage such detestable wars on these people who dealt quietly and peaceful-ly on their lands? Wars have destroyed an infinite number of them by homicides and slaughters never heard of before. Why do you keep them so oppressed and exhausted, without giving them enough to eat or curing them of sickness. Tell me by what right of justice do you hold these Indians in such criminal and horrible servitude? On what authority do you wage such detestable wars on these people?"*
> *(Text excerpt, www.PBS.org/conquistadors)*

For their efforts, Montesinos and his confreres were recalled to Spain and replaced by missionaries more attuned to the rapacious conquistadors. Montesinos was so upset that he reported the inhumane conditions in Hispaniola to the king, who tried to rein in his avaricious subjects. Alas, Hispaniola was far away from Spain. The colonizers could ignore their king with impunity as long as treasures enriched their nation and an aristocracy that included the bishops.

Antonio de Valdivieso (1495–1549), the first bishop of Nicaragua, was not fortunate enough to be recalled. A staunch defender of native rights, Valdivieso was stabbed to death by the son of the governor. Neither Valdivieso nor Montesinos and his companions were ever regarded as saints for fulfilling the gospel to love neighbor as self.

As a result of Las Casas' book, Spain became the first imperial power to recognize the humanity of the Indigenous people of the Americas and the Spanish crown did enact some laws to protect them from abuse. However, the crown still fully expected the people to accept Spanish rule, pay tribute in the form of labor, and accept Catholicism under pain of punishment. All native babies had to be baptized, and children older than thirteen were taken away from their parents to be educated as Christians. While the people could not be forced onto the encomiendas, once there, they could not leave and were forced to work under the threat of violence for little or no pay. In practice, if not in name, the people remained slaves of their Spanish masters.

While it is true that many Indigenous people died from European diseases, it is also true that the population could have bounced back as did the population of Europe after the Black Death. However, illness partnered with slavery, imprisonment, and extermination caused the native population to precipitously drop by 90 percent in some areas of the Caribbean.

Many apologists are quick to dismiss Las Casas' description of the horror he saw unfolding all around him in the West Indies as an exaggeration. However, Hispaniola was not the only island that lost its native population. In one generation, almost all of the native Tainos from the island of Jamaica died or were killed by Spanish invaders. Indigenous people in Cuba met the same fate.

Current research estimates that there were anywhere from 60.5 to 80.3 million Indigenous souls in the Americas prior to 1492. Some of them built Machu Picchu in Peru. Others built great cities and pyramids in Mexico and Guatemala. The mound builders lived in the planned city that is now called Cahokia in Illinois. This native metropolis was the largest city in what became the United States until 1781 when it was surpassed by Philadelphia.

The native encounter with the Europeans killed 95 percent of the Indigenous peoples in parts of North America, Central and South America between 1492 and the early 1600s. This translates into a 10-percent reduction in the human population at the time. It is no wonder that Las Casas, Valdivieso, and Montesinos were appalled by the human tragedy unfolding around them. (Koch et al., 2017)

While Las Casas has not been canonized, he is an important witness to what has been called the Great Dying. The scope of the death and destruction visited upon native peoples in North and South America is second only to the casualties in World War II. Entire civilizations collapsed, some in little more than a decade, never to be rebuilt or restored. Residents of complex agricultural societies were reduced to being hunters and gatherers as the decimated populations could no longer support farming. Ancient wisdom, including medicines, was lost. Lands that once sustained vibrant, healthy communities were turned into plantations that benefitted a few slave-holding Europeans.

The effects of the Great Dying were not reserved for the Americas. The huge tracts of farmland left fallow in the Americas by the deaths of their occupants led to reforestation. This in turn led to a significant decrease in carbon dioxide levels that cooled the entire planet, leading to severe winters and famines in the lands of the conquerors (Koch et al 2017). This drop in carbon dioxide in the early 1600s is reflected in samples of ice cores from Antarctica (Koch et al., 2017).

Some of the remaining Indigenous people engaged in wars against their conquerors that lasted until the late 19th century. The United States Army was tasked with attacking native people, killing their livestock, and driving survivors onto reservations. This was the milieu that created the mantra, "The only good Indian is a dead Indian."

The government and the white citizens of the nation never could understand why the native people were so angry with the innocent white Christian settlers who marched onto native ancestral lands and claimed them as their own, evicting the original inhabitants without mercy. For the settlers, the violence of the Indian wars was one-sided. The native people were wicked savages while the newcomers were just searching for the legendary Promised Land to which they felt entitled to take by force. Thus, encounters between the Indigenous people of the Americas and the European colonists included invasion, war, conquest, grand theft of lands and labor, as well as enslavement, murder, and cultural genocide. There were no exceptions. Even the so-called "civilized" tribes in Georgia were forcibly removed from their land by the U.S. government under Andrew Jackson to be replaced by wealthy white slave owners. American politicians continue to oppress native Americans by enacting laws that hinder residents of reservations from voting and appropriating tribal lands to extract their natural resources.

Aside from the voices of prophets like Montesinos, Las Casas, and de Valdivieso, one must wonder what the missionaries and the colonists thought as the native people began to die en masse. Were the deaths of fifty-three million people a necessary evil or the collateral damage of progress? Very few then or now look back. When I relate this horror, many of my listeners comment that the native Americans engaged in warfare or religious practices that also resulted in death, as if this redeems genocide.

If the genocide of Indigenous people in America was the original sin of European colonists, slavery was a close second. The Christians who landed on the shores of the Americas embraced the horror of buying and selling human beings to make money with alacrity. Church attendance, personal piety, scripture, ordination, and membership in a religious order offered no protection from evil. Greed trumped Christian charity.

In the many histories written about their order, the Jesuits omit the fact that they were once the largest slave owning institution in the world. Slavery, in fact, is the basis of their great wealth. Despite the order's pride in following the spiritual practices of their founder, and the decade long preparation for the priesthood, one of the very first practices in which the Jesuits participated was the enslavement of their fellow human beings. Within ten years of the order's founding, they used enslaved Africans to build the first Jesuit college in Coimbra, Portugal (Chamberline, 2018). By the 1600s, they used enslaved Africans as house staffs in China and Japan. The Jesuits were so invested in the use of Black slave labor that it silenced those brave members of the order who spoke out against it (Chamberlin).

In addition, their blood-stained missionary history honors priests who forcibly converted people or inured them to their new lives in America as slaves.

Peter Claver was one such white, Spanish Jesuit priest who was revered for tending to the thousands of slaves who were brought into the city of Cartegena, Colombia by Catholic slave catchers to be sold to Catholic owners of haciendas (plantations). Through the tireless efforts of Peter Claver (1580–1654) and his sidekick Alonso Sandoval (1576–1652), human beings whom Claver labeled "poor savages" were freed from "the devil" by baptism and declared "sons of God," which, for the church and its representatives, was a greater liberty than freedom (Grimes, 2017). The care these priests provided for dying slaves transported across the ocean in horrific conditions has long disguised the fact that they were neither abolitionists nor humanists, but racists.

The white Catholic slave owners used Claver and his twisted theology to keep the slaves docile and obedient. Regarded by his peers as a gloomy ascetic, Claver beat Africans with a large crucifix or whipped them for activities he regarded as sinful while excusing the behavior of the Spanish men who used rape as an instrument of control over native and African women.

In a classic case of white hubris, Jesuit John Laures wrote in 1928 that the slaves regarded the words of Claver as "tidings from heaven." After listening to Claver, the kidnapped Africans dropped to their knees, resigned to their fate and thankful for their new faith. Catholicism was an unmitigated good for masters and slaves alike because it taught slaves "due deference to authority" (Von Germeten, 2005). Since the white colonizers did not occupy Black spaces, they had no idea what the enslaved people really thought and believed about Claver and company. As enslaved people, they would say what they thought their persecutors wanted them to say to garner favor or escape punishment.

Conversions came with a financial incentive awarded by the crown. The missionaries were obliged to teach the catechism for an hour a day to non-Spanish-speaking people, through the medium of enslaved interpreters, including some owned by Claver. We have no idea what the Spanish-speaking slaves said to their newly arrived sisters and brothers. Did they tell the poor souls to agree to convert lest even more be taken away from them? Did they warn them of further torture if they spurned conversion? Did the interpreters advise the newly arrived to pay attention to what the white people did to slaves rather than what they said about God?

Alonso Sandoval happily (and incorrectly) bragged that he baptized three hundred thousand slaves, sometimes giving them sweets in order to put the faith "into a positive light" (Chamberlain, 2018). Like missionaries in other parts of the Americas, Claver and Sandoval were agents of destruction who never questioned the existence of slavery or the activities of the colonial powers of whom they were an integral part. Contrary to the 2015 pronouncement from the Eastern Province of Jesuits, neither Sandoval nor Claver were abolitionists (Chamberlin).

Sandoval wrote a missionary treatise exalting the white Europeans who were running the slaving enterprise where human beings were kidnapped, raped, imprisoned, and then transported in filthy ships to be sold as human workhorses as "the most noble, virtuous, magnificent, and civilized people on earth" (Quoted in Chamberlin, 2018). The squalor, pain, death, disease, and sadness inflicted upon the Africans by the Spanish apparently made no impression upon any of these men. Using Thomas Acquinas's hierarchy of beings to justify their inhumanity with Europeans at the top and Indigenous people at the bottom, it was God's will that the white, Christian Europeans enslave the Africans and steal the land of the Indigenous people.

When the kings of Spain and Portugal were beginning to question the morality of slavery in the Americas, it was the priests of religious orders who reassured them that their investments in the new colonies could not exist and continue providing revenue without slavery. It was Claver and de Acosta's "humanistic" approach to slavery that convinced the monarchs that Catholics could buy and sell human beings with clear consciences (Chamberlin, 2018).

The French, like the Spanish, did not have a high opinion of the people they found in what they declared was New France. The explorer Jacques Cartier (1491–1557) called the native peoples he found "savages" and asked his king for help in converting them. The philosopher Montaigne wrote that the duty of colonization is "to gentle" natives whom other explorers described as having "marvelous dispositions" and who practiced hospitality and honesty (Jaenan,1983)

Fresh from the wars of the Protestant Reformation and practitioners of nascent French nationalism, French explorers and missionaries wished to imbue the native people with the French language and culture. The more zealous among them, called the Companie des Tres Sant Sacrament, believed that in the Indigenous peoples of Canada they had found a fresh medium to restore the purity of the early church (Jaenan, 1983). To accomplish both the Frenchification and Christianization of Canada, the French undermined First Nations communal practices and tribal authority, introduced alcohol, and repudiated tribal agreements. With their culture weakened and Jesuit segregationist practices breaking apart families and tribes, the native people came to be viewed as bloodthirsty, filthy, barbaric, and depraved.

Francis Xavier Laval (1623–1708) became the bishop of Quebec at age thirty-six. The first thing he did upon arriving in New France was to set up an ecclesiastical council to establish his authority although there were not yet existing parishes. He repeatedly provoked controversy with the governor to the point that some of his fellow priests feared violence between the church and the government.

Laval began his tenure in New France with a positive view of the native people, joyfully baptizing one the day he set foot in New France. He excommunicated those who sold alcohol to the native people and is described as being both generous and humble. Yet like his fellow missionaries, he could not seem to understand why the native people would reject Christianity and engage in warfare to repel what they perceived as invaders. Thus, the missionary venture was largely a failure, as few native people chose to convert to Christianity. In spite of taking children away from their parents to educate them as proper and pious French Christians, there were no native vocations to the priesthood or to the women's religious orders. Eventually, Laval labeled the native people "Turcs" and declared them worthy of annihilation. For his work in New France, Laval was canonized a saint.

On the other hand, large numbers of Laval's fellow Frenchmen found the freedom of indigenous life salutary and left their civilized counterparts to live with the native people. Few chose to return to white settlements.

Isaac Jogues (1607–1646) and his fellow Jesuits were part of a French church-state venture in New France that was obsessed with conversion and martyrdom. Like the Spaniards before them, the blind arrogance of the missionaries led them to both disregard and disrespect the cultures they had come to save. Jogues' self-indulgent fixation on martyrdom instead of upon understanding caused the French to miss the chance to peacefully co-exist as equals in God's family.

The native people regarded Jogues as an interloper rather than as a savior. For his efforts to convert, Jogues had his hands mutilated by members of the Iroquois. He went home to recover from his wounds in France, where the pope gave him a dispensation to say Mass. Determined to end his life as a martyr, Jogues returned to New France, where the Iroquois obligingly carried out his suicide mission.

The murder or martyrdom by "blood-thirsty" savages of allegedly saintly, innocent missionaries whose only purpose was to save those benighted souls who did not know Christ led to more European violence. After forty hard years of contact with native people who invariably rejected their advances, the Jesuits decided that the peoples of the Americas who refused to convert had something wrong with them, much like the early Christians came to despise the Jews for being too stubborn to accept Jesus. The reasons why their fellow human beings might reject conversion to Christianity remained a great mystery that missionaries and their fellow Catholics never cared to explore.

After many abortive missionary expeditions, the Jesuits came to place the recalcitrant Native peoples without writing and hierarchical states on the bottom rung of civilization, with the pirating genocidal Europeans occupying the "most civilized" level. By the end of the sixteenth century, Jesuit notables like Jose de Acosta had written that the indigenous way of life was "an unfit vessel for Christianity" that could not be preserved if conversion were to "take" (Chamberlin, 2018). Acosta's works became a textbook for Jesuit missionaries all over the world and seeped into the colonial powers' understanding of native peoples. It provided the rationale for sequestering native converts from their communities and families in the Americas and in Asia. Upon this was based the mission system in California and, by extension, the Indian schools in the United States and Canada where native children were forcibly removed from their homes to be both Christianized and civilized by superior white overlords of European descent.

The Jesuits were founded in 1534 by a soldier of sorts, Ignatius Loyola, who was born one year before Columbus landed in the West Indies. After being seriously wounded in battle and suffering a long convalescence complicated by surgical procedures done without anesthesia, Loyola found God. He approached his new dedication to

God in the same manner that he once had pursued war, with zealous devotion and fortitude. Just as he could once bear all during war, he could now bear all for Christ. A man who knew no compromise, he expected members of his new religious order to do the same, pledging allegiance to the pope in Rome as they marched off to save the world for Christ.

It was Loyola's Jesuits who launched the missionary juggernaut in what they believed was the empty, fallow ground of North and South America. There, in obedience to their founder, who ended his letters with the directive, "Go, set the world on fire," they (along with European soldiers) did their very best to burn away the culture and religious beliefs of the native people and replace it with white European Christianity.

While Loyola's devotion to God and the discernment of divine will as exemplified in his *Spiritual Exercises* written between 1522 and 1524 remain a source of inspiration and comfort to Catholics as well as people of other faiths, his role in conquering the world for Christ left millions of people dead. One can be the founder of a religious order and an inspired spiritual advisor without being a saint.

Kateri Tekawitha, (1656–1680), a member of the Mohawk tribe in upper New York State, was given the title the "Lily of the Mohawks" for her refusal to marry. Canonized by Benedict XVI in 2012, she is a poster child for missionary excess. As a child, Tekawitha experienced multiple and repeated traumas that reflect the upheaval of the times in which she lived. At age four, she lost her parents and siblings in a smallpox epidemic that scarred her face so badly that she felt obliged to cover her face with a blanket in public. The village to which she then moved with her aunt and uncle was burned by the French when she was ten. When she was thirteen, her village experienced a three-day siege by Mohicans where she was expected to care for the wounded and bury the dead. The French forced the village to accept Jesuit missionaries as a condition of peace.

It was from these Jesuits that the teenaged Tekawitha learned about Christianity and the need for repenting for sin, the sin that allegedly caused the destruction of her family and her people. She left her village in New York and moved to a mission near Montreal, where she lived with other native women converts. It was in this mission where she met her friend Marie Therese, in whose arms she died at age 23.

Tekawitha's Jesuit biographer gave her a left-handed compliment by describing her as a well-behaved girl, surprisingly pious for an Indian. In spite of her exemplary behavior, another Jesuit had introduced her to whips, hair shirts, and an iron girdle to enhance her repentance. Tekawitha came to be obsessed with suffering. She ate little and slept on a mattress with thorns, which contributed to her overall poor health and premature death. The churchmen in charge of her life seem to have reveled in her suffering. Her tombstone reads, "The fairest flower that ever bloomed among red men."

In the late twentieth and early twenty-first centuries, some Catholics and native people petitioned the Vatican to formally revoke the Doctrine of Discovery, which had justified land theft as the modus operandi of the Christian European colonists in the Americas. Instead, Benedict XVI canonized Kateri Tekawitha in 2012 against the wishes of Indigenous peoples, some of whom regarded it as a canonization of colonialism. (It took until 2023 for Francis I to revoke the offending doctrine). While Tekawitha is beloved by some native people, she was canonized because she was a poster child for the traditional European Catholic values imposed upon women: purity, obedience, piety, and humility. Like Maria Goretti, Tekawitha is more a victim than she is a saint. Her canonization, like that of Maria's, ignored rather than addressed the societal and religious beliefs that directly harmed them and eventually killed them. Canonizing her for living up to the colonial ideals that destroyed her family, her village, and most of her people is cheap grace that brings no redemption to her people. She is a victim and not a saint.

The peripatetic Jesuit missionary Francis Xavier, a confrere of Ignatius Loyola, earned the title "Apostle to the Indies" for his herculean attempts to convert the people of the East to Catholicism. There was a reason for Xavier's frequent moves. Missionaries in East Asia experienced the same problem converting the native people as did their Western confreres. The local people were not enthralled with either him or his message. As he wore out his welcome in one country, he moved to another hoping to find fertile soil to plant his message about Jesus and eternal salvation. Even those who converted remained eclectic in their beliefs, continuing to celebrate Muslim and Hindu holidays and participating in local religious customs. His missionary tactics explain why the faith rested so lightly upon his converts.

When Xavier arrived in a village speaking his newly acquired Malabar, he presented a foreign faith without any context. Beginning with rote prayer and moving on to credal statements and the ten commandments, he omitted Jesus' commandment to love one's neighbor as oneself. When he finished teaching, he asked his listeners if they believed what he taught them. After answering in the affirmative, Xavier duly baptized the native people. Xavier commented that his baptizing arm ached from overuse at the end of the day.

Xavier strove mightily to destroy native culture while trying to convert the Indians. In a letter to the Society of Jesus in 1543, Xavier wrote:

> *"Following the baptisms, the new Christians return to their homes and come back with their wives and families to be in turn also prepared for baptism. After all have been baptized, I order that everywhere the temples of the false gods be pulled down and idols broken. I know not how to describe in words the joy I feel before the spectacle of pulling down and destroying the idols by the very people who formerly worshipped them. Even children show an ardent love for the Divine law, and an extraordinary zeal for learning our holy religion and imparting it to others. Their hatred for idolatry is marvelous. They get into feuds with the heathens about it, and whenever their own parents practice it, they reproach them and come off to tell me at once. Whenever I hear of any act of idolatrous worship, I go to the place with a large band of these children, who very soon load the devil with a greater amount of insult and abuse than he has lately received of honor and worship from their parents, relations, and acquaintances. The children run at the idols, upset them, dash them down, break them to pieces, spit on them, trample on them, kick them about, and in short heap on them every possible outrage"* (Letter to Rome, 1548).

When his multitudinous baptisms looked more like diversions

than real conversions, Xavier decided to bring in the big guns of the European Inquisition to the city of Goa to enforce belief. As a result, Hinduism, Islam, and the speaking of the local language were outlawed on the threat of death. Hindu children were taken from their parents, and those who refused to follow the dictates of the invading colonizers were tortured and burned at the stake by the Inquisition.

While some Jesuit apologists laud the love, self-awareness, ingenuity and heroism of their missionary predecessors, Indigenous people are not as sanguine. Neither the Hindus, whose faith was far older than Christianity, nor the native Americans were anxious to be saved by foreign missionaries.

There will be those who claim that the missionaries were acting upon their deeply held beliefs and, therefore, deserve to be excused for their actions. They meant well in spite of the harmful outcome of their work. Because they were men of their time, we in the twenty-first century should not condemn them, even though they always had the gospel of Jesus who said, "Whatever you do to the least of my people, that you do unto me" at their disposal. Apologists will claim that "everybody" behaved like the missionaries, as if they had no moral compass aside from the mores of their time—although many of their contemporaries like Erasmus did not share their enthusiasm for violence and forced conversion. As the historical record in the Americas and elsewhere proves, some of the most terrible deeds in history are committed in the name of deeply held religious beliefs that too often have flown right in the face of Jesus' kingdom values. How much good did men like Pius V, Junipera Sera, Peter Claver, Alonso Sandoval, Isaac Jogues, and Francis Xavier need to do to in order to make up for the sheer number of lives they helped to destroy?

In every culture, in every time, there *have* been people who pointed to another way. North American Indigenous culture, with its respect for the land and tolerance for differences was one way, a way the colonists and their progeny rejected out of hand as they slaughtered buffalo, beaver, elk, and wolves with impunity, polluted waterways, and wantonly leveled virgin forests across northern Pennsylvania and New York. Antonio Montesinos and his Dominican confreres, Antonio de Valdivieso, and the transformed Bartoleme Las Casas supported and protected native rights, sometimes at great risk to themselves. They, and not Isaac Jogues, Francis Xavier, Peter Claver, and Junipera Serra are the true heroes and saints.

On November 17, 2018, twenty-seven-year-old American missionary John Chau tried to force himself on a group of native people on the remote Sentinel Island located in the Bay of Bengal. These people had repeatedly rejected all contact with the outside world. The government of India respected their wishes and forbade contact. Without knowing anything about the Sentinese people, Chau pronounced the island, "Satan's last stronghold," and decided he would convert the inhabitants to Christianity, even if they killed him (*The Guardian*, 2015). And kill him they did, on his third attempt to enter their country.

Chau insisted that his deeply held beliefs were more important than the wishes of the Sentinelese people to be left alone. While some looked upon Chau's efforts with scorn, his friend John Ramsey defended Chau's suicidal act. "Well, my ancestors were savages (in Europe) that wanted to be left alone. I'm sure glad missionaries like St. Boniface stepped up and were willing to give their lives and that I don't live in a society like that anymore" (Quoted in *The Guardian*, 2015).

Ramsey's question begs the question of who the savage is. The society that formed as a result of the efforts of Boniface and his fellow missionaries set the stage for the colonial enterprise in the Americas that led to the deaths of some fifty-three million souls and the enslavement of millions.

Augustine of Canterbury, Boniface, Peter Claver, Columba, Gall, Isaac Jogues and his fellow French Jesuits, Francis Laval, Francis Xavier, and Junipera Serra were agents of destruction, not saints. Kateri Tekawitha was a victim of colonialism and Clothide, the wife of a violent man. I leave it to the reader to decide if Ignatius Loyola should be considered a saint.

Followers of the Way of Jesus

Antonio Montesinos
Antonio de Valdivies
Francisco Vitoria

Chapter 11:
VISIONARIES

"For in the darkest hours of this world's history, when godlessness is rife or immorality parades itself before men's eyes, it pleases God to summon certain souls to sacrifice themselves freely in imitation of the crucified for the advantage of the church and the salvation of the world."

Abbe Paul Giloteaux, 1922.

I was six and playing in the middle of a tiny urban street in working-class Philadelphia where my maternal grandmother and three of her sisters lived. For no obvious reason, I looked at the sky and saw a vision of Jesus above the steeple of a nearby Protestant church. I duly noted the vision and went back to playing in the street with my little friends. Years later, I understood that I had had a vision of Jesus. Although the vision is almost as real today as it was all those many years ago, I have my doubts as to the cause. Had Jesus appeared above that church steeple just for me? Or did I imagine it?

At a time when kindergarten was not mandatory, my mother had sent me to public school for kindergarten with the understanding that I would transition to our local parish school for first grade the following year. It was in that public school that I had the grace to meet Richard, whose father was the minister of the church in my vision. When we were playing together after school one day, Richard brought me inside the small, dark church, which was quite unlike my cathedral-size parish church with its cream-colored Corinthian columns, ornate crucifixes, richly colored stained-glass windows, and wide marble aisles. I liked Richard so much that I came to believe that Jesus must have lived in his church like he lived in mine, although believing that the Divine took up residence in a Protestant church was heretical in the pre- Vatican II church. I believed that my vision gave Richard's church—and my little friend—a divine stamp of approval. Had God opened my heart to ecumenism when I was six years old? Or did I just backfill the details as I got older? The truth is that I did believe in ecumenism from a very early age—although whether that was because of the vision, my Protestant uncle, my open-minded Girl Scout leader, or my own father, who had attended public school in the 1930s along with Black, Jewish, and Protestant boys he had liked and admired—I cannot tell. The church that inspired my vision figured prominently in my childhood for reasons other than Richard who, much to my chagrin, suddenly moved away sometime during the school year. The church used its large grassy yard to host a neighborhood carnival every summer, an event I eagerly anticipated.

Despite its friendly overtures, the church must have had trouble surviving in our overwhelmingly Catholic community. After it closed in the early 1960s, we would climb the low wrought-iron fence and play in the deserted church yard.

Several years later, a Catholic organization founded in the name of Venerable Anna Catherine Emmerich purchased the church. A huge banner promised the grand opening of an academy founded in her name, despite the fact that the neighborhood was already filled with five Catholic schools and two public ones. The plan for the academy never came to fruition despite the size and promise of the banner which hung outside the church for twenty years, becoming the butt of jokes as the church fell into disrepair and was finally torn down.

Neighbors steeped in Catholic hagiography had never heard of Venerable Anna Catherina Emmerich (1774–1824). Most Catholics never heard about her until the film "The Passion of the Christ" made its debut in 2004. Mel Gibson appropriated the visions of Anna, a sickly German farm girl and later nun whose visions were recorded by Clemens Brentano (1778–1842) in a book entitled *The Dolorous Passion of Our Lord Jesus Christ* (Bretano, 1833).

It is difficult to parse out the alleged visions of an uneducated sick woman from the words of her poetic biographer who was steeped in the *sturm* and *drang* of German romanticism that reveled in suffering, passion, and the death of the innocent.

Since Brentano did not speak or understand Anna's language, he could only imagine what Anna was saying when she mumbled through sickness and fever. Nor did he take notes during the times he spent at her bedside. After consulting his atlas and reference books in the tranquility of his home, wondrous visions emerged from Clemens' pen. Although Anna had never traveled beyond the boundaries of her town, Brentano claimed she provided him with descriptions of the Himalayas, detailed maps of Jerusalem, unicorns prior to the flood, and Mary's house high on a hill outside of the ancient city of Ephesus. ("Mary's house," clearly of recent construction, is now a favorite excursion site of cruise ships that dock in the nearby city of Kusadasi, Turkey. (When I visited what was clearly a tourist trap in 2009, I wondered how anyone could believe that Mary would choose to live so far away from the early Christian community of believers in Ephesus).

Anna devoted herself to personal suffering in the hope of alleviating the suffering of others. This suffering included vicariously taking on the sufferings of Jesus. By age thirty-eight, an undetermined illness accompanied by great pain confined Anna permanently to her bed. While her fellow nuns commented upon Anna's strict adherence to her order's rules, which could have included ascetic practices, ill health was a common and debilitating occurrence in the early nineteenth century. However, as we have seen with other canonized saints, intense ascetic practices often exacerbated pre-existing illness, sometimes leading to disability and death. Interestingly, Anna's pain increased precipitously on Fridays, reaching a peak on Good Friday. Like Stanislaus Kostka, Aloysius Gonzaga, and Rose of Lima, Anna's caretakers reveled in her sufferings rather than trying to alleviate them.

Anna's reception of the stigmata— wounds in her hands, feet, and side matching those of Jesus—confirmed the churchmen's assessment of her holiness. Although there is no explanation why Jesus would reward those who loved him with painful, bleeding wounds when he spent his life curing the sick and the suffering, the stigmata became a badge of honor after Francis of Assisi (1181-1216) received it five hundred years earlier. The stigmata set the stage for a new level of miracles. Gregory IX (1170—1241), he of the Inquisition fame, regarded Francis's wounds as marvelous and singular, more important than any miracle performed by any saint before him. Those who wished to emulate Christ now sought pain, suffering, and even death as a means to achieve holiness. Freeing the oppressed was a poor second.

Nine papal bulls were written about Francis and his stigmata. After Gregory devoted three of them to Francis, the Dominicans became jealous and put forth members of their order who they claimed had also received the stigmata. Other religious orders did the same thing. The great amount of attention led to even more stories, more examples of holy people receiving the stigmata, and more religious iconography to dispel the naysayers who were dismayed by the efforts of the pope and the Franciscans to identify Francis with Jesus, a belief that bordered on heresy. Over the last centuries, the Catholic Church has been careful not to equate the stigmata with sanctity. When the church beatified Anna, there was no mention of the stigmata. Instead, she was beatified for the charitable deeds she performed before the onset of her illness.

Apparitions with their divine messages from Jesus, Mary, or the saints usually occur during times of political and religious division that sparked a personal crisis for the visionary. My vision of Jesus, for instance, occurred during a stressful time when my family was preparing to move.

Visionary Margaret Mary Alacoque (1647–1690) was another sickly nun who claimed to have received a stigmata— this one invisible—as a reward for the gruesome tortures she inflicted upon her already stressed body. She was born at the end of the long and bloody Thirty Years War (1618–1648) where violence, disease, and starvation had reduced the population of central Europe by approximately seven million people. The catastrophe caused many people to despair.

Margaret Mary was one of many canonized women who believed that their suffering could take away the suffering of the world and make reparations to a chronically angry God who kept a celestial score, noting who was naughty or nice, and punishing the good along with the bad with war and disease in endless divine snits of retaliation. No amount of suffering, no pain, and no bloodshed was too much for the God created by the churchmen who had sacrificed his only son to atone for sin. Rather than working to change the world, the saints chose to wallow in personal pain in expectation that their endless suffering would persuade God to ease the suffering of the world.

Like Teresa of Avila and Catherine of Siena, Margaret Mary had violent, erotic visions of a brutal Jesus who tore out his heart, placing it within her own. In another vision, she said that Jesus allowed her to place her head upon his chest.

Like Joan of Arc, Alacoque was given inside political information from the Divine about the future of her own country whom God seemed to favor above others. If, Alacoque learned from Jesus, King Louis XIV consecrated France to the Sacred Heart, he would triumph over his enemies. Both Louis and his successors failed to follow the saint's advice. As a result, Louis XIV's third great grandson, Louis XVI, lost his head during the French Revolution.

A male confessor fostered Alacoque's devotion to the Sacred Heart, doing nothing to stop her physical self-destruction. As Margaret Mary spiraled downward to death, the Blessed Virgin is said to have thanked the confessor for his support of Margaret Many and the Sacred Heart. One should wonder why the confessor did not encourage Margaret Mary to walk outside in the sunlight and smell the flowers.

Along with political advice, Jesus gave Alacoque specific instructions on circumventing purgatory, a twelfth century creation unknown to Jesus. Those who attended Mass and received communion on the first Friday of each month for nine consecutive months would go directly to heaven and bypass punishment in purgatory. Catholic schools took these divine instructions very seriously. Throughout the 1960s, our school dutifully took us to Mass and communion on first Fridays during the school year, thus guaranteeing our place in heaven If we died during the summer. The practice had to be renewed every nine months in order for it to remain in effect.

One of Jesus's many promises included a blessing for those who placed a picture of his Sacred Heart on the wall of their home. My grandmother dutifully hung this picture to siphon some of God's blessings into the unhappy home she shared with my alcoholic grandfather.

As someone who once regularly attended daily Mass, I would be loath to dismiss the religious practices of any believer who wanted to become a more faithful follower of Jesus. Nor would I dispute the comfort religious iconography brings to the believer. Few would disagree that prayer does often lead to major and substantial change in those who offer the prayers. While some may be comforted and sustained by the fact that others think enough about them to pray for them during times of trial or illness, God does not require encouragement to act on the behalf of the sick and the suffering. God does not favor one human being over another or answer the prayers of one person and ignore or refuse the prayer of another. God does not personally "give" anyone a cross to bear. Nor does God have a list of favored nations. That kind of god is a capricious human being, not the Divine.

Vicarious, gratuitous suffering does not and never has assuaged the sufferings of others. The ascetic practices of the saints did not reduce the suffering of humanity by one iota. Nor did it ease the suffering Jesus experienced during his horrendous death. Nor does it please or appease God, who does not seek suffering or impose it. While the lives of those who follow Jesus sometimes are placed in danger because of the demands of the gospel, God does not require that believers suffer or die to prove love and devotion. Instead, Jesus wants us to use our lives to mitigate the pain and suffering of others as he did. A loving God always walks with those who suffer, offering grace, peace, comfort, and strength, not pain and suffering.

Devotion to the Sacred Heart led, unfortunately, to generations of Catholic "victim souls," people who punished themselves for the sins of the world and the perceived slights that wounded the Sacred Heart of Jesus. Some churchmen touted the rewards of those (usually women) who were willing to suffer for unrepentant sinners and advised idealistic women in religious life that intimate relations with Jesus required suffering and atonement. As a result, some young women burdened their families and religious orders with the constant care as they, like modern day cutters, deliberately injured themselves, broke their own teeth and bones, refused to eat or sleep, made themselves vomit, or refused medical treatment.

Some religious orders engaged in overtly harmful practices in order to toughen up their novices and postulants, encouraging victim soul theology. One former member of a religious order told me she was forced to wear a woolen nightgown and sleep in a hot attic during the summer months while being told to offer up her discomfort to Jesus.

The establishment of suffering as a feminine virtue has persisted to the present time. The anti-abortion movement has sanctified women's suffering, declaring it right and just. Women are expected to bear the results of rape, incest, bad health, and lifelong care of children with life-threatening abnormalities because that is what God expects and demands of them. No health, social, economic, or social problem is too great for women to bear. Suffering is holy, even desirable to those who would regard pregnant women as God's chosen victim souls.

Most canonized female visionaries were victim souls. Unresolved childhood trauma often leads to serious manifestations of post-traumatic stress disorder. The hagiography of these young saints glibly glides over the horrors that often marked their early lives: parental death, abandonment or abuse, the death of siblings, poverty, war, illness, disease, religious persecution, or bullying by family members and religious superiors. The church treated these tribulations as pre-conditions for sainthood, rejoicing as the young people increased their capacity for suffering and lifting them up as role models with the implication, "Look what these young people will suffer for Jesus! You should be willing to do this as well."

The young, impressionable teenagers who lived amid this trauma observed the sins of their respective world unfold around them and believed with a teen's passionate nature and self-absorption that they might somehow have been responsible. They heard that the suffering of Jesus took away the sins of the world. They would emulate Jesus and do the same. Churchmen obsessed with sin and purity encouraged and canonized the young people's obsessive penitential practices.

The mother of Catherine Laboure (1806–1876) died when the little girl was nine years old. Like many a motherless child, Catherine lost more than her mother. When her father sent Catherine and her sister to live with an aunt, she also lost her father, her other siblings, and her community of friends and neighbors. There is a legend that is quite possibly true that in her grief, the little girl picked up a statue of Mary and told the mother of Jesus that she would now be Catherine's mother. It was at her aunt's house that Catherine's dreams of Mary began.

At age twenty-four, three months after becoming a postulant in the Daughters of Charity, Catherine saw three visions of the heart of her order's founder, Vincent de Paul. She also saw an apparition of Jesus as described in the liturgy of the day. When the superior gave the novices part of de Paul's vestments to hold, the young nun was determined to behold a vision of Mary that very night. Mary granted her wish. That very night, a young child led her to the chapel to meet Mary in person.

Like Margaret Mary's vision of the Sacred Heart, Catherine's vision of Mary commented on the political situation in France. Mary also understood nineteenth century gender relations. She told Catherine that she needed a man to help her. Several months later, Mary again appeared to Catherine in a stance that would be later imprinted upon what is known as the Miraculous Medal. All who wear the medal, Mary said, would receive great grace. Her confessor would help her cast and distribute the medal.

Like many religious talismans, the Miraculous Medal became a smash religious hit. Originally called the Medal of the Immaculate Conception, the name changed to the Miraculous Medal because so many wearers experienced miracles while wearing it. Even now, at the beginning of devotions to Mary at the Shrine of the Miraculous Medal in Philadelphia, the priest will list the miracles believers experienced since the previous week just by wearing the medal and praying, "O Mary conceived without sin, pray for us who have recourse to thee."

Catherine never told anyone except her confessor about her role in the origin of the Miraculous Medal until just before she died at age seventy after a life devoted to the care of the poor and sick. Like many saints before and after her, the church violated her corpse by exhuming her body to check for decay. Their efforts were rewarded by a body that had not decomposed, thus proving Catherine's sanctity, as if a life of dedicated service was not enough to canonize her.

We do not know if Catherine's confessors or her superiors modified her vision. We do know that the colors attributed to Mary are blue and white, the colors favored by royalist France. The serpent whose Mary's feet crush on the medal represents the perennial enemies of the church: the secular, godless, satanic, materialistic, or just the plain disobedient.

Another French visionary, Bernadette of Lourdes (1844–1879), was the eldest child of nine born into a desperately poor family in France. Her life, like the lives of other visionaries, was marked by trauma. Poverty had reduced the family to living in a one-room basement of what once was a jail. Five of Bernadette's siblings did not survive to adulthood and Bernadette herself battled severe illness her entire life.

In 1858, when she was fourteen, Bernadette had a vision in a grotto near a stream (the eponymous Lourdes) of a "small young lady" (like her) wearing a blue girdle and a yellow rose on each foot, a vision that could not be confirmed by the other children who accompanied her. On her second visit to the grotto, the vision instructed her to return every day for fourteen days. Bernadette pressed the vision to identify herself. The vision finally announced that she was the Immaculate Conception, a dogma defined by Pius IX (1792–1878) four years earlier. Unlike every other human being who must weep and mourn in their respective valley of tears on Earth because of sin, the church declared that Mary was conceived without original sin and lived without committing even one sin.

While God protected Mary from the effects of sin, the rest of humankind was not so fortunate. The omnipresence of sin rankled the young lady in the vision who instructed the sickly young teenager (who stood only four-feet-seven as a result of severe and unrelenting illness exacerbated by chronic starvation) to subject herself to acts of repentance. No adult questioned why the mother of Jesus, whose own child died an excruciatingly painful death, would encourage a sickly young girl to engage in repeated acts of penance that damaged her frail health to atone for sins she did not commit. Bernadette obliged the pretty young lady dressed in blue. After entering the convent, she spent the last fourteen years of her life in the convent infirmary refusing treatments that might have helped improve her health, declaring that she was happier in her bed than a queen was sitting upon her throne. Her job, she once informed an exasperated superior, was being ill. Only by engaging in self-denial could she rack up the merits necessary to please the lady in her vision.

Bernadette's young lady demanded the erection of a chapel dedicated to her near the stream endowed by believers with healing powers. Today, a chapel big enough to accommodate twenty-five thousand believers stands at the site, and tens of thousands visit every year hoping for a miraculous cure. Although many have prayed devoutly for healing, only about seventy allegedly have been blessed by Our Lady of Lourdes with a cure, the last in the 1970's. Although these seventy cures defy scientific explanation, the cruelty of that pathetically low statistic should indicate that they are not of divine origin. How could a loving God be so stingy with divine blessings?

While agents of the church repeatedly exhumed Bernadette's body to determine the extent of decomposition and thus verify her saintliness, none of them bothered to examine the life of abject poverty Bernadette had lived in the dank basement room with her parents and many siblings. No one questioned the penitential practices that made Bernadette sick unto death.

When rigorously examined about her vision by both secular and religious authorities, Bernadette never changed her story. The repetition of details, however, does not make a story true.

While the faithful believe that visions come from heaven (or hell), there are other possible explanations. When I was nineteen, I awoke in utter terror. While I had had nightmares before, this was of a much different caliber. Though wide awake, I could neither move nor breathe. Something heavy seemed to be pressing upon my chest. As I lay gasping for breath, a man with a black top hat appeared by the side of my bed, his entire body outlined by flowing cartoon-like bolts of lightning. He was bending over my bed, and I could not move away from him. What was he going to do to me? After several moments of sheer terror, I realized that I could move my little finger. That tiny movement broke the spell. The vision disappeared and I could move again. Attributing the vision to a very bad dream, I went back to sleep.

I was in my thirties when a radio program dealing with sleep disturbances finally explained my random and very strange sleep experiences that had continued to occur infrequently in the intervening years. What I now know is that I suffered from an unfortunate glitch in my sleep cycle called sleep paralysis. About twenty percent of all people have had at least one episode of sleep paralysis. Less than eight percent of the population regularly experience the phenomenon which occurs among people of every religious faith in all parts of the world.

Others have had far more disturbing experiences with sleep paralysis than I had, hence its folk designation, "Hag's Syndrome." Some sleep paralytics feel as if they are floating in the air or moving to another location. They see visions, hear hissing noises and roars, or see lights. Like Job, they hear voices they attribute to God who during deep sleep, "while they slumber on their beds, he opens their ears and terrifies them with warnings" (Job 33:14-16). Like Catherine Labore's Mary and Margaret Mary's vision of the Sacred Heart, the paralytic describes a presence in great detail. Those who meditate or daydream can slip into sleep paralysis and, like Bernadette, experience visions. The powerful, uncomfortable, and frightening experiences of sleep paralytics lend credibility to stories of visions, angels, witches, demon possession, devils, goblins, and alien abductions. Scientists who have studied sleep paralysis believe that the sufferers define their own physical and psychological experience (Jalal, 2020). Within this context, stories of saints levitating, hearing voices, talking to Mary, or fighting off Satan and his minions during sleep make perfect sense.

Sleep paralysis can be exacerbated or caused by stress, anxiety, and PTSD. Anna Catherine Emmerich, Margaret Mary Alacoque, Catherine Labore, and Bernadette of Lourdes were traumatized by war, sickness, death, and starvation. Were these women holy, mentally ill, or suffering from chronic PTSD or any combination of the three?

Do we want to canonize the women the Catholic Church made into victim souls?

Chapter 12:
NINETEENTH CENTURY SAINTS

"If I were to meet a priest and an angel, I should salute the priest. The latter is a friend of God, but the priest stands in His place."

John Vianney

"If you love the pope, you do not debate his dispositions. You do not set limits to his authority."

Pope Pius X.

"I feel that Jesus demands of the two of us that we quench his thirst by giving him souls, most of all, the souls of priests. Our mission is to lose ourselves, to annihilate ourselves...the salvation of souls depends upon our sacrifice."

Therese of Lisieux to her older sister Celine.

In their infinite wisdom, my Catholic elementary school decided that all seven-year-olds would make their Confirmation, first Penance, and First Communion. Since I turned seven in February during first grade, I was a member of that select group. Those who turned seven after May would have to wait another year. In spite of our tender age and rudimentary reading skills, we were not spared from memorizing what was a very long list of complicated questions, some containing vocabulary words that even my mother did not know. As we embarked upon our journey into the world of practiced faith, we were essentially lost in a sea of theological jargon.

My mother sat patiently with me every night, reading over the Confirmation questions until I had them memorized. One of my fears was the "slight blow on the cheek" that would serve as a reminder that I could be martyred by the godless Communists in Russia for practicing my faith. An even greater fear was that I would laugh out loud if the bishop asked me the question about the Twelve Fruits of the Holy Spirit, as my mother did when she tried to pronounce the word "benignity."

Like many fears, mine were in vain. The bishop had mastered the tricks of his ecclesiastical trade. When faced with the prospect of confirming a hundred seven-year-olds and still making it to the rectory in time for a fancy dinner, the bishop asked no questions. Several eighth-grade girls sponsored all of the girl *confirmandi*, their right hand moving quickly and deftly from white clad shoulder to shoulder as the bishop gave us that tiny slap on the cheek while mumbling my confirmation name: my mother's name, Marie. The process was quick—and painless—for everyone. Within an hour or so I was a newly minted soldier for Christ.

Two months later, I received the next two sacraments, Penance and First Communion. I went to confession the day before I made my communion and was so nervous that right after I got out the words "Bless me, Father, for I have sinned," I threw up all over the confessional.

St. John Vianney (1786–1859) spent a great deal of time in the confessional with nervous little girls like me. Although he is regarded as the patron saint of priests, one must wonder what kind of confessor he was since his homilies were filled with vitriol directed against the very people he was forgiving. I wonder how young girls felt as he, like so many churchmen in whose footsteps he willingly followed, declared them occasions of sin rather than human beings and children of God.

Like many of the canonized, Vianney's life was filled with trauma. When he was a child, France suffered through the violent anti-religious Reign of Terror, where priests were forced to hide and administer the sacraments in secret. Vianney, in fact, received his First Communion in a farmhouse where the windows were covered with the rural version of blackout curtains. Because of the fear associated with his religious upbringing, Vianney came to regard priests as heroes and aspired to be one.

The education Vianney needed to become a priest was repeatedly interrupted by war. When he finally entered the seminary, his seminary professors found him functionally illiterate and too far behind everyone else to be ordained. A tutor persuaded the rector that Vianney's piety compensated for his lack of intelligence. At age twenty-nine, Vianney was finally ordained and was made the parish priest of a small town where he found mortal sin embedded in his parishioners' activities of daily living.

Like many stupid and ill-prepared but overly pious priests before and after him, Vianney took his unresolved psychosexual issues straight into his parish, which he regarded as a hotbed of fleshy sin. His homilies were consumed with his flock's sexual peccadilloes that he learned from first-hand contact in the confessional and broadcast in sermons. He also must have spied on them.

"Tell me, my dear brethren, what are the penances that are given to you? Alas! /a few rosaries, some almsgivings, a few little mortifications. Do all of these things, I ask you, bear any proportion to our sins which deserve eternal punishment? There are some who carry out their penance walking along or sitting down; that is not doing it at all. Unless the priest tells you that you may do it while walking along or sitting down, you should do your penance on your knees. If you do perform your penance while walking or sitting down, you should confess it and never do it again. In the second place, unless you are not able to do it as required, in which event you must tell that to your confessor when you go to confession the next time, I must tell you that the penance should be done within the time indicated; otherwise, you commit a sin. For example, the priest might tell you to make a visit to the Blessed Sacrament after the services because he knows that you go around in company which will not bring you any nearer to God; he may order your to mortify yourself in something which you eat because you are subject to gluttony; to make an act of contrition if you have the misfortune to fall back into the sin which you have just confessed"(Homilies of St. John Vianney, 6).

The huge decrease in number of priests during the French

Revolution had led to a lack of pastoral care and religious instruction for several generations, a fact that also emboldened people to think for themselves. Some of the once largely obedient French Catholics now practiced birth control, married during Lent, and danced on Sundays, much to the dismay of the post-revolution priests like Vianney who refused to give them absolution for engaging in what is objectively an innocent activity. Vianney also condemned the personal practice of enjoying life as a normal part of one's sojourn on Earth, ignoring his fellow wealthy clergymen, who dressed, ate, drank, and played like the nobility. One wonders if Vianney would have preached the words below to a group of nobles instead of to his congregation of peasants.

> *"What harm can there be in enjoying oneself for a while? I do no wrong to anyone; I do not want to be religious or to become a religious! If I do not go to dances, I will be living in the world like someone dead! My good friend, you are wrong. Either you will be religious, or you will be damned"* (St. John Vianney, Homily No. 7).

Like all voyeurs and sex-obsessed clerics, Vianney graphically pointed out the shapes and clothing of the women in his parish. He also had a knack for tracking down nakedness. The culprits? Nursing mothers with exposed breasts and naked babies whose diapers were not changed quickly enough for his liking. According to Vianney, naked babies "offend the angels." The solution of the man who never had to comfort a crying baby with a dirty diaper was to limit diaper changing so that the baby would get used to being covered with feces and not come to enjoy his or her nakedness and use it for evil.

Fixated upon sins of the flesh, Vianney criticized those families who slept together in the same bed, oblivious to the fact that members of his flock might not have had enough beds for everyone. According to confessor, mothers who slept with their children, including those with nursing infants who might feed every two hours during the night, committed a great sin.

He directed his most poisonous invectives at the young, impressionable girls sitting in the pews of the parish church, attacking their youthful beauty as a near occasion of sin for men, including him. Covering their physical beauty with repellent spiritual imagery to ward off his own impure thoughts, he announced that devils surrounded the heads —and breasts —of young women. Like Medusa of Greek mythology, all who look upon these hideous girls would die. He extended his soulless, joyless misogyny to the girls' mothers whom he described as equally disgusting.

All his homilies drip with hate, malice, and condemnation covered with a patina of certain damnation and punishment. Under his aegis, all were guilty. Only by confessing their many sins to him would they be saved. Not only were his words mean and spiteful, so were his actions. When hungry parish children stole apples from his rectory orchard to supplement their sparse diets, Vianney chopped down the trees.

Vianney also targeted the Jews:

> "We cannot dwell upon the conduct of the Jews, my dear people, without being struck with amazement. These very people had waited for God for four thousand years, they had prayed much because of the great desire they had to receive Him, and yet when He came, He could not find a single person to give Him the poorest lodging. The all-powerful God was obliged to make His dwelling with the animals" (St. John Vianney, Sermon 3).

Information about Vianney was written in the late nineteenth and early twentieth century as part of his hagiography, so it remains difficult to separate the real man from the myth of the tireless and compassionate confessor created by the church. Like any corporate entity, the church needed to build itself back better with new messaging after the twin insults of the Reformation and the French Revolution. What better way to do it than to popularize the stories of an uneducated priest in a remote village whose good works attracted the attention of thousands of the newly reconverted faithful? Not only is Vianney portrayed by the church as following a prodigious schedule of hearing confessions eleven to sixteen hours a day, but he is also described as engaging in nightly battles with Satan, probably caused by sleep paralysis, as mentioned in the previous chapter.

Twenty-first-century believers should ask why popes, bishops, and priests offer a man who preached hate and condemned nursing mothers and teenaged girls from the pulpit as a model priest whose acts should be not only admired but also emulated.

In its long history, the church had accumulated a stable of scams that revved up the base after periods of disillusionment and decline. Magical men like John Vianney, who nightly wrestled with Satan; the visions of Margaret Mary Alacoque, Catherine Laboure, and Bernadette of Lourdes; coupled with tales of suffering of faithful young people like Rose of Lima, Stanislas Kostka and Aloysius Gonzaga, stimulated belief in the thrilling days of Catholic yester-year when all members of the faithful purportedly believed and acted in concert to fulfill God's will. The world was but a place of expected and unrelieved suffering, a dismal prelude to eternal life in heaven with the Beatific Vision. Within this context, it made no sense to fix the world so that people did not suffer, although Jesus tried to fix it repeatedly throughout his ministry.

The divine will was defined by the luxuriously dressed white men who sat around the food-laden gilded tables in Rome and other glittering cities of Europe who wanted believers to know their place and remain there without question or complaint. The men at those tables set the gold standard for reactionary, illiberal, and unchristian behavior that has characterized the church and the societies in which it has been embedded since the establishment of Constantinian Christendom. In its centuries-long struggle to maintain ordained privilege, members of the clergy were quick to condemn the individual actions of their parishioners while miserably failing to address their own sin and the structural sin that oppressed and impoverished their flocks. Incense and miraculous cures, the charmed relics of saints, fear of hell, and the hocus-pocus of priests kept the people pious and obedient and in their place. Thus, Vianney and other French saints should be seen as part of the restoration of the church in France after the hiatus forced upon the faithful by the French Revolution.

The French Revolution had attempted to dismantle Roman Catholicism in response to the church's reactionary association with the *ancien regime*. As with most religious upheavals, a good portion of the population did not agree with the government's heavy-handed anti-religion policy. Arbitrarily banning religious practice is as useless and stupid as forcing religion down people's throats.

Although some priests—and nuns—were executed during the Reign of Terror, most priests were deported, leaving a few who, along with women, continued services in secret. Like twentieth-century Ludmilla Jarorova, who presided at Mass and distributed communion in Czech prisons during the Communist takeover of her country, women in France kept the church alive when priests were forced into hiding, executed, or deported. Jeanne Artide Thouret received a letter of thanks from the ordained man who returned to lead the parish she saved during the Revolution. "I owe you a great debt," he wrote, "You have supported my parishioners during my absence; you have been the priest and the vision in doing our work" (Kselman, 2013). Women also led liturgies in the forests while the men kept guard.

Once Napoleon reinstated Catholicism, the remaining bishops reopened parishes and rebuilt seminaries. Due to decades without church services or religious education, the church began to focus upon the education of children as a means of re-Christianization. One of the unintended consequences of the Revolution was the rise of feminism, as the public rights of man spawned the nascent rights of women. The nineteenth century literally exploded with French religious orders of uncloistered women dedicated to the education of children and care of the sick. The invention of the bicycle, interestingly, enabled the mobility of large numbers of women.

Therese of Lisieux (1873–1897), who wanted so badly to save souls for Christ, did not choose to join one of the religious orders of women that actively worked in the world to better the lives of children and the sick. Instead, the fifteen-year-old Therese received special permission to follow her three older sisters into the Carmelite order, which was dedicated to solitary prayer and contemplation rather than to direct action in the world.

Therese's parents, Zelie Martin and her husband, Louis, were also canonized saints. This seems to be a strange way of honoring marriage since the couple regarded marriage as a poor substitute for their primary vocation to religious life. Zelie wrote that her wedding day was the worst day of her life. Their parish priest had to talk them into having sexual relations, which they apparently later did with great gusto, producing nine children in thirteen years. Three children died before their first birthday; the fourth died at age five. The remaining five girls all eventually entered the convent, including Leonie, who had tried to resist her mother's overbearing religious personality. In spite of these tragedies, to which should be added Zelie's death when Therese was four, Therese painted a romantic picture of an ideal family in her autobiography, *The Story of a Soul,* a book heavily edited and published by her two older sisters and an ordained editor in 1899.

Zelie was, apparently, a stern religious taskmaster, expecting the girls to make a nightly examination of conscience before bedtime at their mother's knee as she "nurtured them for Heaven." She wrote to her two oldest girls, urging them to be good but expecting them to be saints. As a toddler, little Therese repeatedly promised her mother that she would be good.

Like many proper middle-class French Catholic families, the Martins' life revolved around church, private devotions, and the sacraments. They attended the daily 5:30 A.M. mass with those wearing work clothes and aprons, people with rough hands and no voice. Other than this brief and impersonal contact with the working poor, the family and future saint had nothing to do with the political and social concerns of the day, choosing instead to live in splendid isolation from the world, allowing very few outsiders into their inner circle. Consequently, Therese grew up in profound alienation from the people that Jesus loved. Like her older sister Leonie, Therese experienced psychological difficulties during her childhood. Her struggles are glossed over and explained away by her hagiographers.

The death of her mother and her four siblings, and her sisters' move to the convent soured Therese on interpersonal relationships whose impermanence caused so much pain. It should come as no surprise that she desperately wanted to follow her beloved older sisters into the Carmelites, an order that did not suit the spirited Therese from the very beginning.

Rather than considering that God might have wanted something different from a contemplative order for a young and energetic person with big ideas, the young Therese stayed with the Carmelites, drifting in and out of depression as her cloistered life did not fulfill her religious yearnings. Turning her dissatisfaction instead onto herself, Therese decided that she alone was the cause of her discontent. She was simply disobedient and did not work hard enough. Suffering through an ill-suited life and misplaced vocation in order to please a Jesus who, as her bridegroom, demanded pain from those who loved him, became her goal. She even regarded the onset of the symptoms of consumption as "a visit from her bridegroom," and the severe pain of her impending death at age twenty-four "transported her with joy" (Quoted in Losel, 2008).

Hans Von Baltasar, a friend and associate of John Paul II, was enthralled by Therese's self-described "little way" of self-abnegation. For von Baltasar, no humiliation was too great for a young woman who described herself as a plaything of the child Jesus who threw her to the ground, kicked her, and poked holes in her. Therese was the archetypical Catholic woman who was ordained to a life of suffering by God. Her "thirst for suffering," according to Von Baltasar was like "heaven on earth." (Quoted in Losel, 2008). Psychologists would now regard the joyful pursuit and self-infliction of suffering as masochism. The depraved indifference of those who inflict suffering, praise it, or do nothing to stop it are sadists.

Nothing Therese did was extraordinary. Reading parts of her book is like reading a teenager's diary. No, she wouldn't ask for another blanket even though she suffered from the cold. Yes, she would eat her vegetables even if she did not like them. She would bear with her fellow dishwasher who accidentally splashed dirty water into her face.

None of her fellow Carmelites recognized her as living saint. Instead, the saintly reputation of Therese of Lisieux was created by the churchmen who canonized her little way because it fit well with their low opinion of women. Women should shut themselves up in the cloister for God, cover their bodies up with the Catholic version of the chador, make themselves as small as possible, and accept the exigencies of life without complaint. Oblivious to their own role in creating the sins of the world, the churchmen sanctified Therese's suffering with a halo and the august title of Doctor of the Church

Like many religious orders with saints, the Carmelite order that included her adoring older sisters and cousin helped to elevate a very ordinary young woman into the annals of the saints, fulfilling their mother's dream. They published her autobiography in lieu of an obituary and saved all of Therese's belongings, and indeed, anything that touched her, to be sold as relics. Therese, who would be also known as the "Little Flower" augmented their efforts by tearing her trademark rose petals apart before she died (Pope, 1988).

By 1909, the Carmelites were getting a hundred fan letters a day attesting to miracles performed in Therese's name. Making herself and her devotees small did nothing to help save the world from a catastrophic war. Not twenty years after Therese's death, the Europe that purportedly received the heavenly gifts of Therese was torn apart by the Great War in which forty million men, women, and children perished.

Dominic Savio (1842–1857) was a male version of Therese, a teenager plucked from oblivion by his mentor, the also canonized John Bosco (1815–1888). According to the hagiography that led to the teenager's canonization, Bosco, the founder of the Salesians, found the very young Dominic to be so appealingly holy at such a tender age that the older man began recording incidents from his protégé's very short life, nudging him toward canonization. Like Therese, however, nothing Savio did was extraordinary. According to Bosco, Savio refused to swim naked with his classmates in order to protect his purity and declined to look at naughty books. At home, he said his prayers faithfully and helped his mother around the house. After the dogma of the Immaculate Conception was proclaimed, Savio began a sodality devoted to Mary. His cause for canonization was promulgated by what appears to be an overly involved father and a well-placed Bosco. Like another child saint, Maria Goretti, Savio was a lesson to be learned rather than a real boy.

Savio's hagiographer, Bosco, was an orphan who learned juggling, magic, and acrobatics from street performers to augment his family's income. At age ten, he is described as having the power to see into the souls of his classmates and mediate fights. Ordained at age twenty-six, Bosco began taking in wayward and orphaned boys, sheltering as many as eight hundred at a time. In spite of his charitable impulses during desperate times, his hagiography includes a list of people or groups who are described as deliberately trying to interfere with his vocation and mission. Some of the people of Turin were not thrilled with his shelters filled with young boys.

Like some other nineteenth-century French saints, Bosco repudiated the ideals of the French Revolution and the Enlightenment. As the church in France clawed its way back from the constraints of revolutionary secularism, its priests and bishops invested themselves and their parishioners in the Ultramontane movement. Ultramontanism was devoted to expanding and deepening the authority of the papacy with its promise of peace via absolute obedience, a pathway that had never worked in the past. It was the adherents to this movement that foisted the idea of papal infallibility upon the Catholic world.

The promulgator of this august power was Pope Pius IX, beatified in 2000 by another adherent of papal power, the sainted John Paul II. Like many popes before and after them, both men tried their best to create a church that stood in opposition to an always emerging and developing secular world which they regarded as the source of all evil.

In spite of various popes throughout the centuries who claimed universal power over both spiritual and temporal realms, it was not until Vatican I (1869–1870) that Catholics all over the world actually bought into the idea of an infallible ruler. As the rest of Europe, including Italy, was dismantling the divine right of kings, unifying realms into nation states, and changing monarchies into representative governments, Pius IX and his lackey bishops established the papacy as the voice of God and the pope as a divine-right king. As such, Catholics were obliged to obey.

Armed with infallibility, Pius IX and subsequent popes did battle with all who challenged their reactionary world view. Modernism, socialism, trade unions, the free press, republicanism, liberalism, and the separation of church and state, indeed, any movement toward justice and equality became verboten under the baleful eye of the popes and the bishops they appointed. Pius IX opposed religious rights for anyone who was not a Roman Catholic. He refused to accept the unification of Italy that required the dissolution of the Papal States which ended his political power.

Along with promulgating the dogma of papal infallibility, Pius IX, like so many churchmen before him who perseverated upon the purportedly virginal body of Mary, declared that she was conceived without sin, unlike the rest of the human race. The unfortunate dogma of the Immaculate Conception confirmed the inherent sinfulness rather than the beauty and wonder of a newborn baby. The churchmen consigned the innocent babes who had the misfortune of dying before being absolved of original sin to a place they plucked from their sin-obsessed imagination called limbo where they were never to be reunited with their parents in heaven. The stigma attached to these unbaptized babies was so strong that they were consigned to graves in unconsecrated ground in Catholic cemeteries, much to the lifelong distress of their families.

Repulsed by the rise in secularism that accompanied the expansion of literacy and the development of the modern state, Pius IX issued the encyclical *Quanta cura* in 1864 which condemned freedom of conscience, religious liberty, liberalism, socialism, communism, and modernism. To the encyclical, he attached the *Syllabus of Errors,* a compilation of papal defined heresies. While apologists like Cardinal John Newman claimed that the encyclical was misinterpreted, the evidence of its meaning and message played out in Catholic political and religious positions.

The encyclical and the syllabus and resulted in freezing the theological milieu theology and philosophy study for generations. Students and professors were obliged to ask for permission to read philosophical treatises by thinkers like John Locke, Immanuel Kant, and David Hume. Novelists like Victor Hugo, Honore Balzac, and Emile Zola appeared on the Vatican hit list. All books written by Catholics needed a stamp of approval from their local bishop called an imprimatur.

Decrees made by men with observable character flaws who chose to endow themselves with absolute power did not sit well with people of other faiths and contributed to ongoing Protestant prejudice against Catholic immigrants in America. The fact that infallibility was limited to theological matters did not diminish Protestant suspicion, especially for those who knew European history.

Pius IX, like many popes and churchmen, had no faith in the

ability of the faithful to make their own decisions. By extension, he had no faith in God to effect change in believers. Instead, he chose to operate by the force of his own beliefs, committing the sin of presumption. He was a bully and not worthy of beatification.

Sandwiched between the beatified Pius IX and the canonized Pius X was Leo XIII (1819–1903), author of the encyclical *Rerum novarum*, the basis for the belated and sparse body of instruction regarded as Catholic Social Teaching. Leo, unlike his predecessors and successors, engaged with the modern world. He encouraged the pursuit of biblical studies, archeology, and science. Although he was not a liberal, he believed that workers had the right to form trade unions, earn a living wage, and toil in safe working conditions. The church did not share his insight. There has been no move to canonize him.

Leo's successor, Pius X, a man who opposed individual rights and forced all clerics to take an oath against what he called Modernism, was canonized a mere forty years after his death by another pope who failed to use his authority to combat the Nazis.

Pius X was hardly a saint. He advocated the use of violence against clerics who opposed him. He also forbade Italians to vote in national elections because Italy's annexation of the Papal States deprived him of a temporal power Jesus would never have understood. The lure of temporal power was so strong that in the late 1950s, American Catholics were still fervently praying for the restoration of papal territory to the Roman pontiff every Sunday after Mass.

To the chagrin of backward-looking institutions like the Roman Catholic Church, change remains an integral part of life. While Pius X insisted that Modernism was the synthesis of all heresies, it was rather a natural progression of thought that occurred as a result of the Enlightenment, the French Revolution, the rise of socialism, the industrialization of society, and the spread of literacy. Modernism had its own share of prophets. Faithful Catholic scholars like Lord Acton, Albert Loisy, and Ignaz Dollinger dared to propose that God did not interfere directly in human affairs, that scripture should be understood metaphorically, and that the church has, in spite of assertions to the contrary, evolved over the centuries. These scholars understood that the Vatican march back into a mythological golden age was at odds with a modern, literate society. It was also ahistorical.

Popes and bishops resisted their efforts to reconcile the church with the modern world with every ounce of their ecclesiastical might. In 1907, Pius X began forcing clerics, theologians, philosophers, and Catholic university professors to take the antimodernist oath. Ignoring the grave ecclesiastical heresies that led to the Crusades, the Inquisition, the witch hunts, and the endless European wars, Pius fixated instead upon miracles, prophecies, and the unchanging nature of dogma, placing questioners into a theological straight jacket. The oath was not rescinded 1967.

Pius also intruded into the personal lives of believers declaring that marriages not performed by priests were sacramentally invalid. Priests could refuse to marry a mixed-faith couple. His interference in the marriages between Catholics and Protestants caused ongoing political problems in places like Northern Ireland which had large Protestant minorities and many couples of mixed faith who rightfully feared the arbitrary dissolution of their marriages by a foreign entity.

Pius extended his understanding of papal infallibility into the social and political realm, declaring democracy a perversity. Contrary to democratic principles of equality, there was, Pius insisted, a natural inequality between rulers and subjects that Catholics were obliged to recognize. Pius favored rule by the superior classes of white men, Catholic clerics, and Machiavellian nobles. In the new era of newspapers, Pius's undemocratic diatribes were broadcast all over Europe and the United States.

If one considers the decades-long papal vendetta against the rulers of the newly unified kingdom of Italy, Pius's vehement disagreement with the modernist theologians and his malignant condemnation of trade unions that were improving living conditions for large numbers of people, American Protestant suspicions of Catholics were warranted. Anti-Catholic sentiment in America, however wrong-headed and mean-spirited, did not exist in a vacuum.

One hundred and twenty-six years later, John Paul II and Josef Ratzinger (later Benedict XVI) were instrumental in issuing *Ex corde ecclesiae*, an encyclical that insisted that Catholic theologians who teach in a Catholic institution apply for a mandatum, an acknowledgement that a Catholic professor is in full communion with the Roman Catholic Church. In a 1990 letter on the duty of Catholic theologians to conform their teaching to the magisterium and by extension to the hierarchy, Ratzinger claimed that a "juridical bond" existed between the mandate to teach theology and the teaching authority of the church. The mandatum should be seen as another attempt by the papacy to control believers from above rather than from within.

The ecclesiasts who had often and visibly fallen short of the glory of God tried mightily to reinsert the faithful back under their dirty thumbs. These men perceived themselves as representatives of a sinless institution who alone could prevent the world from sinking into a culture of death and the dictatorship of relativism. Their consciences were clear even as they failed to consider the damage their faulty theology had unleased upon the world throughout the centuries. Salvos launched during the papacy of John Paul II denied Catholic citizens the right to follow their own consciences during elections and vote for candidates who supported abortion rights. Creating and maintaining the divide between faithful and cafeteria Catholics, they subjected believers to the dictates of an institution with a diminished and often blinkered understanding of the social, political, health, and gender realities that are endemic to the world they condemned.

John Paul II and his loyal and subservient bishops practiced their own version of moral relativism and engaged in a culture of death when they deliberately chose not to apply the universally accepted moral law to protect children from the harm of sexual abuse. Instead, they willingly and knowingly allowed their obviously ill-formed consciences to protect adult male clerics who preyed upon innocent children, grievously harming the psyches of young people, and destroying their souls. John Paul II, like those he so roundly condemned, was perfectly willing to make deals with his conscience to protect those he regarded as redeemed in spite of the fact that his self-understood exalted position as Vicar of Christ allegedly guaranteed truth. This moral blindness to fact, morality, and human kindness should dissuade anyone from pledging allegiance and obedience to mere mortals who have repeatedly proven over the course of two thousand years that unaccountable power accompanied by great wealth breeds corruption of the worst sort. There is no greater sin than the abuse of children. Because of his refusal to see, condemn, and correct sin in his own priestly caste, John Paul II should never be regarded as a saint.

It is a myth that the church worked throughout the ages to eliminate the evil of owning human beings. Augustine (354–430) never condemned slavery and placed enslaved human beings in the same category as an owner's other valuable possessions like a horse. Respect for authority and obedience to the state rather than the freedom of his fellow human beings dominated Augustine's thought. Paul did not request freedom for the slave Onesimus. Thomas Aquinas taught that higher orders of beings had power over lower orders. Pope Saint Gregory the Great (540–604) gave slaves to his friends as gifts and the medieval church enslaved women who had sexual relations with priests. While several popes condemned the trans-Atlantic slave trade, none condemned the buying and selling of human beings until Leo XIII in 1888. It was only then that the Catholic country of Brazil decided to free their slaves.

The Catholic Church in America was born in the slave-owning South. Like a dementor from the *Harry Potter* series, slavery sucked out the soul of the church leaving an institution that idolatrously worshipped mammon. Contrary to popular belief, the church did not immediately recognize the evils of slavery or establish religious orders to tend specifically to slaves. Instead, the Catholic Church, like other Christian denominations, had no comprehensive plan to address slavery and the ensuing evils of Jim Crow and ongoing racism largely because they did not regard it as evil. As a result, Catholic institutions of higher learning, churches, and religious orders were all tainted with this egregious crime against humanity.

Slaves helped grow Catholic institutions and so were factored into the bottom line. Most religious orders, including the Jesuits, the Vincentians, the Sulpicians, Capuchins, the Daughters of Charity, Ursulines, Carmelites, and the Visitadines unabashedly bought and sold human beings in the firm belief that all was right with their slaveholding souls. Like their fellow secular slave owners, the religious orders of nuns and priests operated with the same darkened consciences, selling off young couples with small children to pay off debts or finance building projects as if there was no other way of conducting business. The Catholic Church thus became the biggest corporate slave owner in Florida, Kentucky, Maryland, and Missouri. It has continued its racist policies into the modern area by closing down Catholic parishes in urban African American neighborhoods and rebuilding itself in the mostly white suburbs.

The Jesuits were the midwives of slavery in the one state founded by a Catholic— Maryland. In spite of their decade-long theological educational preparation, recitation of the Daily Office, and engagement with the *Spiritual Exercises* of their founder, the order experienced no twinges of conscience as they enslaved the people in both North and South America not long after their founding. Two of their members, Louis Molina (1535–1600) and Francisco Suarez (1548–1617), justified slavery while ignoring the ghastly horror that uprooted and destroyed generations of families. According to Andrew Dial (2021), the Jesuits were among the most successful slave owners in the Americas, buying, selling, owning, and using the bodies of over twenty-thousand human beings to work their missions. After all, the ordained wrote, who else would "hew the wood, draw the water, and bake our daily bread?" (Sweet, 1978).

In 2021, Georgetown University in Washington, DC reported having an endowment of 2.59 billion dollars on its website. Much of that wealth associated with the university can be traced back to the free labor of slaves who built the university in 1790 under the aegis of the Catholic slave-owning Carroll family of Maryland, of which John Carroll, the first Catholic bishop in America, was a member. Enslaved men and women also fed the students and cleaned and maintained the grounds for Georgetown students from 1790 to 1860. The Jesuits' shameless use of slaves to build and maintain their new university instructed and justified the ways of enslavement to impressionable young minds and formed the slave-owning consciences of generations of young Catholic men who attended Georgetown.

The Jesuits also owned three hundred and twenty-three slaves who worked the thirteen thousand acres of land in tobacco plantations in nearby Maryland. Apologists claim that the order practiced a kinder, gentler form of slavery. Indeed, the order consoled themselves for their slaveholding behavior by baptizing the slaves, thus granting them access to the white man's idea of salvation in the next life. Like their secular neighbors on other Maryland plantations, however, the Jesuits placed the hardworking slaves on strict rations and crammed them into small, squalid quarters. They were also not averse to breaking up families. When the British sacked one of the Jesuit plantations during the War of 1812, a number of the "well-treated" slaves chose to escape their ordained slave masters, whose tender mercies were not quite as warm and caring as apologists like to cite.

Like Molina and Suarez, the Maryland Jesuits wrote that it was perfectly possible to serve God faithfully while buying and selling human beings. The very first bishop, John Carroll (1735–1815), advised his confreres to sell "a few unnecessary Negroes, 3 or 4" to garner some necessary funds (Georgetown Slavery Archive). In 1838, the Jesuits followed Carroll's financial advice and sold off three generations of faithful, baptized, enslaved people to Catholic owners of rice plantations in Louisiana to pay off their financial debts. The blood money enabled the Jesuits to expand their mission throughout the United States and fund the building of other Jesuit universities like Loyola in Baltimore (Svrluga, 2024) and St. Joseph in Philadelphia (O'Connell, 2021).

The good the Catholic Church accomplished in the Americas was accomplished at a great price. Enslaved Africans erected the buildings that enabled the Jesuits to educate subsequent generations of slave owners. The enslaved tilled the fields that grew food for the order. Slaves cooked and served the food for both the Jesuits and their students. Freed from manual labor, the hands of the priests remained clean and smooth as they held up the Body of Christ to the enslaved people. Slavery corrupted the very heart of the priesthood. Priests betrayed the baptized Catholic slaves who relayed their intention to run away under the seal of confession by ratting them out to their masters (Schmidt, 2022).

The buying and selling of human beings by both Catholic and Protestant clergy modeled slave-owning behavior for their flocks, who adopted it with alacrity. No religious or political barrier stood between Christian entrepreneurs and the accumulation of great wealth via the free labor of slaves. Owning human beings was the business plan of action for those who sought wealth as no man could make a great fortune without the direct or indirect use of slaves. Churchgoers learned from their preachers that the providence of God designated Black people as a slave class just for them. Everybody owned slaves, a fact the Jesuit apologists use to excuse their behavior, as if the ordained slave owners had no choice but to participate in the status quo. If it was anyone's fault, it was Adam and Eve's and the concomitant omnipresence of evil in the world, and not the deliberate choice of people who had studied the gospel and should have known better than to participate in unspeakable evil.

It was the slave-owning Jesuits of Maryland who traveled to southeastern Pennsylvania and tended to the souls of the area's growing Catholic population in Philadelphia (O'Connell, 2021). For bishops like Francis Kendrick, the third bishop of Philadelphia, owning slaves was the collateral damage that the accumulation of wealth required (O'Connell, 2021). Although churchmen were always quick to interfere win the sexual lives of their flocks, bishops like Francis Kendrick directed the priests in his diocese not to interfere with workings of slavery. His brother Peter, the bishop of St. Louis, owned slaves. Churchmen like the Kendrick brothers proffered nonsensical reasons to maintain slavery. Both bishops worried that advocating for slavery's abolition would overturn the social order and interfere with the growth of the church. According to Peter, his fellow human beings in the South had been in bondage for so long, they could not even remember freedom. This lack of memory would preclude their enjoyment of personal liberty. Consequently, enslavement remained the better condition. In addition, freeing the slaves would make his white parishioners nervous and fearful since both men, like the white people they pastored, feared that freed Black people would seek to endanger white society in retribution.

The evil of colonialism and accompanying racism continued unto the generations. According to historian Katie Walker Grimes, slavery has bestowed the evil fruit of a "racialized" society upon America from which it has yet to recover (Grimes, 2017). The colonizers and their priests were among the architects of this racialized society. Many 21st-century Americans who have directly or indirectly benefitted from the genocide of the Indigenous people and the enslavement of Black people regard the past as a necessary step to the future. Why question the past? Why criticize people who were representative of their time? Why question Thomas Acquinas' egregious assumption that some people are superior and born to rule over others? Few even try to imagine that there could have been a better or a different way exemplified by the vast majority of people who did not own slaves.

Like many saints, Elizabeth Ann Seton (1774–1821), founder of the Daughters of Charity, was intimately acquainted with grief. When she was three, her mother died in childbirth along with her newborn sister. Her father remarried and later separated from her stepmother after having five children together, leaving Elizabeth and an older sister with an uncle. Her father, a physician, lost his life to yellow fever in 1802 and her husband died of tuberculosis the following year, leaving her a widow with five small children and little means of financial support. Two of her children and two beloved sisters-in-law would later die of tuberculosis, which would also claim her life at age forty-six.

Seton was raised as an Episcopalian and like many socially conscious wealthy married women in New York City, she was educated to care for the sick, the suffering, and the poor. Seton and her family became a part of the last group after her husband lost his company and then his life. Seton refused to succumb to despair, and instead relied upon her faith in God to sustain her. This faith included converting to Catholicism, an act that alienated her from the financial support of family and friends. Anti-Catholic bias blocked the success of schools she tried to start in New York City. Poverty forced her to move with her children to Baltimore, where she was commissioned by the Bishop John Carroll to open a school for poor Catholic girls and found a religious order, the Sisters of Charity, the first religious order to be founded in the United States. Seton proved to be an organizing genius. Prior to her death in 1821, she established schools, orphanages, and hospitals in Pennsylvania, New Jersey, Ohio, New York, and Missouri, all staffed by her new order of sisters.

Although no one has proven that Seton or her order owned slaves, original members of her order in Emmitsburg, Maryland, a slave-owning state, personally owned slaves. There is no record of

Seton's personal opinion on slavery or slave owners. Students of slavery Kelly L. Schmidt, Shannen Dee Williams, and Rachel Swarms have written that the American Catholic Church, born and nurtured in the slave-owning South, would not have survived without the free labor of enslaved Black people. The greater anomaly, according to Schmidt, was the religious order that did *not* own slaves.

The 2022 newsletter of the Sisters of Charity contained this sentence, "It is confirmed that the original Sisters of Charity of St. Joseph, beginning with their founding by Elizabeth Ann Seton in 1809 and their successors, had some involvement with slavery until its cessation in the United States in 1865."

The legacy of Katherine Drexel (1858–1955), the founder of the Sisters of the Blessed Sacrament, remains mixed. There is no doubt that Drexel's intense desire to educate and convert freed African Americans and Native Americans was heartfelt. She donated millions of dollars of her considerable fortune to founding, supporting, and staffing schools for Indigenous children in the Midwest and West. In spite of stories of the sisters and priests and their benevolent self-sacrifice to save the Indians from their culture and religion, recent history has proven that most of the schools for Native American children were a horror.

Drexel was one of many fervent Christians who wore the "white person's burden" with its sense of moral and spiritual superiority on her sleeve. The plight of the other fueled her missionary zeal and compelled her to rescue the Native people from themselves, earmarking them for God by baptizing them. By educating and converting the children, the missionaries hoped to destroy native culture and build up a new generation of adults who repudiated native ways and acted and believed like the white American Christians. Drexel believed that Native American children educated in Catholic schools would bring their new faith and morality home to their pagan parents. Authoritarian countries would later use this mode of education model to teach children to repudiate the values and beliefs of their parents.

Education by white missionaries led to the widespread abuse of Native American children and their parents. Policies to forcibly convert children meant cutting their hair and forbidding them to speak their native language. Regarded as savages, the children were beaten for small infractions. They were housed in overcrowded dorms where they often became ill from Western diseases like measles and tuberculosis. The children were forced at an early age to engage in heavy farm work that enabled the schools to function without paying for outside help. Priests and nuns urged the children to give up what the white people labeled as native superstitions for rosaries and scapulars. When Seton visited a reservation, she decided that the Native Americans were crying out for Roman Catholicism. In fact, we really have no idea what they were thinking as Drexel passed out her own superstitions in the form of holy cards and miraculous medals, statues, and crosses to non-English speaking people recently traumatized by being forced onto reservations who had no Catholic frame of reference.

Elizabeth Schoffen (b. 1861) was a sister of Charity of Providence for thirty-one years who worked in Catholic orphanages, hospitals, and mission schools in the latter part of the nineteenth century and the early twentieth century. In her autobiography entitled *The Demands of Rome* written in 1917, she described the lives of poorly educated, overworked, and often sick sisters who were ill-equipped to teach and care for Native children. She corroborated the beatings and the cramped dormitory conditions without adequate ventilation or sanitation described by former students that led to illness and death for both the children and the sisters.

Schoffen's autobiography notes the lack of care and concern shown by church authorities and the heads of religious orders for their own members. This lack of care was subsumed under the rubric of obedience and sacrifice. Schoffen described being sent by her superiors into the wilds of the West with another sister on a begging campaign to raise funds for the order. One of her companions in her thirties died from illness and exhaustion after going on multiple trips to the Alaskan frontier. Schoffen herself suffered from an undiagnosed and untreated illness that caused paralysis in one of her arms, for which she never received care. Large numbers of sisters in their twenties and thirties died from tuberculosis after living in unhygienic conditions. No sacrifice was too great for the women who obeyed a strict taskmaster type of God. The reliance upon the notion of sacrifice as a means of pleasing God filtered down to the children. Crowded dorms and classrooms, lack of washing facilities, and the extinction of culture was the price the children had to pay for their Catholic education.

Although Drexel gave away millions of dollars to start up or fund established missions, many of the mission schools had another funding source. In 1900, Catholic leadership introduced the idea of diverting native treaty and trust funds to pay for the gift of a Catholic education. For much of the twentieth century, the federal government obliged the Catholic mission authorities. The practice ended only in 1970 after the withdrawal of $30.4 million dollars had completely depleted the Native peoples' trust funds (Pember, 2020). The influx of that huge amount of money did little to improve conditions in the Catholic Indian schools.

Signing over their trust fund money to pay for tuition often left Native families without food. When native parents complained of being denied funds guaranteed by their treaty with the federal government, Father Ketchem, the Director of the Bureau of Catholic Indian Missions wrote coldly, "The Indians are indignant over the sacrifices required of them and begin to look at the missionaries and the schools as mercenaries" (Pember, 2020).

The Catholic Church and Mother Drexel usually get a bye on the issue of Indian mission schools since substantial numbers of Native people converted to Catholicism and not Protestant sects, growing the Catholic church in the West. Ketchum wrote glowingly about Drexel, "Had it not been for one devoted woman raised up by Almighty God for the edification of the American people and for the poor abandoned races, the whole system of Catholic Indian schools would have collapsed and the Indian children been given over to schools decidedly anti-Catholic" (quoted in Bresle, 2014).

Survivors of the Indian mission schools do not share Ketchum's enthusiasm. Lakota Sioux Mary Crow Dog (1954–2013), author of *Lakota Woman*, grew up on the Rosebud Reservation and attended St. Francis Mission School. She regarded the mission schools as a generational curse.

Katharine Drexel is admirable on many levels. She repudiated her former life as a wealthy socialite and spent her entire life donating

millions of dollars to those she regarded as less fortunate. She founded Xavier University in New Orleans for Black Catholics. Her sisters
of the Blessed Sacrament staffed Catholic schools for Black children
in Northern and Southern states in the face of intense anti-Catholic
bigotry and virulent racism. She donated large sums of money to
Native people fighting for their rights to their ancestral land. She
refused to hand over her fortune to the men of the church without
accountability, much to their chagrin. Despite taking vows, she lived
her life as she and not the churchmen saw fit. Was Katharine Drexel
a saint? I leave the answer to that question up to the those whose
ancestors attended the mission schools.

The South was not the only region to benefit from slavery.
Many Yankee fortunes were also made on the backs of the enslaved.
According to Eric Williams, author of the seminal book *Capitalism
and Slavery (1944)*, the corruption of slavery depletes the soul
and leads to widespread social depravity that dims the conscience.
Eventually all who come in contact with slavery become inured to
evil in all of its many manifestations. As the choice to commit the
great sin of slavery became habitual and normal, it spread to the
voracious captains of industry in the North, whose fortunes relied
upon the payment of very low wages to their workers. Within the
capitalist system in America that included chattel slavery, child
labor, and unfair and unsafe labor practices, justice and morality
were moot. The market became the god of Christian capitalists, and
it remains their god in the twenty-first century. Nothing is more
sacred than the market. Well-paid churchmen in the United States
and Europe have developed elaborate theologies to support the accumulation of great wealth in a small number of grasping hands under
the aegis of private property.

In large northern cities like Philadelphia, small children worked
long and hard hours at large machines in unsafe factories. A victim
of child labor, my friend's grandmother lost her finger in a loom. The
foreman took her finger and threw it out of the window, coldly ordering the traumatized child to return to work as if nothing serious
had happened. Owners of the railroads actively worked to prevent
the installation of safety equipment on rail cars such as air brakes and
automatic couplers because of the cost to management. It was easier

and cheaper to replace workers than it was to install new equipment. Impoverished miners who went on strike in Pennsylvania mines were shot at by machine guns wielded by the precursors of the F.B.I. In all of these situations, it was the victims of the wealthy who were named as villains.

Into the nineteenth-century morass of poverty and violence marched a woman dressed in black called Mother Jones (1837–1930). The early life of Mary Harris Jones was marked by tragedy. At ten, she fled with her parents from the potato famine in Ireland. After marrying George Jones, a union organizer in Memphis, Tennessee, Jones gave birth to four children. She lost her husband and her children, all under the age of five, in a yellow fever epidemic in 1867.

Jones then moved to Chicago and opened her own dress making shop that catered to rich women. From the windows of her workplace, she saw her wealthy patrons prancing along Lake Shore Drive in their finery while the poor shivered and begged along the margins of Lake Michigan. Jones lost her shop and all of her possessions in the great Chicago fire of 1871.

Instead of taking to her bed and honing her considerable suffering into a vocation, Harris Jones dedicated the next sixty-three years of her life to trying to dismantle the structures of injustice. Harris Jones joined the Knights of Labor, the first major union in the United States that organized across racial and gender lines. She organized the wives and mothers of striking mine workers in Pennsylvania. Armed with mops and buckets of cold water, and banging spoons against wash basins, the women spooked donkeys carrying coal and stopped the influx of scabs. During a 1902 strike in West Virginia, she ignored an injunction against the right of mine workers to assemble freely and was arrested. At her trial, the state attorney general bestowed upon her the title, "The Most Dangerous Woman in America" (McGinley, 2021).

Jones railed against both church and state. Although she was raised a Catholic, Harris Jones had no time for any churchmen's opposition to labor unions and their fatalistic acceptance of poverty and low wages as the will of God. She repeatedly debunked Theodore Roosevelt's assertion of American prosperity by pointing out the large numbers of children working in factories and called out senators for taking bribes from businessmen who hoped to block legislation to protect children.

During a 1903 strike of textile workers in Philadelphia, Mother Jones assembled a group of child workers with missing fingers and crushed hands on a platform, displayed their injuries to the assembled crowd, and announced that the great mansions in Philadelphia were built upon the broken bones and lost futures of the maimed children. She then accused the state and city officials of ignoring the shocking conditions in Philadelphia's many factories.

Statistics backed up her accusations. In 1901, there were 1,161,524 children enrolled in school in Pennsylvania. Only 847,445 attended. The rest were employed, mostly illegally, in factories. My great-grandfather, my grandmothers, great aunts, and uncles were among this number. They worked in the hosiery and glass factories in Kensington, the manufacturing district in Philadelphia, after leaving school in the fifth grade to supplement their family's meager income.

Mother Jones saw all of life through the lens of God's love for the world. She had witnessed religious institutions' fixation with private virtue and personal salvation while ignoring or explaining away society's grievous structural sin with the mythical story of Adam and Eve, Satan and the will of God which always seemed to favor the rich. Consequently, Mary Jones understood that systemic sin was neither inevitable nor irremediable, but rather repairable through action and organizing for good. Unlike the men who stood each Sunday in pulpits all over the world, Mary Harris Jones understood that confessing one's faith in Jesus Christ meant working to better the lives of all who live in an interrelated world created by a loving God.

Mother Francesca Cabrini, like Mother Jones tried to provide solace and support to immigrants who left the impoverished countries in Europe only to find similar conditions in the United States. The youngest of thirteen and one of only four siblings to survive childhood, Cabrini wanted to become a missionary in China. She was dissuaded by Leo XIII who advised her to work with impoverished immigrants in New York City.

Against great odds, including the lack of support from the Irish archbishop of New York City, Cabrini arrived in America in 1889 and quickly went to work founding orphanages, schools, and hospitals with sisters from the order she founded, the Missionary Sisters of the Sacred Heart of Jesus. By the time she died in 1917, Mother Cabrini and her order had founded sixty-seven institutions that served the sick and suffering. All were run by women.

John Vianney, Zelie and Louis Martin, John Bosco, Pius IX and X were zealots, not saints. Therese Martin's "Little Way" was a recipe for the self-abnegation of women promoted by churchmen. Dominic Savio was a sick young man whose illness was ignored by adults who surrounded him.

I leave it to readers to decide if Katharine Drexel and Elizabeth Ann Seton are saints.

Follower of the Way of Jesus
Marry Harris Jones
Mother Francesca Cabrini

Chapter 13:
A CAVALCADE OF SAINTLY NUNS AND PRIESTS

*"Padre Pio is a man with a restricted field of knowledge,
low psychic energy, monotone ideas, and little volition."*

Agostino Gemelli, O. F.M. founder of the Catholic University of Milan.

*"Today, Christianity stands at the head of this country. I pledge that I
will never tie myself to those who want to destroy our culture again...
We want to burn out the recent immoral development in literature,
theater, the arts, and the presss... In short, we want to burn out the
immorality that has entered our whole life and culture as a result of
liberal excess in the past few years."*

Adolph Hitler.

*"If you touch the idea of sainthood especially in this country (US)
people feel you've taken something from them personally. I'm
fascinated because we like to look down on other religious beliefs as
being tribal and superstitious, but never dare criticize our own."*

Christopher Hitchens on CSPAN.

St. Paul tells us that the trumpet shall blow and in the twinkling of
an eye, we shall be changed. So, what the afterlife really looks like is
anyone's guess. Traditional church teaching advises us that we shall
spend eternity gazing at the Beatific Vision, something that always
sounded quite boring to me. Sister G. in third grade assured us that
heaven would be more like a continuation of life on earth with all

the bad stuff excised. That description was more to my liking.

Sister G. had replaced Sister J. mid-year, a most uncommon occurrence in 1960 Catholic schools. I don't know what happened to Sister J. but I was ecstatic that she left. I had always loved school and my teachers. Having Sister J. as my third-grade teacher changed all that. At age eight, I experienced the dislike of a person who had power over me during most of my waking hours. I prayed every night that Sister J. would just go away.

Sister G. explained Sister J.'s absence with a quick flick of her hand. Sister J. had been transferred to a neighboring parish school, a policy often followed by church officials when they received complaints against priests or nuns. From her unkind and unchristian behavior towards her eight-year-old charges whom she regularly called "bold, brazen articles" in a hateful tone of voice, it seems as if parents might have made their share of complaints, especially when their children, like me, began to hate school and claimed to be sick on Sunday night.

Sister G., who was older than Sister J., was far more fun. She obviously liked being both a teacher and a nun. She told us stories and played math games. She also read books to us. One book portrayed heaven as a suburban paradise where St. Patrick's front lawn was shaped like a shamrock. For someone like me who lived in an industrialized area of Philadelphia filled with cement and asphalt, having a front lawn equaled paradise. This was a heaven where I could spend eternity playing in the grass instead of in the street. I wanted to hear more stories about that kind of God who lived in that kind of heaven and provided that kind of amenities.

Most people never grow out of their love of stories. I never did. It was through the efforts of teachers like Sister G. and others that I became a veteran reader at a very early age who would go on to devour five library books per week all through elementary school.

Stories are exciting, inspirational, and tragic whether in print or in the movies or on television. Americans pay a small fortune for streaming services each month to bring their favorite kinds of stories into their homes. Binge watching a series has become a favorite American pastime. Likewise, believers never seem to tire of stories about purported divine intervention and magical, miraculous women and men who are believed to have been chosen by God to defy the rules of science, even in twentieth and twenty-first centuries where humanity has walked on the moon and powerful telescopes have taken pictures of space phenomena called nebulae and galaxies thousands of light years away.

Padre Pio (1887-1968) is one of these magical men. He is also a member of a divine elite club who were allegedly rewarded by God with the stigmata, although there is evidence from church investigators dating back to the 1920's that his stigmata were self-inflicted. When confronted by the evidence that he had purchased large amounts of a sterilizing agent and a pain killer indicating that his wounds came from a place other than heaven, Pio, who was a showman on par with P.T. Barnum with his public displays of bloody mittens covering the wounds in his hands, piously explained them away. The carbolic acid sterilized needles, he claimed, and the pain killer was used as a joke to cause his fellow friars to sneeze. Pio explained his reception of the stigmata by plagiarizing the work of a woman who had also allegedly received the stigmata, claiming to investigators that he never read the book or heard of the woman. These unfortunate facts never detracted from his saintly reputation.

Instead, his chronically bloody hands endeared him to a society traumatized by two wars. For veterans missing fingers and hands and civilians with war injuries, he was their fellow sufferer, their companion on the journey of chronic pain. The stigmata led to even more elaborate stories. He could bi-locate and levitate. People claimed to see him fly up into the sky to repel bombs during World War II. He could predict the future and knew the inner workings of people's hearts and minds. While never claiming to have performed a miracle, Pio never denied the stories, lending veracity to the outrageous claims. (Stille, 2012)

An apostolic visitor sent to examine the marks of Pio's stigmata asked a question more befitting a non-believer than a member of the clergy. How do people like Pio continue to attract large numbers of followers with fantastical stories that seem to usurp the power of God? The reality that this ordained doubter could not or would not recognize is the fact that the church has always cultivated this circus-like attraction to magical people with its insistence upon miracles as a qualification for canonization. If believers need a miracle, they will find one, as representatives of the Vatican insure on a regular basis. The same apostolic visitor who had qualms about the veracity of Pio's stigmata had no problems accepting the stigmata of St. Francis. Apparently, some stigmata are more miraculous than others.

Eventually Pio and his bloody hands went too far for the top echelon of the church. Popes Benedict XV, Pius XI, and John XXIII expressed deep reservations about a man whose ostensible miraculous acts of alleged holiness were performed while participating in Fascist activities in Italy prior to World War II. Pio had a long-term relationship with a scam artist who made a fortune on the black market during the war. Building a hospital in Pio's name with huge amounts from the Marshall Plan and writing a book about Pio saved him from jail. Pio willingly handed over the blood-soaked rags and mittens that covered his bleeding hands to be sold as relics in the marketplace established near his living quarters. The sale of relics of a living saint raked in so much money that the Vatican released him from his vow of poverty.

Like many churchmen before and after him, alleged sanctity did not protect Pio from misogyny. Pio felt obliged to address and then publicly humiliate women who violated his definition of feminine modesty. Like many sexually immature churchmen, Pio fixated upon women's dress and refused to hear the confessions of women wearing short dresses or slacks.

Pio also did not like movies or television and referred to the media as "the propagation of evil." Nor did he like the reforms of Vatican II, applying to the Vatican for a dispensation to say the Tridentine Mass where a priest in ornate and expensive vestments prays with his back to the people in a language they could not understand. To his followers, Pio's reactionary ideas and behavior were signs of reverence and sanctity.

Paul VI plucked him from obscurity in the 1960's after Pio publicly congratulated the pontiff on his controversial encyclical *Humanae vitae* which outlawed the use of artificial birth control. John Paul II also worked hard to redeem and rehabilitate the outwardly pious Pio to the point of calling him "the image of the suffering risen Christ" and canonizing him a mere thirty years after Benedict XV and Pius XI forbade him from saying mass. John Paul apparently did not get the memo about the carbolic acid and the pain killers.

The cult of Padre Pio remains the largest cult in Italy. People from all over the world have flocked to his village, transforming it from a poverty- stricken, sleepy town to a stop on the tourist circuit. There pilgrims can still purchase bloody rags that once touched his hands and kneel before pictures of his wounds. They, too, see the suffering of Jesus in a charlatan rather than in the poor, the sick, and the suffering.

To his credit, Padre Pio was instrumental in building that first-class hospital staffed by credentialed doctors in his remote village. Mother Teresa, the elderly nun dressed in a simple sari who raised enormous amounts of money to care for the sick and suffering of Kolkata, warming the hearts and opening the wallets of Americans, could have built a similar world-class hospital. In spite of the tens of millions of dollars at her disposal, she chose not to. Instead, as she explained to an admirer who regarded her as a living saint, "I think it is very beautiful for the poor (in India) to accept their lot, to share it with the passion of Christ. I think the world is very much helped by the suffering of the poor people," rendering the people of India into victim souls for a Christ in whom they did not believe (quoted in Rajput, 2018).

For Mother Teresa, illness came from God in the form of a teaching moment— to those unafflicted by disease and had modern hospitals at their disposal. In 1988 Mother Teresa announced, "Leprosy is not a punishment, it can be a very beautiful gift from God if we make good use of it. Through it we can learn to love the unloved" (Quoted in Prashad, 2002). For those whose skin is rotting away, a cure— which was well within the ability of modern medicine— was in order. Mother Teresa could have loved the lepers by sending them for proper treatment and returning them to their community healed as Jesus did.

She chose not to follow the example of Jesus. Instead, her institutions were marked by practices that were not second or third best, but draconian and downright mean lest, as Mother Teresa said, the hospices and orphanages drift towards her tortured understanding of materialism. The belief that the poor benefitted from their poverty and poor health superseded patient need and led to the implementation of questionable institutional, medical, and nursing procedures.

Mother Teresa used her untrained sisters to care for vulnerable people with complex needs and complicated conditions. The sisters' lack of nursing education prevented them from differentiating the considerable needs of the sick. Those at death's door and those with mild illnesses were treated the same way. Because Mother Teresa valued suffering, those in pain were given few to no analgesics. The sisters refused to sterilize needles, gave cold baths, and washed dishes and contaminated linen in the same room. An integral part of her care plan was the reliance upon divine providence rather than human action including standard medical and nursing practice to effect a cure (Prashad, 1997).

Poverty, Mother Teresa insisted, was "beautiful" at least for the poor, as she flew in private jets owned by wealthy American scammers like Charles Keating who contributed 1.5 million dollars to her charity and hobnobbed with despots like the Duvaliers of Haiti who escaped Mother Teresa's criticism even as they impoverished the citizens of their country by stealing government funds. Haiti is the poorest country in the western hemisphere. More than fifty per cent of the population live below the poverty line and lack basic services like housing and running water. However, Haiti, unlike India, is a Catholic country and does not need to be saved by foreign missionaries.

In spite of subjecting the residents of Kolkata to the redemptive values of suffering and the value of simplicity, Mother Teresa did not check into one of her own hospitals when she developed heart disease. She chose not to be treated by untrained personnel or receive cold baths or eat from questionably cleansed plates. Instead, she chose to fly to California to receive first class health care from one of the best cardiologists in the world, care that prolonged her life by fourteen years after a heart attack. Her actions stood in stark contrast to a young teen in her care with a treatable kidney infection who was denied antibiotics and transport to a hospital that would have saved his life.

Although she and her admirer, John Paul II regarded abortion as murder, neither chose to criticize the excesses of capitalism. Mother Teresa never recognized that British imperialism caused much of the poverty she saw in India. In addition, neither she nor John Paul II adequately addressed the death of eight thousand and the injury of over five hundred thousand in Bhopal after western owner negligence caused a massive leak of poisonous gas. Both regarded the incident as an unfortunate accident rather than the result of a deliberate policy of long-term neglect to increase corporate profits. While abortion was unforgiveable, the callous refusal to repair equipment in a factory making a lethal pesticide resulted from "man's efforts to make progress," according to John Paul II ("Around the World," 1986).

Global praise and multiple awards including the Nobel Peace Prize covered up the fact that, as critic Christopher Hitchens wrote, Mother Teresa opposed the one known cure for poverty— the empowerment of women.

Historian Vijay Prashad is one of many Indians who have found fault with what he calls the western mode of industrial charity. What Mother Teresa did, he said, was less important than how she made donors feel. The exaltation of the poor's status enabled white, western donors to believe that the primary purpose of the poor was to enable those who lived comfortably and received first class health care to feel virtuous and generous (2003). When Robin Fox, the former editor of "The Lancet," a peer reviewed British medical publication, visited a home for the dying in Kolkata, he found volunteers, "drunk in their own philanthropy" while ignoring the primitive and unhygienic conditions around them. No one apparently ever asked the sick and the poor what they wanted for themselves. Critics labeled Mother Teresa's theology a "plantation religion" where suffering is dished out to the poor to serve the egos of the rich (Cook, 1997).

Mother Teresa was a representative of a foreign church with foreign ideas living in a land that neither shared her disdain of modern science nor her faith in Jesus. Kolkata was not a "black hole" requiring the intervention of western missionaries to save its population from themselves but a vibrant international city that like all major world cities, including those in the United States, was beset with intractable poverty and homelessness where people lived and died on the streets. This is a statement of fact, not acceptance. Would the

Americans who contributed so generously to Mother Teresa's charity for the destitute in India have contributed the same huge sums to eradicate homelessness and poverty, American style? The presence of tent cities in places like Washington D.C., Philadelphia, Portland, and San Francisco answers my question.

Facts about Mother Teresa and her homes for the dying were immaterial as she slipped into the mythological realm of saints during her lifetime. Although the physical care of the sick and the suffering lay completely outside her purview, admirers poured tens of millions of dollars into a ministry with no financial oversight or accountability thinking they were providing medical care to the poorest of the poor. They had no idea that the facilities they thought they were supporting did not deign to hire even one trained nurse or doctor or that the recipients of their funds were not relieved of their suffering because Mother Teresa believed that "agony brought one closer to God" (O'Brien, 2021).

By the end of her life, Mother Teresa's charities collected seventy-two million dollars a year in annual donations. Only 7% of it was used for charitable activity (Gillette, 2016). Her order has never given an accounting of the money it received because as Mother Teresa's successor, Sister Nirmalda Joshi said, "God is our banker" (Hines, 2021).

From her own personal experience, Mother Teresa obviously knew what a modern hospital looked like and what it should do to provide care for the sick and the suffering. She rejected that model for the poor of Kolkata even as she chose a modern hospital with highly trained doctors to provide her with expert medical care that saved her life. This makes her a hypocrite.

To those unacquainted with history, violence perpetrated against the redeemed seems to arise from the evil intentions of Satan rather than from events and circumstances created by human beings. What kind of evil person would want to kill a priest or a nun who had given their lives for God? What kind of wickedness inspired people to overthrow a government ordained by God?

The answers to these questions appear to be self-evident. They are not.

As mentioned in Chapter ten, the conquest of Mexico, Central and South America was a joint venture of the Spanish government and the Roman Catholic Church. Both entities quickly acquired great wealth and power as the native people died off by the millions, leaving vast areas of land in the hands of the European marauders. In Mexico, the church owned vast amounts of real estate and collected tithes on the entire agricultural output of the country, making it the most prosperous enterprise in the country. (Matson, 1979). The wealth of the church and the clergy stood in stark contrast to the poverty of the people. Mexicans, like the people in Europe, noted the discrepancy between the gospel and the status and wealth of the church.

As the move for Mexican independence grew in the nineteenth century, the people recognized the church as a reactionary force aligned with the status quo that was oppressing them. This belief was bolstered by pontiffs like Pius IX who viewed liberalism in any form as destructive to the faith. Under his aegis, unions, voting rights, freedom of religion and of the press— indeed anything that would improve the lives of the poor— were verboten. As a result, the revolutionary forces in Mexico saw the church as a barrier to change and began confiscating church property for distribution to the people, much to the chagrin of Mexican bishops who argued repeatedly that the right of the church to own property originated with Jesus and the apostles. It was Jesus, himself one archbishop argued, who gave the church the right to acquire wealth (Knowlton, 1965). Because of the church's close association with the wealthy and powerful, anticlericalism in one form or another persisted through-out the remainder of the nineteen century and into the twentieth.

In the late 1920's, the president of Mexico began to confiscate church property, and required priests to register with the govern-ment. In response, the bishops of Mexico closed all of the churches throughout the country, using the blunt instrument of interdict to assert its power and enforce its position. Those who found that their salvation was now in question without the sacraments and the Mass rose up in a bloody rebellion named after the Prince of Peace, the Cristero War. The Mexican church supported the seditionists rather than the poor. Some ninety thousand people died in the Cristero War where the rallying cry of Catholic loyalists was, "Long live Christ the King" as they massacred their fellow citizens. Entire hamlets were plundered and then leveled by bombs, impoverishing populations already living on the edge of society. Large numbers of Mexicans fled to the United States. Priests were among those murdered during a time of violence that could have been avoided had the church behaved in a more pastoral manner. When John Paul II and Benedict XVI canonized the priests murdered during the war, they allegedly omitted those members of the clergy who took up arms against their own parishioners in the holy name of Jesus. The murdered campesinos did not receive a martyr's crown.

The ordained who were murdered were victims, not saints, as were all the ninety thousand who lost their lives to terrible, useless violence aided and supported by an institution trying to maintain its power and authority at the expense of the people it was supposed to serve.

Many of the countries conquered by Spanish colonial forces and the Catholic Church remain in turmoil today. While Canada and the United States are far from perfect, the early enactment of religious liberty into law and the separation of church and state has protected their citizens from the worst incursions of religious absolutism and sectarian warfare.

Spain, Mexico's mother country, followed its former colony into chaos and violence during the Spanish Civil War (1936-39) and its aftermath, the Franco regime. Determined to block reforms like universal suffrage instituted by the Republic established in 1931, military groups regarded the legally elected officials of the Spanish Republic as a Jewish-Masonic-Bolshevik plot to destroy Christianity and Spanish civilization. In the words of the general who unleashed what became what historian Paul Preston called "the Spanish Holocaust," those who disagreed with the right were to be eliminated "without scruple or hesitation" (Preston, 2012).

The Spanish generals viewed the peasants and factory workers as an inferior race that needed to be subjugated by terror and death. Teachers, doctors, lawyers, trade union leaders, free thinkers, non-church goers, and women who had dared to vote under the new constitution fared no better. Under the banner of the leading Catholic party and some members of the clergy who were regarded as mouthpieces of God, hundreds of thousands of innocent victims were murdered under the mantra of "Religion, Fatherland, Family, Order, Work, and Property." According to Preston (2012), the clergy justified the military call to eliminate "those who do not think as we do." One bishop justified the civil war and the death of thousands as "a battle between the children of light and the children of darkness, between Catholicism and Judaism, between Christ and the Devil" (Preston).

Although the Spanish had driven out their Jewish citizens five hundred years earlier, the country became obsessed with conspiracy theories of Jews trying to take over the country. The Jesuit conspiracy theorist Juan Tusquets Terrats, a man regarded favorably for what appeared to be his deep piety, published the parent of all fake news, the *Protocols of the Elders of Zion*, to prove to his fellow Catholics that the Jews were trying to destroy their faith and their country through the redistribution of wealth (Preston, 2012). After visiting Dachau, Tusquets favorably regarded the idea of concentration camps to contain Jews, liberals, Freemasons, Communists, and Socialists. An inspiration for the vicious extermination campaign of Franco, Tusquets was one of the architects for the evil that was the Spanish Civil War.

In the beginning of the coup by the right wing, the left responded in kind and set loose a violent reaction born of centuries of exploitation by the wealthy that included the clergy. Almost seven thousand priests and three hundred nuns were murdered in horrifying orgies of reactive violence to the murderous activities of the rebels (de la Cuerva, 1998). While the Republican government was finally able to quell the violence against the clergy, the generals had just begun their descent into the hell of sectarian brutality where Franco engaged in a war of annihilation that would eventually solidify his forty-year dictatorship. While Catholic people were appalled by the violence against the clergy, the church was not appalled enough to excommunicate the generals who caused the violence in the first place. These Catholic generals, most particularly Franco, have been treated much too kindly by both history and the church.

The status and power of the church was more important than the gospel where followers of Jesus were to love all of their neighbors as they loved themselves. When wages dropped by 60% in 1930's and Spanish landowners were reducing their farm workers to abject poverty and starvation, the church supported the landowners and civil guards that were inflicting terrible violence upon those advocating for unions. According to one union leader,

> *"The same owners who would spend 400,000 pesetas on a shawl for the statue of the Virgin or on a crucifix for the Church stinted the olive oil for the workers' meals and would rather pay a lawyer 25,000 pesetas than an extra 25 cents to the day-laborers lest I create a precedent and let the workers get their way. In Baiena, there was a master who put cattle in the planted fields rather than pay the agreed wages to the reapers. A priest who had a farm, when the lad came down to get olive oil, had made dents in the tin jug so that it would hold less oil" (Preston, 2012).*

It was these peasants and advocates for change who died by the thousands under the Catholic generals who led the rebellion against the Spanish Republic.

In his quest for saints, John Paul II chose to ignore the hundreds of thousands of innocent people who were tortured, murdered, sent to work camps in Nazi Germany, or who died in Spanish concentration camps and in prisons and instead canonized priests and nuns who might have supported Franco. He also omitted the many who were executed during Franco's repressive forty-year regime. While Franco was buried with all the honors of the church under a gigantic crucifix, many of his victims were buried in mass graves all over Spain, the records of their deaths destroyed by the government. The papal exaltation of the ordained and those in religious life discounts the lives of the thousands of the disappeared.

The action of the Spanish seditionists is instructive for modern day America. When the right did not win the election of 1934 by parliamentary methods, they supported the use of force to malign and then exterminate their opponents. (Casanova, 2017) In 1930's Spain as in twenty-first century America, the Catholic Church remains a force of division rather than unity, fomenting culture wars revolving around abortion and human sexuality, excommunicating opponents, and working to elect and appoint judges who support their position while trampling upon the rights of those who are not Catholic. The Thomas More Society, a Catholic public interest group which is formally recognized by the United States Conference of Catholic Bishops, filed cases in support of Donald Trump's failed coup to overturn the 2020 election. While the United States Conference of Catholic Bishops (USCCB) did issue a condemnation of the attempted coup on January 6, 2021, they have failed to condemn the animus that sparked the attempted coup in the first place.

Today, a little over 50% of Spaniards consider themselves to be Catholic and less than a fifth actually practice their faith. In Spain, like in many other Catholic countries, a clergy shortage has closed down many parishes as the number of vocations has fallen precipitously. Yet, the bishops continue to regard the widely supported socialist government which has enacted liberal abortion and gender laws with suspicion. Like conservative (and Fascist) citizens in other countries, such legislation is still regarded as destroyers of traditional values and customs (Luxmoor, 2023).

The editor of a Spanish Catholic weekly newspaper is one of the few who has proposed that the church examine its conscience. "It is important that we, as Catholics, ask ourselves why these ideological tendencies have found a place in our society-and what prevented the Gospel message from reaching so many of our contemporaries" (Luxmoor, 2023). One can only hope that he and his fellow believers examine the Catholic ideology that has aligned religious with political power, effectively blocking the adoption of gospel values by the majority of Catholics, including the Catholic hierarchy, since the church forged its bonds with the resident state and the ruling classes in the fourth century.

World War II led to the canonization of those in religious life almost to the exclusion of the thousands of people who worked to protect their Jewish sisters and brothers during the Holocaust.

Some members of the clergy who were canonized were vocal opponents of the Nazis. Vilmos Apor (1892-1945), a Hungarian bishop not only criticized the Nazis but also lost his life for trying to protect women from being raped by invading Russian soldiers. While individual bishops like the future John XXIII managed to save the lives of thousands of Jews by issuing fake baptismal certificates and immigration certificates to Palestine, most bishops, including the Bishop of Rome, Pius XII, remained silent in the face of Nazi horror.

The eleven Polish Sisters of Nazareth, collectively called the Martyrs of Nowogrodek, exchanged their lives for those of condemned people with families. Like ordained priest Maximilian Kolbe who is widely touted, their names deserve to be mentioned individually to honor their courage: Eugenia Mackiewicz, Paulina Borowik, Leokadia Matuszewska, Veronika Narmontowicz, Adelaid Mardosewicz, Jadwiga Zak, Anna Kukolowicz, Eleonara Jozwik, Jozefa Chrobot, Helena Cierpka, and Julia Rapiej.

Edith Stein (1891-1942), a Jewish convert to Catholicism who converted to Catholicism and became a Carmelite nun after experiencing the trauma of World War I, was canonized a saint and martyr in 1998. Critics claim that Stein was killed because she was Jewish and not because of her Catholic faith. While baptized Jews were, indeed, rounded up and executed by the Nazis after the Dutch bishops condemned their policy of extermination, it was her racial identity as a Jew, and not her Christian faith, that directly led to Stein's death. Stein was a victim rather than a saint.

John Paul II canonized more saints than his seventeen predecessors combined, claiming that anyone could be a saint. While that is true, being a nun or especially a priest greatly increased the chances of canonization, even as the conditions for canonization might remain murky.

Teresina Mainetti (1939-2000), for instance was a nun who worked with adjudicated youth. In the tortured logic of the Vatican, she was beatified and declared a martyr for being stabbed by three teenaged girls in a purported satanic ritual. Apparently, the victim of troubled adolescents is holier and more compelling than are those who were murdered by agents of the government for trying to improve the status of the poor.

There is one group of souls that the Catholic Church has completely ignored despite the fact that they willingly offered up their lives in acts of heroic virtue and extraordinary love. Mary Sherlach, Anne Marie Murphy, Rachel D'Avino, Jean Kuczka, Irma Garcia, and Eva Mireles are among the many teachers and school personnel who were murdered while trying to protect their students from school shooters armed with automatic rifles. While staring at the barrel of a gun, these brave women placed their bodies between certain death and their students. These exemplary brave and dedicated women were buried as Catholics. They are surely both saints and martyrs.

Padre Pio was a charlatan, and Mother Teresa, a hypocrite. Edith Stein, Teresina Mainetti, and the Mexican and Spanish clergy were unfortunate victims.

Followers of the Way of Jesus

Vilmos Apor
Eugenia Mackiewicz
Paulina Borowik
Leokadia Matuszewska
Veronika Narmontowicz
Adelaid Mardosewicz
Jadwiga Zak
Anna Kukolowicz
Eleonara Jozwik
Jozefa Chrobot
Helena Cierpka
Julia Rapiej
Eva Mireles
Irma Garcia
Mary Sherlach
Anne Marie Murphy
Rachel D'Avino
Jean Kuczka

Chapter 14:
LIFE, WAR AND, PEACE

Onward, Christian soldiers,
Marching off as to war,
With the cross of Jesus
Going on before!

(Sabine Baring-Gould, 1865).

"Every time I went to Mass in my uniform and put the vestments
on over my uniform, I couldn't help but think of the words of Christ
applying to me: Beware of wolves in sheep's clothing."

Spoken by Father Dave Becker after leaving the Trident
submarine base in 1982 and resigning as Catholic chaplain.

My Aunt Diane was a diabetic. She gave birth to five children in
the late 1950s, two of whom were stillborn due to the effects of her
disease. Her doctor told her not to have any more children.

Maternal disease was once an ongoing and serious problem for
practicing Catholic mothers who were forbidden to practice birth
control even to save their lives. Using birth control was a mortal sin
that damned women like my aunt to hell for all eternity. Catholic
couples were taught to either be completely open to life or totally
abstain from sexual relations, not an easy practice for young couples.
I do not know what pathway my aunt and uncle chose, but they did
not have any more children.

From my late grandfather's chair in the sitting room, my paternal
Aunt Nellie regularly and negatively pontificated about the church's
position on birth control. Prior to the 1960s, families regularly lost
baby after baby to hemolytic disease of the newborn caused by what

is known as the RH factor. Rh-negative women are now given an injection during pregnancy and after the birth of Rh-positive babies (and after a miscarriage) to prevent the buildup of antibodies that can later destroy the red blood cells of Rh-negative newborns, causing their death. Aunt Nellie railed against a church that would insist that mothers continue to bear children doomed to die and then blame the parents for their lack of self-control.

Not only did the church not have a problem with dead newborns, but it also had no problem with mothers dying in childbirth. One of my classmates was the oldest of nine children. Her mother, like my Aunt Diane, was advised not to have any more children or risk death. Unfortunately, my classmate's mother became pregnant again, delivered the baby, and died, leaving her fourteen-year-old daughter, according to one of the parish priests, as "the mother of the house" to take care of the family. Another classmate, the oldest of ten, was twelve when she lost her mother in childbirth. Four of her siblings had cystic fibrosis. She was left with the burden of caring for them.

When I first heard the story of Gianna Molla (1922–1962), who was canonized for allegedly refusing to have medical treatment during pregnancy that might have harmed her fetus, I thought she had cancer and declined to have chemotherapy. The truth is very different. What Molla had was a fibroid tumor, a benign condition that never posed any threat to her life. Molla did what most pregnant women would have done to allow her fetus to grow—she had the fibroids removed even though the surgery could have resulted in premature labor and the death of her fetus—not her. The remainder of Molla's pregnancy was uneventful and she went on to deliver a healthy ten- pound baby girl.

Molla's hagiography sets her up for canonization. She had aunts and uncles who were in religious life. She received her sacraments. Like many saints before and after her, Molla suffered from poor health that prevented her from fulfilling a dream to be a missionary. In fact, her chronic stomach and back pains could have resulted from the uterine fibroids that led to her surgery. Far too many women suffer excruciating pain caused by fibroids and endometriosis that sharply curtail their lives. Like the church, the medical establishment has too often dismissed female suffering as inevitable and, therefore, untreatable.

Pregnancy and delivery are hardly ever easy and are not risk-free. Describing childbirth as "natural" obscures the danger every pregnant woman faces. How can something natural kill you? During pregnancy, the developing fetus commandeers all of the mother's organ systems to facilitate its growth and development. The mother's blood volume increases by fifty percent, sometimes taxing the heart, lungs, and kidneys. The fetus will extract calcium from the bones and teeth of even a malnourished mother. As the fetus grows, it compresses the mother's stomach and intestines, sometimes causing digestive problems. Back pain is not unusual. Some mothers develop eclampsia, a serious condition where high blood pressure sometimes causes seizures and death. Post-partum hemorrhage, stroke, and blood clots can end the lives of even the healthiest mothers. In addition, there is the ever-present possibility of post-partum infection.

It was postpartum infection and not the fibroid surgery she chose to have seven months prior to her delivery that actually killed Molla. Overwhelming sepsis, once known as "childbed fever," also killed Mary Wollstonecraft, author of "A Vindication of the Rights of Women" and mother of Mary Shelley, author of *Frankenstein*, as well as thousands upon thousands of other women throughout the ages. According to the standard applied to Molla, every pregnant woman who dies in childbirth should be canonized a saint.

At no point in her pregnancy did Molla ever make a decision that led directly to her death. Instead, Molla is like every woman who has suffered from hormonally induced conditions, who has faced tough decisions during pregnancy, who has experienced difficult labors, and who has died in childbirth. She is not a martyr for her faith or even an example of someone who chose death to protect her unborn baby. She is a tragic example of the existential danger that is inherent in every pregnancy. In life and in death Molla was neither exceptional nor heroic but unfortunate.

Rather than misrepresenting the death of one woman as an act of heroic martyrdom and making her the patron saint of the anti-abortion movement, perhaps the better choice is to improve the health of all pregnant women by providing high-quality universal pre-natal and post-partum care so that all the Gianna Molla's of the world can joyfully return to their families after giving birth instead of dying from a preventable condition.

The Catholic Church states that direct abortion is gravely contrary to moral law and a crime against human life. Having or cooperating in an abortion incurs an automatic excommunication (*Catechism*, 2272 and 2273). There is little parsing in the church's campaign to eliminate abortion. According to Mother Teresa, abortion is "the greatest destroyer of peace today," even while countries amass weapons of mass destruction that could eliminate all life on Earth. Military budgets have risen into the trillions of dollars, bankrupting their citizens, and underfunding or eliminating programs that provide basic human needs and services to pregnant women. Reducing the military budget by even a small amount and applying it to maternal and child health would go a long way toward preventing abortion.

The strong language used to condemn abortion has always been conspicuously absent from the church's treatment of war even though millions of innocent people, including babies and fetuses, have been killed during the endless conflicts that have marked human history. According to church policy, "governments cannot be denied the right of lawful self-defense, once all peace efforts have failed" (*Catechism*, 2308). Further, those who are sworn to serve their country in the armed forces are servants of the security and freedom of nations. If they carry out their duty honorably—even as they fire rockets and drop bombs on enemy forces which always causes collateral damage to civilians—they truly contribute to the common good of the nation and the maintenance of peace (*Catechism*, 2310.) Drafting young people to fight is the right and duty of the government. The business of war is left to "the prudential judgment of those with responsibility for the common good" (Ibid, 2309).

In post-9/11 times, the American bishops declared that a military action against terrorists was justified and moral. Even as they danced around the economic and political roots of terrorism, the bishops chose to ignore Detroit Bishop Thomas Gumbleton's plea to return to the non-violence practiced by the early, pre-Constantinian church.

While mothers, doctors, nurses, and politicians are excommunicated under the guidelines of the catechism for having or participating in an abortion, no Catholic general or member of the armed forces has received the same punishment for massacring civilians or bombing cities into dust.

Spanish dictator Francisco Franco, a mass murderer, was never excommunicated. Neither was systemic human rights violator and murderer Agosto Pinochet in Chile. Catholic Nazis were never excommunicated, nor was the Catholic pilot who dropped the atomic bomb on the Catholic city of Nagasaki, annihilating churches, schools, children, babies, and fetuses in a matter of seconds. For many Catholic prelates, current president Joe Biden's support of abortion rights constitutes a far greater sin than does sending weapons of war to Ukraine and Israel, even though war could involve the country in nuclear war and the death of hundreds of millions. (I am not debating the merits of the war in Ukraine or Israel. I am just making a point about Catholic tolerance for violence).

While Catholics are free to make up their minds about participating in wars such as the ones in Iraq and Afghanistan which took tens of thousands of lives and undermined societies throughout the Middle East, they are not free to consider abortion. While the American church provides answers to those who choose to participate in the horror of war, the only answer to having an abortion is not to have one, even if the mother might die. As the possibility of war in Iraq unfolded in the winter of 2003, Wilton Gregory, president of the United States Catholic Conference of Bishops said:

"As pastors and teachers, we understand that there are no easy answers. People of goodwill may differ on who traditional norms apply in this situation. The gravity of the threat and whether force would be preemptive are matters of debate, as are the potential consequences of using or failing to use military force. We urge Catholics, especially lay men and women who are called to be 'leaven' in society, to continue to think deeply about the choices we face, to review carefully the teaching of our church and to speak out strongly in accord with their conscience. Our hearts and prayers go out especially to those who may bear the burden of these terrible

*choices-the men and women of our armed forces and their families,
the people of Iraq, and the leaders of our nation and world who
face momentous decisions of life and death, of war and peace:
(Wilton Gregory, 2-26-03).*

The choices Gregory empowers Catholic women and men to make about participating in war are denied to women with a problem pregnancy. The churchmen's criticism of war pales beside the marshalling and unleashing of all ecclesiastical forces against abortion, which the bishops have determined to be the greatest sin of all. While giving governments that teeter upon legitimacy a wide berth, the church does not recognize the legitimate authority of medical doctors who may have determined that a fetus is causing the death of its mother. All mothers are forbidden to act in self-defense. The life, security, and freedom of a mother and her right to participate in the common good remain meaningless to the churchmen in their unqualified support for the fetus's right to life. The Catholic Church has moved the United States towards a nation-wide ban on abortion as the lives of women as brave as Gianna Molla have callously been placed in mortal danger.

Long before an aborted fetus became the church's number one priority, the institution had developed a name for the wars it has supported, the often misused and misnamed "just war." From its inception, the just war theory created a huge abyss in Catholic moral thought and action. Catholic leaders repeatedly invoked it to lead their flocks into a void of unspeakable evil.

The just war theory was developed by Augustine, whose ultimately facile assertion that Christian soldiers would fight only in just wars declared by a legitimate authority for a just cause and as a last resort was further fleshed out by Thomas Aquinas. It provides just the right amount of theological obfuscation to justify the extinction of millions. It also absolves its adherents from sin. Augustine used it against the heretical separatist Donatists in North Africa. Subsequent popes adopted the concept with alacrity, declaring Crusades against those they called heretics or the infidel. Rebels, witches, Jews, Communists, Socialists, trade unionists, and anarchists were fair game, earmarked for elimination. The notion of a just war validated the European invasion of the Americas. It sunk its malevolent tentacles into the American doctrine of Manifest Destiny that led to the deaths and internment of Indigenous people on reservations. It provided the foundation for the wars against "godless Communism" and the propping up of vicious Catholic dictators in Central and South America. The just war has been waged against women in the United States, where fundamentalist Catholics and Protestants have enacted vigilante laws including long prison sentences that harm the most vulnerable members of society to reach their goal of no abortions anywhere on American soil. Those who have feared what they might have called "papism" or "popery" throughout the ages have been wise to do so. Catholic governors and Catholic justices have pushed the anti-abortion agenda of the bishops into American civil life, levied Catholic belief upon unbelievers, and curtailed the rights of those who are not Catholic.

The criteria for a just war are instructive for their profound lack of clarity. There is no mention of Jesus, the Prince of Peace amid the discussion of just causes, proportionality, good intentions, and legitimate authorities. The Catholic Church, which acknowledges the Jesus who directed his followers to put down their swords as their Lord and Savior, has failed to develop a comprehensive theology of peace that addresses the reams of paper that too often justify the rush to shed innocent blood in war.

John XXIII, John Paul II, Benedict XVI, John XXIII, and Francis have condemned war and promoted peace. John Paul II informed U.S. President George W. Bush in a letter that the war in Iraq was hardly a just war. Benedict mused if any war could be considered just. Francis has preached that with war, everyone loses, a position for which he was harshly condemned by American Catholic hawks. While the Catholic Church has worked toward peacebuilding since John XXIII's encyclical *Pacem in Terris* (1963), it is not a peace church like those of the Quakers, Mennonites, Amish, and Seventh Day Adventists who actively discourage service in the armed forces. George Fox, the founder of the Society of Friends, expressed his faith's understanding of war to Charles II of England in 1660: "We utterly deny all outward wars and strife and fighting with outward weapons for any end or under any pretense whatever; this is our testimony to the whole world" (The Quaker Testimony for Peace). The Quakers' repudiation of war as a violation of the spirit and doctrine of Christ sometimes came at great cost. Many had their property confiscated, were imprisoned, or executed.

Some brave, mostly forgotten souls throughout the centuries have recognized the church's hypocritical support of war and developed their own resistance to violence based upon the gospel of Jesus.

Father George Zabelka, the chaplain who blessed the crews who dropped atomic bombs on Hiroshima and Nagasaki, later came to believe that he had betrayed the basic tenets of his faith by legitimizing mass murder. He later repudiated the mandates of war that demanded the deaths of innocents and renounced the "ethical hairsplitting" of the just war theory which he asserted makes the teachings of Jesus and, in fact, Jesus himself, "irrelevant." "Militarized Christianity," he said, is a lie because "when Jesus disarmed Peter, he disarmed all Christians" (quoted in *The Plough*, 2022).

Upon learning of the carnage caused by the bombing of Japan, Zabelka said,

"If a soldier came to me and asked if he could put a bullet through a child's head, I would have told him, absolutely not. That would be mortally sinful. But in 1945 Tinian Island was the largest airfield in the world. Three planes a minute could take off from it around the clock. Many of these planes went to Japan with the express purpose of killing not one child or one civilian but of slaughtering hundreds and thousands and tens of thousands of children and civilians – and I said nothing" (Ibid, 2022)

Benjamin Salmon (1888–1932) was a working-class American man whose Catholic faith inspired him to refuse to sign up for the draft in World War I. At the time, his pacifist stance was so unusual and so hated that he was sent to a hospital for the criminally insane after first being tried and sentenced to death. When his sentence was commuted to twenty-five years at hard labor, he spent time in various prisons where even his fellow prisoners disagreed so vehemently with him that they tried to lynch him. During his imprisonment, he went on a hunger strike and was force-fed for over a hundred days.

While near death from starvation, he asked for a priest, who refused to give him the last rites and communion for resisting the war. A second priest who finally did give him communion was relieved of his duties in Washington, DC and sent to a frontier town by the bishop as a punishment for dispensing pastoral care to the dying conscientious objector. After two years of terrible trauma, Salmon was released. He never recovered his health and died penniless.

The name of Benjamin Salmon has never been submitted for canonization.

Unlike Benjamin Salmon, the American bishops fully embraced the First World War that had already claimed millions of European lives in the two and a half years prior to America's entry, establishing a War Council that grew into the U.S. Council of Catholic Bishops. Cardinal John Farley of New York said in 1918, "Criticism of the war irritates me. I consider it a little short of treason. Every citizen in this nation, no matter what his private opinion or his political leaning, should support the president and his advisors to the limit of his ability" (quoted in Dear, 2017). The United States would suffer over 320,000 casualties. Overall, forty million souls perished in what could never be described as a just war that was supposed to end all future wars. This war, of course, set the stage for another war twenty-one years later that would claim the lives of seventy to eighty million people.

Many members of the Catholic clergy continue to embrace the just war theory. One third of the American military is Catholic. Many Catholic campuses sponsor ROTC programs that continue to train young Catholics for war rather than for peace. My daughter attended the College of the Holy Cross on an Army ROTC scholarship. The Navy paid for my second son's undergraduate and graduate degree. Our family falls neatly into this category.

Gertrud Luckner (1900–1995) and Margarete Sommer (1893–1965) were two German women who worked to save Jews prior to and during the war. Luckner, a social worker with the international Catholic charitable organization Caritas, helped to transport Jews over the Swiss border and disabled trucks transporting Jews to concentration camps. She was arrested by the Gestapo and spent two years in a concentration camp. Sommer was discharged from her job as a teacher for refusing to promote Nazi policies in school. She then worked for various Catholic organizations trying to find exit strategies for German Jews and then hiding those who were left behind. While working for the Berlin Diocese welfare office in 1943, she and the bishop, Konrad von Preysing, drafted a letter of resistance from the German bishops criticizing the deportation of Jews to concentration camps. It began, "With deepest sorrow—yes, even with holy indignation—have we German bishops learned of the deportation of non-Aryans in a manner scornful of all human rights. It is our holy duty to defend the inalienable rights of all men guaranteed by natural law" (quoted in Faulkner, 2015).

The collective body of German bishops refused to issue this strongly worded criticism of a crime against humanity and God. The number of ordained and members of religious orders canonized during World War II disguises the acute lack of concern too many Catholics both ordained and lay felt toward the fate of the Jews. Unfortunately, the church's ancient and pervasive anti-Semitism provided the framework for the Holocaust and hardened the hearts of devout Catholics, most of whom did little to save their Jewish sisters and brothers from death. Not only did ordinary people participate in barbarous acts of evil during World War II, but prelates from the pope to the European bishops also refused to speak out against the murderous acts of the Nazis. As French Jews were being rounded up and transported to concentration camps, only six of the seventy-six French bishops condemned the action. The ecclesiasts were, however, quick to condemn the French resistance, whose actions disturbed the Vichy government, which, like all Fascist regimes, promulgated God, Catholic education, family values, and the church. In 1943, an assembly of French archbishops and cardinals roundly condemned the French resistance for its "deplorable attitudes of personal judgment and independence," reminding the few brave souls who stood up to the murderous fascists of the "exclusive authority of the hierarchy" (quoted in Henry, 2008).

John Paul II, the architect of rapprochement between Christians and Jews, inexplicably proffered Pius XII for canonization, a man who stood by silently as six million Jews were led to their deaths. Some have tried repeatedly to rehabilitate Pius, claiming that he saved hundreds of thousands of Jews. Pius never directed his flock to save Jews and did not do so personally. Instead, Pius warmly congratulated pro-Nazi Petain's Vichy government for its efforts to renew religious life in France (Henry, 2008). One can only imagine the effect Pius might have had on European Catholics if he had spoken out as forcefully against Nazis depredations as the current members of the hierarchy speak out against abortion.

Neither are the hands of Paul VI clean. As a diplomat close to Pius XII, in 1941, the future pope informed the Vichy regime that the Vatican would not oppose the statutes against the Jews or start any quarrel with the Nazi collaborators who were actively perse-cuting French Jews. As a result of this hands-off policy, seventy-six thousand Jews, including eleven thousand children, were deported by the Vichy regime, and sent to concentration camps. As pope, Paul would try to redeem and absolve himself by publicly stressing the heritage Jews and Christians shared and condemning anti-Semi-tism. Meanwhile, six million men, women, and children lay in their graves.

It took over fifty years for the French church to apologize for their lack of action during the Holocaust. In September of 1997, the bishop of Saint-Denis, Olivier de Berranger said, "The majority of the spiritual authorities, entangled in loyalty and docility that went beyond traditional obedience to established power, remained confined in an attitude of conformity, prudence and abstention... They did not become aware of the fact that the church, at that time called upon to play a substitute role in the dismembered social body, possessed in fact, considerable power and influence and that, given the silence of other institutions, her word, by its impact could have held back the irreparable" (quoted in Henry, 2008)

Apologists for the church claim that it was steamrolled by the power of the Nazis, who, if they had put up objections, would have destroyed the Vatican and its treasures or gone on an extermina-tion campaign against the clergy and members of religious orders. Thousands of members of the lower clergy, nuns, and ordinary citizens, however, exercised no such caution and often gave their lives and the lives of their families to protect their Jewish sisters and brothers. Meanwhile, not one bishop in any European country was arrested or spent any time in a concentration camp. Not one died a martyr for the faith (Phayer, 2001).

Although Dorothy Day (1897–1980) has not been canonized, she was a staunch advocate of peace and a defender of the poor. While much time has been devoted to her peripatetic, "bohemian" early life, her abortion, and her out-of-wedlock child, Day's record of discipleship is peerless. She was a member of suffragist Alice Paul's "Silent Sentinels" who picketed for women's suffrage outside of the White House during World War I. When the women charged President Woodrow Wilson with hypocrisy as he sent armies to war to fight for freedom abroad while denying women the right to vote at home, they were arrested and charged with obstruction of traffic. Day served fifteen days in jail, ten of them on a hunger strike.

Most of Day's positions were, and remain, unpopular. Over the course of her life, she praised the dictators Lenin, Castro, and Ho Chi Minh for overthrowing the powers of a corrupt government. She also rejected the American hierarchy's support for the Catholic mass murderer Franco during the Spanish Civil War and urged people to put away their flags and stand for peace at the outset of World War II. As the world spun for six years in a maelstrom of death, she maintained her pacifist stance even as Catholic Worker houses closed. Twenty years and tens of millions of dead later, she hoped that Vatican II would endorse pacifism as a pillar of Catholicism only to be disappointed. Her prophetic words stand against the hedging by members of the Catholic hierarchy like Francis Cardinal Spellman (1889-1967) of New York City who regarded the Vietnam War as a war for civilization.

Day, along with the Catholic Worker movement she and Peter Maurin founded, stood with the poor and the right of workers to form trade unions. Here she and Spellman differed again. When poorly paid New York cemetery workers went on strike for higher wages in 1949, Spellman brought in lay brothers and seminarians as scabs to dig the graves, teaching future pastors an unfortunate lesson in clerical-lay relations. Day wrote to Spellman, who lived in an opulent New York City mansion and rode around town in a limo, asking him to meet with the strikers and grant their demands. Spellman refused to concede. The strikers were forced to accept the archdiocese's original offer of a six-day, forty-eight-hour week.

Dorothy Day's sharp tongue and refusal to fall into ecclesiastical categories stand in the way of any impulse the church might have toward official canonization. The church could not contain her during her life, and she consistently rejected any attempt to be sanctified by her admirers. Perhaps she understood that she did only what is expected of all Catholic Christians: to be a witness to the Prince of Peace. Canonizing her would place her under the control of a church that has not been above twisting the messages of the canonized to push their own agenda of institutional power and purity of intention. While remaining a faithful, practicing Catholic, Dorothy Day worshipped God, not the Catholic Church.

Like Mother Jones and Dorothy Day, Paul Farmer (1959–2022) never accepted the status quo as the will of God. Rather than putting the sick in homes to suffer and die like Mother Teresa, Farmer cured them and returned them to their families. He also tried to address the structural sins of unjust economic and social policies and the unfair allocation of resources that made people in poor countries sick. For Farmer, bringing health care with all of the benefits of modern science to those most in need not only cured the body but also the soul. His program to combat drug-resistant tuberculosis had the highest cure rate in the world, even better than at hospitals in the United States.

Farmer's non-profit Partners in Health grew out of liberation theology, a Catholic movement that began in Central and South America that believed in justice for the poor and oppressed. As a medical student, he traveled to Haiti and witnessed the people's abject poverty, severe malnutrition, and overall poor health. Like Jesus and the Buddha, he was transformed. While still in medical school, he founded a clinic to serve the Haitian people. Over the years, his one-room clinic blossomed into a hospital with operating rooms, a blood bank, and a nursing school. The hospital also dispensed food, water, and provided housing assistance. Instead of using the poor to teach the rich a lesson or regarding illness as a blessing, Farmer developed programs to combat HIV and vaccinated children against communicable diseases. Paul Farmer, the apostle to the poor, died in his sleep in Rwanda in 2022 at age sixty-two. Farmer was able to manage his health care mission while married with children.

The brothers Daniel (1921–2016) and Phillip Berrigan (1923–2002) not only spoke and wrote prolifically against war, but they also organized and participated in burning draft records and destroying weapons of war during the Vietnam War, acts today that would be regarded as domestic terrorism. For his acts of property destruction, Phillip spent eleven non-consecutive years in jail and Daniel's face was plastered on the FBI's most wanted list.

Six months after burning the draft records of young men in Baltimore, Phillip, along with brother Daniel and seven others, poured homemade napalm on six hundred draft records in Catonsville, Maryland, proclaiming:

> *The time is past when good men can remain silent, when obedience can segregate men from public risk, when the poor can die without defense. We ask our fellow Christians to consider in their hearts a question which has tortured us, night and day, since the war began. How many must die before our voices are heard, how many must be tortured, dislocated, starved, maddened? How long must the world's resources be raped in the service of legalized murder? When, at what point, will you say no to this war? We have chosen to say, with the gift of our liberty, if necessary, our lives: the violence stops here, the death stops here, the suppression of the truth stops here, this war stops here (Daniel Berrigan, 1968).*

Bishop Thomas Gumbleton (1930—2024) was the auxiliary bishop of Detroit, Michigan from 1968 until 2006 when the Vatican asked him to resign for advocating for the victims of clergy sexual abuse and violating the communion of bishops. A tireless worker for peace, Gumbleton was arrested for protesting against the testing of atomic bombs in Nevada, the bombing of Kosovo, and the US invasion of Iraq. In 2012, he declared that Catholics should not participate in war. *The National Catholic Reporter* regularly published his homilies about peace.

None of the admirable and loyal disciples mentioned in this chapter would approve of an attempt to canonize them. All would assert that they did only what those who claim to follow Jesus should do: love their neighbors as themselves to its logical conclusion.

Gianna Molla was not a saint or a martyr, but unfortunate. Pius XII refused to speak out against genocide.

Followers of the Way of Jesus

All mothers who died in childbirth.
All peacemakers, known and unknown.

EPILOGUE

Like those who were persecuted and/or executed for criticizing the unholy alliance between church and state, twentieth-century Protestant theologians William Stringfellow (1928-1985) and Walter Wink (1935-2012) were suspicious of governments, corporations, and institutional churches of all denominations. Both men called these entities "the powers," a term used by Paul in his letter to the Ephesians (6:12) to represent the attractions of the world. Those who become entranced by the glamor of evil cleverly embedded in the powers too often slide into hypocrisy, idolatry, and violence.

It was the hermeneutic of the powers that bastardized the message of the Prince of Peace and led to the violence described in this book.

Wink, however, bequeathed a message of hope in his book *Engaging the Powers*. Because societies need organizations like governments to exist, the powers are good. Because of their frequent descent into the abyss of violence, the powers have fallen. The good news is that the powers can be redeemed.

Those who live within the paradigm of the powers and refuse to be mastered by any of it are the true saints.

BIBLIOGRAPHY

Abulafia, David, Franklin, Michael, and Rubin, Miri. (1992). *Church and City, 1000–1500*. Cambridge: Cambridge University Press.

Adamson, W. L. (2014). "Fascism and Political Religion in Italy: A Reassessment." *Contemporary European History, 23*(1), 43–73.

Agócs, S. (1973). "Christian Democracy and Social Modernism in Italy during the Papacy of Pius X." *Church History, 42*(1), 73–88.

Ahlgren, Gillian T. W. (1995). "Negotiating Sanctity: Holy Women in Sixteenth-Century Spain." *Church History, 64*(3), 373–388.

Alexander VI. (1443). *Division of the Undiscovered World Between Spain and Portugal.*

Ali, R. U. (2012). "Medieval Europe: The Myth of Dark Ages and the Impact of Islam." *Islamic Studies, 51*(2), 155–168.

Ambrose of Milan. (377). *Concerning Virgins*. https://cudl.lib.cam.ac.uk/view/MS-TRINITYHALL-00026/65.

Ambrose of Milan. (377). Epistle 42, 4. XVI.

Amar, Joseph Phillip. "Anatomy of a Tragedy." *Commonweal, 151*(4). 20-27.

Ames, C. (2005). "Does Inquisition Belong to Religious History?" *The American Historical Review, 110*(1), 11–37.

Anderson, E. (2016). "'White' Martyrs and 'Red' Saints: The Ongoing Distortions of Hagiography on Historiography." *American Catholic Studies, 127*(3), 9–13.

Anderson, M. W. (1986). "William Tyndale (d. 1536): A Martyr for All Seasons." *The Sixteenth Century Journal, 17*(3), 331–352.

Andreani, A. (2016). "Between Theological Debate and Political Subversion: Meredith Hanmer's Confutation of Edmund Campion's Letter to the Privy Council." *Aevum, 90*(3), 557–573.

Annals of Worms. 24, 405.

Anstey, R. T. (1968). "Capitalism and Slavery: A Critique." *The Economic History Review, 21*(2), 307–320

Apocryphal Acts of Peter and the Twelve Apostles. https://www.earlychristianwritings.com/text/actspeter.html.

Appleby, S. (2000). "Pope John Paul II." *Foreign Policy, 119*, 12–25.

Aquinas, Thomas. (c. 1273) *Summa Theologica*. https://www3. nd.edu/~afreddos/summa-translation/TOC.htm

Argodale, Jane. (2016]). "A Gift of God: Mother Teresa's Canonization and Her Complicated History."

Around the World. (1986). *New York Times Archive*. https://www. nytimes.com/1986/02/07/world/around-the-world-pope-in-india-prays-for-the-bhopal-victims.html

Athanasius. (367) Defense of the New Testament. https://christianhistoryinstitute.org/magazine/article/ athanasius-defines-new-testament

Augustine, Letter 105:16. Http://Wesleyscholar.com.

Augustine. (1958) *On Christian Doctrine*. New Jersey: Prentice Hall.

Baigent, Michael, and Leigh, Richard. (2000.) *The Inquisition*. London: Penguin Books.

Ball, David P. (2014) "Mary Brave Bird, Author of 'Lakota Woman' Walks On." *Tulalip News*.

Barnes, Timothy David. (1981). *Constantine and Eusebius*. Cambridge: Harvard University Press.

Barnes, Timothy David. [2008]. "The Date of Ignatius." *The Expository Times*. 120 (2),119-130.

Barr, Jane. (1990). "The Influence of St. Jerome on Medieval Attitudes." The Wijinggaards Institute. www.womenpriests.org/ the-influence-of-st-jerome-on-medieval-attitudes.

Barstow, Anne Llewellyn. (1988). "On Studying Witchcraft as Women's History: A Historiography of European Witch Persecutions." *Journal of Feminist Studies in Religion, 4*(2). (Fall), 7–19.

Basil of Caesarea "Letter to a Fallen Virgin." Basil, Letters. Vol 1: Letters 1-158. https//www.loebclassics.com.

Bauer, Eberhard. (2003) *The Archaeology of Religious Hatred in the Roman and Early Medieval World*. Gloucestershire, U.K.: The History Press.

BBC.com. (2016). "Pope Urged to End Catholic Church 'Just War' Theory." 4-14. http://BBC.com/news/world-Europe 36050229. Accessed 2023.

Bedford. S. (2014) "Mother Teresa's Troubled Legacy." *New Internationalist*, (September).

Benedict XV. (1920). *Divina disponetes.* www.papalencyclicals.net.

Ben-Yehuda, Nachman. (1980). "The European Witch Craze of the 14th–17th Century: A Sociological Perspective." *American Journal of Sociology,* (July), 1–31.

Betros, Gemma. (2010). "The French Revolution and the Catholic Church." *History Today,* (68) December.

Bettenson, Henry, and Maunder, Chris, eds. (1999). *Documents of the Christian Church.* Oxford: Oxford University Press. Third Edition.

Bireley, R. (2009). "Early-Modern Catholicism as a Response to the Changing World of the Long Sixteenth Century." *The Catholic Historical Review, 95*(2), 219–239.

Blake, Matt. (2013). "The Desecration of the Temple at Timbuktu." *Daily Mail.* 1-28.

Blaydes, L., and Paik, C. (2016). "The Impact of Holy Land Crusades on State Formation: War Mobilization, Trade Integration, and Political Development in Medieval Europe." *International Organization, 70*(3), 551–586.

Bolt, Robert. (1962) *A Man for All Seasons: A Play in Two Acts.* New York: Random House.

Boniface VIII. (1302) *Unam Sanctam.* www.papalencyclicals.net.

Bonner, Raymond. (2016) "The Diplomat and the Killer." *The Atlantic.*

Borg, Marcus. (2003). *The Heart of Christianity.* San Francisco: Harper.

Bowskill, S. E. L. (2009). Women, Violence, and the Mexican Cristero Wars." *The Modern Language Review, 104*(2), 438–452.

Boyer, P. (1997). "Praise the Lord and Pass the Ammunition: Evangelicals and the Military since World War II." Review of *American Evangelicals and the U.S. Military 1942–1993,* by A. C. Loveland. *Reviews in American History, 25*(4), 686–691.

Brent, A. (1998). "Ignatius of Antioch and the Imperial Cult." *Vigiliae Christianae, 52*(1), 30–58.

Bresie, A. (2014). "Mother Katharine Drexel's Benevolent Empire: The Bureau of Catholic Indian Missions and the Education of Native Americans, 1885–1935." *U.S. Catholic Historian, 32*(3), 1–24.

Brett, E. T. (2017). "The Beatification of Monsignor Romero:

A Historical Perspective." *American Catholic Studies, 128*(2), 51–73.

Brooke, Rosalind B. (1975). *The Coming of the Friars*. London: Routledge Press.

Brown, Peter. (1995). *Authority and the Sacred*. Cambridge: Cambridge University Press.

Brown, Peter. (1981). *Cult of the Saints*. Chicago: University of Chicago Press.

Brown, William. (2017). "Early Judaism." https://www.ancient.eu/artiste/1139/early-judaism/10-25-17. Accessed 1-23-2022.

Bryen, Ari. (2014). "Martyrdom, Rhetoric, and the Politics of Procedure." *Classical Antiquity, 33*(2), 243–280.

Bunch, Will. (2007). "Different Wars, Different Reactions." *Philadelphia Daily News*. 10-3.

Burns, J. H., ed. (1988). *Cambridge History of Medieval Political Thought*. Cambridge: Cambridge University Press.

Burson, J. D. (2018). "An Intellectual Genealogy of the Revolt against 'Esprit de Système'": From the Renaissance to the Early Enlightenment." *Historical Reflections / Réflexions Historiques, 44*(2), 21–44.

Butler, A. M. (2005). "There Are Exceptions to Every Rule: Adjusting the Boundaries—Catholic Sisters and the American West." *American Catholic Studies, 116*(3), 1–22.

Butturini, Paula. (1986) "Pope Prays for Phopal Gas Leak Victims." https://www.upi.com/Archives/1986/02/06/Pope-prays-for-Bhopal-gas-leak-victims/4510508050000/ph.

Bynum, Carolyn Walker and Freedman, Paul. (2000). *Death and Apocalypse in the Middle Ages*. Philadelphia: University of Pennsylvania Press.

Bynum, C. W. (2002). "The Blood of Christ in the Later Middle Ages." *Church History, 71*(4), 685–714.

Bynum, C. W., & Gerson, P. (1997). "Body-Part Reliquaries and Body Parts in the Middle Ages." *Gesta, 36*(1), 3–7.

Cahill, L. S. (2001). "Using Augustine in Contemporary Sexual Ethics: A Response to Gilbert Meilaender." *The Journal of Religious Ethics, 29*(1), 25–33.

Canavan, T., O'Mahony, G., and McNamara, C. (2013). "Mother Jones, 'The Most Dangerous Woman in America.'" *History Ireland, 21*(4), 6–8.

Candela, G. (1998). "An Overview of the Cosmology, Religion and Philosophical Universe of Giordano Bruno." *Italica, 75*(3), 348–364.

Carrington, Selwyn H.H. (2003). "Capitalism and Slavery and Caribbean Historiography: An Evaluation." *The Journal of African American History, 88*(3), 304–312.

Cassidy, J. (1933). "St. Ignatius of Loyola and Militant Christianity." *The Irish Monthly, 61*(723), 543–549.

Catechism of the Catholic Church. (1995). Washington, D. C. USCCB Publishing.

Catholic News Agency. (2012). "Cardinal George Warns U.S. That Secularization Is More Serious Than Elections." 10-23.

Catholic News Agency. (2020). "Cardinal Dolan: Stories of Persecuted Christians Should Move Hearts." 11-22.

Chakravarti, Ananya. (2020) "Architects of Empire." Aeon. https://aeon.co/essays/how-the-jesuits-cultivated-the-idea-of europe an – empire.

Chamberlin, W. (2018). "Silencing Genocide: The Jesuit Ministry in Colonial Cartagena de Indias and its Legacy." *Journal of Black Studies, 49*(7), 672–693.

Chamedes, G. (2016). "The Vatican, Nazi-Fascism, and the Making of Transnational Anti-communism in the 1930s." *Journal of Contemporary History, 51*(2), 261–290.

Chenard, Genevieve. (2016) "Mother Teresa Doesn't Deserve Sainthood." *New York Times.* 3-25.

Chevedden, P. E. (2011). "The View of the Crusades from Rome and Damascus: The Geo-Strategic and Historical Perspectives of Pope Urban II and 'Alī ibn Tāhir al-Sulamī." *Oriens, 39*(2), 257–329.

Christiansen, Eric. (1997). *The Northern Crusades,* 2nd ed. London: Penguin Press.

Christie-Murray, David. (1976). *A History of Heresy.* Oxford: Oxford University Press.

Chrysostom, John. (c. 400) *In Epist ad Hebraeos homiliae.* 2(3) CPG, 63-93.

Church, R. Forrester. (1975). "Sex and Salvation in Tertullian." *The Harvard Theological Review, 68* (2), 83–101.

Clarke, P. D. (2009). "Between Avignon and Rome: Minor

Penitentiaries at the Papal Curia in the Thirteenth and Fourteenth Centuries." *Rivista Di Storia Della Chiesa in Italia, 63*(2), 455–510.

Cloutier, D. (2017). "Cavanaugh and Grimes on Structural Evils of Violence and Race: Overcoming Conflicts in Contemporary Social Ethics." *Journal of the Society of Christian Ethics, 37*(2), 59–78.

Cluny, Roland. (1963). *Holiness in Action*. New York: Hawthorn Publishers.

Coatsworth, J. H. (1978). "Obstacles to Economic Growth in Nineteenth-Century Mexico." *The American Historical Review, 83*(1), 80–100.

Coffey, John. (2020). *The Oxford History of Protestant Dissenting Traditions*. Volume 1. Oxford: Oxford University Press.

Cogley, John. (1966). "The Spellman Dispute." *The New York Times*. 12-29.

Conger, Cristen. (2012). "Sex Myth Exposed: What They Don't Tell You About Your Hymen." *Huffington Post,* 2-19.

Cooney, John. (12015) "Thomas Merton: the Hermit Who Never Was, His Young Lover and Mysterious Death." *The Irish Times*. https://www.irishtimes.com/culture/books/thomas-merton-the-hermit-who-never-was-his-young-lover-and-mysterious-death-1.2422818

Cooperman, Alan. (2001). "Roman Catholic Bishops Declare U.S. War Is Moral After September 11." *The Washington Post*. 11-16.

Coppa, F. J. (1995). "From Liberalism to Fascism: The Church-State Conflict over Italy's Schools." *The History Teacher, 28*(2), 135–148.

Cornwell, John. (2010). "The Pope's Priestly Model: A Rabid, Self-Harming Tyrant." *The Guardian*. 9-10.

Courtenay, W. J. (1989). "Inquiry and Inquisition: Academic Freedom in Medieval Universities." *Church History, 58*(2), 168–181.

Cox, Rory. (2014) *John Wyclif on War and Peace*. London: Boydell and Brewer, Ltd.

Cummings, Kathleen Sprows. (2012). "American Saints: Gender and the Re-Imaging of U.S. Catholicism in the Early Twentieth Century." *Religion and American Culture: A Journal of Interpretation, 22*(2), 203–231.

Cunningham, Lawrence. (1980). *The Meaning of Saints*. San Francisco: Harper & Row.

Dalarun, J. (2005). "Francis and Clare of Assisi: Differing Perspectives on Gender and Power." *Franciscan Studies, 63,* 11–25.

Dalberg, John. (1907). *Lord Acton: Historical Essays and Studies.* London: Macmillan.

Dallmayr, F. R. (2006). "A War Against the Turks? Erasmus on War and Peace." *Asian Journal of Social Science, 34*(1), 67–85.

D'Althann, R. (1972). "Papal Mediation during the First World War." *Studies: An Irish Quarterly Review, 61*(243), 219–240.

D'Alton, C. W. (2002). "Charity or Fire? The Argument of Thomas More's 1529 Dyaloge." *The Sixteenth Century Journal, 33*(1), 51–70.

Daniel-Hughes, Carly and Kotrosits, Maria. (2020). "Tertullian of Carthage and the Fantasy Life of Powers." *Journal of Early Christian Studies, 28*(1), 1-31.

Davidson, A. I., and Fritz-Morkin, M. (2009). "Miracles of Bodily Transformation, or How St. Francis Received the Stigmata." *Critical Inquiry, 35*(3), 451–480.

D'Avray, David. (2014). *Dissolving Royal Marriages*. Cambridge: Cambridge University Press.

Dean, Sidney. (2015). "Felling the Irminsul: Charlemagne's Saxon Wars." *Medieval Warfare.* 5(2). Pp. 15-20.

Deane, Jennifer Kolpacoff. (2011). *A History of Medieval Heresy and Inquisition*. New York: Rowman and Littlefield.

Dear, John. (2010). "Ben Salmon and the Army of Peace." *National Catholic Reporter.* 2-23.

Debby, N. B.A. (2012). "St. Clare Expelling the Saracens from Assisi: Religious Confrontation in Word and Image." *The Sixteenth Century Journal, 43*(3), 643–665.

De Castro Alves, J. (2000). "Rupture and Continuity in Colonial Discourses: The Racialized Representation of Portuguese Goa in the Sixteenth and Seventeenth Centuries." *Portuguese Studies, 16,* 148–161.

Decosse, David E. (2009). "Conscience Issue Separates Catholics into Moral Camps." *National Catholic Reporter*, 11-10.

Decretal Epistle, No. 1. (1853). *The Catholic Layman.* 2(24). Pp. 137-138.

de la Cueva, J. (1998). "Religious Persecution, Anticlerical Tradition and Revolution: On Atrocities against the Clergy during the Spanish Civil War." *Journal of Contemporary History, 33*(3), 355–369.

Devens, C. (1992). "'If We Get the Girls, We Get the Race'": Missionary Education of Native American Girls." *Journal of World History, 3*(2), 219–237.

Diehl, Peter, and Waugh, Scott L. (1996). *Christendom and Its Discontents*. Oxford: Cambridge University Press.

DiGiovanni, S. M. (1991). "Mother Cabrini: Early Years in New York." *The Catholic Historical Review, 77*(1), 56–77.

Dileo, Ilia. (2019). "Theology Needs Radical Revisioning." *The National Catholic Reporter*. 7-1.

Dobnik, Verena. (2019). "Saint John Vianney's 150-Year-Old Heart To Be Venerated in NYC." *America*. 4-8.

Donahue, P. J. (1978). "Jewish Christianity in the Letters of Ignatius of Antioch." *Vigiliae Christianae, 32*(2), 81–93.

Drabble, J. E. (1982). "Mary's Protestant Martyrs and Elizabeth's Catholic Traitors in the Age of Catholic Emancipation." *Church History, 51*(2), 172–185.

Drury, S. B. (2008). "Aquinas and the Inquisition: A Tale of Faith and Politics." *Salmagundi, 157*, 91–108.

Dürr, R. (2000). "Images of the Priesthood: An Analysis of Catholic Sermons from the Late Seventeenth Century." *Central European History, 33*(1), 87–107.

Eagan, Robert. (2004). "The Mandatum: Now What?" *Commonweal*, 6-17.

Einhorn, R. L. (2008). "Slavery." *Enterprise & Society, 9*(3), 491–506.

Emmerich, Anne Catherine, and Bretano, Clemens. (1833) *The Dolorous Passion of Our Lord Jesus Christ*. https://www.ccel.org/ccel/emmerich/passion.html

Enoch, J. (2002). "Resisting the Script of Indian Education: Zitkala Ša and the Carlisle Indian School." *College English, 65*(2), 117–141.Enochs, R. (2006). "The Franciscan Mission to the Navajos: Mission Method and Indigenous Religion, 1898–1940." *The Catholic Historical Review, 92*(1), 46–73.

Enochs, R. (2009). "Native Americans on the Path to the Catholic

Church: Cultural Crisis and Missionary Adaptation." *U.S. Catholic Historian, 27(*1), 71–88.

Erhman, Bart D. (2018). *The Triumph of Christianity*. New York: Simon & Shuster.

Erhman, Bart D. (1993). *The Orthodox Corruption of Scripture*. Oxford: Oxford University Press.

Evans, Roger Steven. (2003). *Sex and Salvation*. New York: University Press of America.

Faust, Avraham. (2019). "Israelite Temples: Where Was Israelite Cult Not Practiced and Why." *Archeology and Ancient Israelite Religion*. 2-7.

Fessenden, T. (2000). "The Sisters of the Holy Family and the Veil of Race." *Religion and American Culture: A Journal of Interpretation, 10*(2), 187–224.

Fette, J. (2008). "Apology and the Past in Contemporary France." *French Politics, Culture & Society, 26*(2), 78–113.

Findlen, P., and Marcus, H. (2012). "Science under Inquisition: Heresy and Knowledge in Catholic Reformation Rome." Review of *Catholic Church and Modern Science: Documents from the Archives of the Roman Congregations of the Holy Office and the Index*, by U. Baldini. *Isis, 103*(2), 376–382.

Finkelman, Paul. (2021). "America's 'Great Chief Justice' Was an Unrepentant Slaveowner." *The Atlantic*. 6-15.

Flesseman-van Leer, E. (1960). The Controversy About Scripture and Tradition Between Thomas More and William Tyndale. *Nederlands Archief Voor Kerkgeschiedenis / Dutch Review of Church History, 43*, 143–164.

Forey, A. J. (2013). "Western Converts to Islam" (later eleventh to later fifteenth centuries). *Traditio, 68*, 153–231.

Fox, Robin. (1996). "The Calcutta Perspective: Mother Theresa's Care of the Dying." *The Lancet*. https://www.thelancet.com/journals/lancet/article/PIIS0140-6736(94)92353-1/fulltext

Francois, B., Sternberg, E. M., and Fee, Elizabeth. (2014). "The Lourdes Medical Cures Revisited." *Journal of the History of Medicine and Allied Sciences, 69*(1), 135–162.

Frend, W.H.C. (1985). *Saints and Sinners in the Early Church*. Wilmington, DE: Michael Glazier.

Frend, W.H.C. (1982). *The Early Church*. Philadelphia: Fortress Press.

Frend, W.H.C. (1985). *The Donatist Church*. Oxford: Clarendon Press.

Galli, Mark. (1997). "The Great Divorce." *Church Institute*, 54. https://christianhistoryinstitute.org/magazine/article/great-divorce-schism/

Gerlach, D. B. (1973). "St. Joseph's Indian Normal School, 1888–1896." *Indiana Magazine of History*, 69(1), 1–42.

Georgetown Slavery Archives. https://slaveryarchive.georgetownuniversity.edu.

Germeten, N. (2005). "A Century of Promoting Saint Peter Claver and Catholicism to African Americans: Claverian Historiography from 1868–1965." *American Catholic Studies*, 116(3), 23–38.

Gibbons, Edward. (1776–1798). *The Decline and Fall of the Roman Empire*. London: Strahan & Cadel.

Gillette, George. (2016). "The West's Big Lie About Mother Teresa: Her Glorification of Suffering Instead of Relieving It." *Salon*. 1-3.

Given, J. (1989). "The Inquisitors of Languedoc and the Medieval Technology of Power." *The American Historical Review*, 94(2), 336–359.

Goel, Sita Ram. (2012). "St. Francis Xavier: A Pirate in Priest's Clothing." *Bharata Bharati*. 12-04. Httsp://hharatagharati.in/2012/12/04/st-francis-xavier-a-pirate-in-priests-clothing-sita-ram-goel.

Gollar, C. Walker. (2010). "Jesuit Education and Slavery in Kentucky, 1832–1868." *The Register of Kentucky Historical Society*, 108 (3), 213–249.

Gonsalves, Francis. (2020) "For God's Greater Glory." *The Asian Age*. http://archive.asianage.com/mystic-mantra/god%E2%80%99s-greater-glory-062

Goodich, M. (1975). "The Politics of Canonization in the Thirteenth Century: Lay and Mendicant Saints." *Church History*, 44(3), 294–307.

Graeber, David, and Wengrow, David. (2021). *The Dawn of Everything*. New York: Farrar, Straus, and Giroux.

Greenblat, Stephen. (2011). *The Swerve: How the World Became Modern*. New York: W.W. Norton & Company.

Gregory, B. (2014). "Christian Ideas in the Sixteenth and Seventeenth Centuries." *Journal of the History of Ideas, 75*(4), 667–675.

Gregory, Wilton. (2003). "Statement on Iraq." www.usccb.org/ resources. 2-26.

Grimes, Katie Walker. (2017). *Fugitive Saints: Catholicism and the Politics of Slavery*. Minneapolis: Fortress Press.

Groff, Frank. (2020) "Evidence Grows. The Lost Colony Split Up." PBSNC. https://www.pbsnc.org/blogs/science/lost-colony-split.

Hallebeek, Jan. (1987). "Thomas Aquinas' Theory of Property." *Irish Jesuit*, 22(1). 99-111.

Hamilton, B. (1997). "Knowing the Enemy: Western Understanding of Islam at the Time of the Crusades." *Journal of the Royal Asiatic Society, 7*(3), 373–387.

Hardstaff, Michael. (2018). "The Long View: Nobody Expects an Account of the Inquisition." *The Oxford Culture Review*.Https:// theoxfordculturereview.com/2018/06/03/the/long/view/nobody/ expects/an/accountable/inquisition.

Harkins, Charles H. (1902). "Robert le Bourge and the Beginning of the Inquisition in Northern France." *The American Historical Review*, Apr., *7*(3), 437–457.

Harmon, K. E. (2012). "Drawing the Holy in the Ordinary: Ade Bethune, the Catholic Worker, and the Liturgical Movement." *American Catholic Studies, 123*(1), 1–23.

Harris, Carissa. (2021) "800 Years of Rape Culture." *Aeon*. https://aeon.co/essays/ the-hypocricies-of-rape-culture-through-medieval-roots.

Hassell, S. (2015). "Inquisition Records from Goa as Sources for the Study of Slavery in the Eastern Domains of the Portuguese Empire." *History of Africa, 42,* 397–418.

Hearden, M. (2005). Catholic America's Love Affair with the Little Flower." *American Catholic Studies, 116*(3), 39–54.

Heisser, D.C.R. (1998). "Bishop Lynch's Civil War Pamphlet on Slavery." *The Catholic Historical Review, 84*(4), 681–696.

Hendrickson, R. M. (1996). "Victims and Survivors: Native American Women Writers, Violence Against Women, and Child Abuse." *Studies in American Indian Literatures, 8*(1), 13–24.

Henry, P. (2008). "The Art of Christian Apology: Comparing the

French Catholic Church's Apology to the Jews and the Vatican's 'We Remember.'" *Shofar, 26*(3), 87–104.

Heston, A. (2003). "Crusades and Jihads: A Long-Run Economic Perspective." *The Annals of the American Academy of Political and Social Science, 588*, 112–135.

Hildegard of Bingen. (1163). *The Book of Divine Works*. www. catholics.org.

Higman, B. W. (2000). "The Sugar Revolution." *The Economic History Review, 53*(2), 213–236.

Hines, Nicklaus. (2021). "Inside the Little-Known Dark Side of Mother Teresa." *All That Is Interesting*. https://allthatsinteresting. com/mother-teresa-saint

Hitchens, Christopher. (2000). "The Devil and Mother Teresa." *Vanity Fair*. October.

Holc, J. (2019). Review of *Against Anti-Semitism: An Anthology of Twentieth-Century Polish Writings*, by A. Michnik and A. Marczyk. *Slavic Review, 78*(2), 506–513.

Hoose, A. (2010). "Francis of Assisi's Way of Peace? His Conversion and Mission to Egypt." *The Catholic Historical Review, 96*(3), 449–469.

Hoose, A. L. (2016). "The 'Sabotati': The Significance of Early Waldensian Shoes, c. 1184—c. 1300." *Speculum, 91*(2), 356–373.

Horowitz, M. C. (2009). "Long Time Going: Religion and the Duration of Crusading." *International Security, 34*(2), 162–193.

Howard, John. (1984). "The German Mystic Mechthild of Magdeburg." in *Medieval Women Writers*. Edited by Katharina M. Wilson, pp. 153–163. Athens: University of Georgia Press.

Hoy, S. (2004). "Lives on the Color Line: Catholic Sisters and African Americans in Chicago, 1890s–1960s." *U.S. Catholic Historian, 22*(1), 67–91.

Hoyert, Donna. (2020). "Maternal Mortality Rates in 2020."

https://www.cdc.gov/nchs/data/hestat/maternal-mortality/2020/ maternal-mortality-rates-2020.htm

Hsia, R. Po-Chia. (1998). *The World of Catholic Renewal, 1540– 1770*. Cambridge: Cambridge University Press.

Huerzo, Stephanie. (2020). "The Murdered Church Women in El Salvador." Origns.osu.edu. December.

Hunter, David G. (2007). *Marriage, Celibacy, and Heresy in Ancient Christianity: The Jovinianist Controversy. Oxford Early Christian Studies.* New York: Oxford University Press.

Ignatius of Antioch, Letter to the Magnesiana.

Ignatius of Antioch, *Letter to the Smyrnaeans* 6:2-7:1.

International Endowments Network/Georgetown University.

Ireneus. (d. 202) *Against Heresies.* http://www.earlychristianwritings.com/text/irenaeus-book4.html

Jaenan, Cornelius. (1983). "The Frenchification and Evangelization of the Amerindians in the 17th Century in New France." Unmanitoba.ca/colleges/st-pauls/ccha.

Jalal, Baland. (2020). "Sleep Paralysis and the Monsters Inside Your Mind." *Scientific American.* July 15.

Janz, Denis R., ed. (2014). *People's History of Christianity.* Minneapolis: Fortress Press.

Janz, Denis R, ed. (2008). *A Reformation Reader.* Minneapolis: Fortress Press.

Jardine, L. (2004). "Gloriana Rules the Waves: Or, the Advantage of Being Excommunicated (And a Woman)." *Transactions of the Royal Historical Society, 14,* 209–222.

Jarrell, L. (1991). "The Development of Legal Structures for Women Religious between 1500 and 1900: A Study of Selected Institutes of Religious Life for Women." *U.S. Catholic Historian, 10*(1/2), 25–35.

Jenkins, Phillip. (2010). *Jesus Wars.* New York: Harper Collins.

Jenkins, Phillip. (2008). *The Lost History of Christianity.* New York: Harper Collins. Jerome. "On Marriage and Virginity." Letter XXIi.

Jerome. "Letter to Eustochium." http://www2.latech.edu/~bmagee/210/jerome/jerome.htm

Jimenez, Jesus. (2021). "CNN Drops Rick Santorum After Dismissive Comments About Native Kamen, Henry. "Confiscations in the Economy of the Spanish Inquisition." *New York Times*, May 23.

John of Salisbury. (1163) Historia pontificalis. https://archive.org/stream/bookofpopesliber00loom/bookofpopesliber00loom_djvu.txt,

Jones, W. R. (1979). "The English Church and Royal Propaganda during the Hundred Years War." *Journal of British Studies, 19*(1), 18–30.

Julian of Norwich. *Revelations of Divine Love*, trans 1999 Elizabeth Spearing. New York: Pengiun Books.

Kane, P. M. (2002). "'She Offered Herself up': The Victim Soul and Victim Spirituality in Catholicism." *Church History, 71*(1), 80–119.

Kehoe, A. B. (1979). "The Sacred Heart: A Case for Stimulus Diffusion." *American Ethnologist, 6*(4), 763–771.

Kellerman, Christopher. (2023) "Slavery and the Catholic Church: It's Time to Correct the Historical Record." *America.* https://www.americamagazine.org/voices/christopher-j-kellerman

Kelly, H. A. (2016). "Galileo's Non-Trial (1616), Pre-Trial (1632–1633), and Trial (May 10, 1633): A Review of Procedure, Featuring Routine Violations of the Forum of Conscience." *Church History, 85*(4), 724–76.

Kennan, Elizabeth. (1967). "The 'de Consideratione' of St Bernard of Clairvaux and the Papacy in the Middle of the Twelfth Century." *Traditio*, 23, 73-115.

Keresztes, P. (1970). "The Emperor Septimius Severus: A Precursor of Decius." *Historia: Zeitschrift Für Alte Geschichte, 19*(5), 565–578.

Kershaw, Sarah. (2016). "The Race to Save Ancient Islamic Manuscripts from Terrorists Who Want Them Destroyed." *The Washington Post.* 1-21.

Kessler, Edward. (2010). *An Introduction to Jewish-Christian Relations*. Cambridge: Cambridge University Press.

Kim, M.A. (2013). "Liberation and Theology: A Pedagogical Challenge." *The History Teacher,46*(4), 601–612.

Kimball, Charles. (2002). *When Religion Becomes Evil*. San Francisco: Harper.

Kirk, J. (1985). "John Paul II and the Exorcism of Liberation Theology: A Retrospective Look at the Pope in Nicaragua." *Bulletin of Latin American Research, 4*(1), 33–47.

Knibbs, Eric. (2017). "Ebo of Reims, Pseudo-Isidore, and the False Decretals." *Speculum*, 92(1). Pp. 144-183.

Knowlton, R. J. (1965). "Clerical Response to the Mexican Reform, 1855–1875." *The Catholic Historical Review, 50*(4),

509–528.

Koch, Alexander, Brierley, Chris, Maslin, Mark M., and Lewis, Simon L. (2017). "Earth System Impacts the European Arrival and Great Dying in the Americas Before 1492." *Quaternary Science Review, 207.* 1 March, 13–36.

Koch, R. M. (1981). "Mechthild von Magdeburg, Woman of Two Worlds." *14th Century English Mystics Newsletter, 7*(3), 111–131.

Koscheski, J. (2011). "The Earliest Christian War: Second- and Third-Century Martyrdom and the Creation of Cosmic Warriors." *The Journal of Religious Ethics, 39*(1), 100–124.

Krahenbuhl, K. (2013). "The Albigensian Crusade: A Twist in the Story of the Crusades." *Medieval Warfare, 3*(4), 6–11.

Kreuter, Joseph, *Guide for Victim Souls of the Sacred Heart of Jesus.* New York: Benzinger Press. 1939.

Krieder, Alan. (2007) "Violence and Mission in the Fourth and Fifth Centuries: Lessons for Today." https://amnetwork.uk/resource/violence-and-mission-in-the-fourth-and-fifth-centuries-lessons-for-today/

Krostenko, B. (2018). "Three Kinds of Ambiguity: Rhetoric and Christian Citizenship in the Martyr Act of Cyprian." *Wiener Studien, 131*, 149–177.

Kselman, T. (2013). "Claude Langlois's Vision of Nineteenth-Century French Catholicism." *Historical Reflections / Réflexions Historiques, 39*(1), 66–81.

Kselman, T. (2006). "Challenging Dechristianization: The Historiography of Religion in Modern France." *Church History, 75*(1), 130–139.

Lampe, Peter. (2003) *From Paul to Valentinus: Christians in Rome in the First Two Centuries.* Minneapolis: Fortress Press.

Las Casas, Bartholome. (1552). *A Short Account of the Destruction of the Indies.*

Latham, A. A. (2011). "Theorizing the Crusades: Identity, Institutions, and Religious War in Medieval Latin Christendom." *International Studies Quarterly, 55*(1), 223–243.

Lawler, Andrew. (2018). "Reimagining the Crusades." *Archeology, 71(6)*, 26–35.

Lea, Henry Charles. (1954). *The Inquisition of the Middle Ages.* New York: The Citadel Press.

Leverle, Blade. (1993). "John Chrysostom and the Gaze." *Journal of Early Christian Studies, 1*(2, 159-174.

Levine, Joshua. (2020). "The New, Nicer Nero." *Smithsonian Magazine.* Oct. 20.

Lewis, Nicola Denzey. (2018). "The Apostle Peter in Rome." *Biblical Archeology Society* Blog. https://www.biblicalarchaeology.org/daily/ancient-cultures/ancient-rome/the-apostle-peter-in-rome.

Libanius. (352). *Pro Templis.* (Oration XXX.8-10).

Lindberg, D. C. (1992). Review of *Galileo, Bellarmine, and the Bible, Including a Translation of Foscarini's "Letter on the Motion of the Earth,"* by R. J. Blackwell. *Renaissance Quarterly, 45*(2), 362–365.

Linder, Douglas. "The Trial of Giordano Bruno." https://Famoustrials.com/Bruno.

Linz, J. J. (1991). "Church and State in Spain from the Civil War to the Return of Democracy. *Daedalus, 120*(3), 159–178.

Lomawaima, K. T. (1996). Preface. *Journal of American Indian Education, 35*(3), 1–4.

Lomawaima, K. T. (1993). "Domesticity in the Federal Indian Schools: The Power of Authority over Mind and Body." *American Ethnologist, 20*(2), 227–240.

Lösel, S. (2008). "Prayer, Pain, and Priestly Privilege: Claude Langlois's New Perspective on Thérèse of Lisieux." *The Journal of Religion, 88*(3), 273–306.

Luthera, V. (1956). "Goa and the Portuguese Republic." *The Indian Journal of Political Science, 17*(3), 261–280.

Luxmoor, Jonathan. (2023) "Spain's Catholic Church 'Soul-Searching' After 3 Years Under Progressive Government." *The National Catholic Reporter*, February 17-March 2.

Mackenzie, L. (1973). "The Political Ideas of the Opus Dei in Spain." *Government and Opposition, 8*(1), 72–92.

MacNicol, Nicol. (1934). *The Making of Modern India.* Oxford [or NY?]: Oxford University Press.

Malo, Robyn. (2013). *Relics and Writings in Late Medieval England.* Toronto: University of Toronto Press.

Marcos, M. (2015). "Religious Violence and Hagiography in Late Antiquity" *Numen, 62*(2/3), 169–196.

Mary, Margaret. (1954). "Slavery in the Writings of St. Augustine." The Classical Journal, 49(8), 363-366.Marshall, Jermaine. (2021). *Christianity Corrupted: The Scandal of White Supremacy.* New York: Orbis Books.

Marvin, L. W. (2001). "War in the South: A First Look at Siege Warfare in the Albigensian Crusade, 1209–1218." *War in History, 8*(4), 373–395.

Mathisen, E. (2018). "The Second Slavery, Capitalism, and Emancipation in Civil War America." *Journal of the Civil War Era, 8*(4), 677–699.

Matson, R. W. (1979). "Church Wealth in Nineteenth-Century Mexico: A Review of Literature." *The Catholic Historical Review, 65*(4), 600–609.

McBeth, Sally. (1983). *Ethnic Identity and the Boarding School Experience of West Central Oklahoma.* Washington, D.C. University Press of America.

McCartin, J. P. (2007). "The Sacred Heart of Jesus, Thérèse of Lisieux, and the Transformation of U.S. Catholic Piety, 1865–1940." *U.S. Catholic Historian, 25*(2), 53–67.

McCoy, B. J. (1942). "St. Vincent de Paul's Letters on Jansenism." *The Catholic Historical Review, 27*(4), 442–449.

McClory, Robert. (2012). "Cardinal George and a Nation State Gone Bad." *National Catholic Reporter.*

McEachern, P. A. (2002). "'La Vierge et la bête': Marian Iconographies and Bestial Effigies in Nineteenth-Century French Narratives." *Nineteenth-Century French Studies, 31*(1/2), 111–122.

McFarland, C. K. (1971). "Crusade for Child Laborers: 'Mother' Jones and the March of the Mill Children." *Pennsylvania History: A Journal of Mid-Atlantic Studies, 38*(3), 283–296.

McGinley, John. (2021) *"Mother Jones*: 'The Most Dangerous Irish Woman in America.'" *The Irish Story.* www.theirishstory.com.

McLerran, Dan. (2020). "The Case for Hatteras: Unearthing a New Clue. *Popular Archeology.* https://popular-archaeology.com/article/the-case-for-hatteras-unearthing-new-clues-to-americas-historic-lost-colony/

McNeil, B. A. (2013). "Daughters of Charity: Courageous and Compassionate Civil War Nurses." *U.S. Catholic Historian, 31*(1), 51–72.

Mejia, Anthony. (2020) "The Revocation of *Inter Caetera*." Unpublished paper. Markkula Center for Applied Ethics. Santa Clara University, California.

Mendenhall, George E. (2001). *Ancient Israel's Faith and History*. Louisville: Westminster John Knox Press.

Mercier, Charles. (2016). "Maybe Nero Didn't Persecute Christians After All." *Crux*. 12-19.

Metz, J. (2005). "Elizabeth Bayley Seton: Extending the Role of Caregiver Beyond the Family Circle." *American Catholic Studies, 116*(2), 19–38.

Mews, C.J. (2002). "The Council of Sens (1141): Abelard, Bernard, and the Fear of Social Upheaval." *Speculum*, 77(2), 3424-382.

Midura, Rachel. (2021). "On Print and Decision Making: The Management of Information by the City Powers of Lyon (ca. 1550-ca. 1580)." *Print and Power in Early Modern Europe 1500-1800*. Eds. Lamal, Crumbly, and Helmer. Brill.

Miles, L. (1965). "Persecution and the Dialogue of Comfort: A Fresh Look at the Charges against Thomas More." *Journal of British Studies, 5*(1), 19–30.

Miller, J. B. (1999). "Eroticized Violence in Medieval Women's Mystical Literature: A Call for a Feminist Critique." *Journal of Feminist Studies in Religion, 15*(2), 25–49.

Miller, Stephen. (2-11). "What Kind of Heresies Were There in the Early Church?" *Christian Bible Studies*. https://christianity today.com/bible/studies/bible-answered theologies/kind-heresies/church.html.

Montgomery, T. S. (1982). "Cross and Rifle: Revolution and the Church in El Salvador and Nicaragua." *Journal of International Affairs, 36*(2), 209–221.

Monyan, Susanne. (2015). "Build by Slaves and Jesuits." *The Hoya*. 1-.

Moore, R. I. (2012). *The War on Heresy*. Cambridge: Belknap Press of Harvard University Press.

More. Thomas. (1516). *Utopia*. https://www.gutenberg.org/files/2130/2130-h/2130-h.htm

Morwood, Michael. (2010). "*Tomorrow's Christianity*." New London: Twenty-Third Publications.

Moss, Candida. (2012). *Ancient Christian Martyrdom*. New Haven: Yale University Press.

Moss, Candida. (2013). *The Myth of Persecution*. San Francisco: Harper One Press.

Moss, C. R. (2012). "The Discourse of Voluntary Martyrdom: Ancient and Modern." *Church History, 81*(3), 531–551.

Mount, Guy Emerson. (2015). "Capitalism and Slavery: Reflections on the Williams Thesis." *Black Perspectives.* 11-21.

Moss, Candida (2010). "On the Dating of Polycarp: Rethinking the Place of the Martyrdom of Polycarp in the History of Christianity," *Early Christianity 1*(4). 539–574.

Mueller, J., and Stewart, M. G. (2011). "Witches, Communists, and Terrorists: Evaluating the Risks and Tallying the Costs." *Human Rights, 38*(1), 18–20.

Mueller, Tom. (2003). "Inside Job." *The Atlantic.* Oct.

Mullen, Peter. (2017). "The First Global Conflict Between Christians." *The Catholic Herald,* 10-19.

Munro, D. C. (1916). "The Popes and the Crusades." *Proceedings of the American Philosophical Society, 55*(5), 348–356.

Neal, D. (1997). "The Beautiful Death of Thérèse of Lisieux and the Sufferings of the Tubercular Self." *New Blackfriars, 78*(915), 218–229.

Newman, M. Sophia. (2016). "The Liberation Theology of Dr. Paul Farmer." https://*Religion and Politics.*

Ng, Su Fang. (2001). "Translation, Interpretation, and Heresy: The Wycliffite Bible, Tyndale's Bible, and the Contested Origin." *Studies in Philology, 98*(3), 315–338.

Nicholas V. (1452) *Dum Diversas.* https://papalencylicals.net.

Notermans, C. (2008). "Local and Global Icons of Mary: An Ethnographic Study of a Powerful Symbol." *Anthropos, 103*(2), 471–4

O'Connell, Gerard. (2019). "Pope Francis Says Commission on Women Deacons Did Not Reach Agreement." *America.* 5-7.

O'Connell, Maureen H. (2021). *Undoing the Knots*. Boston: Beacon Press.

O'Malley, John, S. J. *Catholicism in Early Modern History*. Volume 2. Ann Arbor: Edwards Brothers.

O'Malley, John, S.J. (2018). *Vatican II.* Cambridge: Cambridge University Press.

Origen. (248). *Against Celsus.*

O'Sullivan, D. (1946). "St. Frances Xavier Cabrini: Canonized." July 7. *Studies: An Irish Quarterly Review, 35*(139), 351–356.

Pagels, E. H. (2006). "The Social History of Satan, Part Three: John of Patmos and Ignatius of Antioch: Contrasting Visions of 'God's People.'" *The Harvard Theological Review, 99*(4), 487–505.

Pagels, Elaine. (2003). *Beyond Belief.* New York: Random House.

Pagels, Elaine. (1979). *The Gnostic Gospels.* New York: Vintage Books.

Pagels, Elaine. (2000). *Reading Judas.* New York: Viking Press.

Paul Vi. (1965). Dignitatus humanae. www.papalencyclicals.net.

Pelagius. (d.418) *de Peccato originali*, 14. https://earlychurchtexts. com/augustine_pelagius-de-peccato-originali-13.htm.

Pelagius. (413) *Letter to Demetrius.* https://earlychurchtexts.com/ public/pelagius_letter_to_demetrias.htm.

Panniker, K. M. (1953). *Asia and Western Dominance.* London: Allen and Unwin.

Pember, Mary Annette. (2019). "Death by Civilization." *The Atlantic.* 3-8.

Pember, Mary Annette. (2020). "The Catholic Church Siphoned Away $30 Million Paid to Native People for Stolen Land." *In These Times.* 7-7. https://inthesetimes.com/article/catho-lic-church-mission-schools-investigation-treaty-ojibwe-na-tive-people.

Perera, Katryna. (2016). "St. Joe's, the Jesuits, and Slavery." www. sjuhawknews.com.

Perkins, Pheme. (2000). *Peter: Apostle for the Whole Church.* Minneapolis: Fortress Press.

Perkins, Pheme. (1982). *Ministering in the Pauline Churches.* New York: Paulist Press.

Peters, E. (2005). "Quoniam abundavit iniquitas": Dominicans as Inquisitors, Inquisitors as Dominicans." *The Catholic Historical Review, 91*(1), 105–121.

Petler, D. N. (1985). "Ireland and France in 1848." *Irish Historical*

Studies, 24(96), 493–505.

Petroff, Elizabeth Alvida, ed. *Medieval Women's Visionary Literature.* New York: Oxford University Press, 1986.

Phayer, M. (2001). "Questions about Catholic Resistance." *Church History, 70*(2), 328–344.

Philo, *Legatio and Gaium.*

Pineas, R. (1964). "Thomas More's `Utopia' and Protestant Polemics." *Renaissance News, 17*(3). 197-201.

Pineas, R. (1963). "William Tyndale: Controversialist." *Studies in Philology, 60*(2), 117–132.

Pius X. (1914) *Doctoris Angelici.* https://www.papalencyclicals.net.

Plescia, J. (1971). "On the Persecution of the Christians in the Roman Empire." *Latomus, 30*(1), 120–132.

Pliny. (d.79) *Letters* 10:96-97. https://faculty,georgetown.ed/jod/text/pliny.html

Pollitt, Ronald. (1985). "The Defeat of the Northern Rebellion and the Shaping of Anglo-Scottish Relations." *The Scottish History Review, 64*(177), 1-21.

Pope, B. C. (1988). "A Heroine without Heroics: The Little Flower of Jesus and Her Times." *Church History, 57*(1), 46–60.

Prashad, V. (1997). "Mother Teresa: Mirror of Bourgeois Guilt." *Economic and Political Weekly, 32*(44/45), 2856–2858.

Preston, Paul. (2012). *The Spanish Holocaust.* New York: W.W. Norton & Company.

Ranft, P. (1994). "A Key to Counter Reformation Women's Activism: The Confessor–Spiritual Director." *Journal of Feminist Studies in Religion, 10*(2), 7–26.

Ratzinger, Josef. (1990). "On the Ecclesial Vocation of Theologians." https://www.vatican.va/documents.

Rawlinson, H. G. (1920). *British Beginning in Western India.* Oxford: Clarendon Press.

Reeves, Richard. (2002). "On Presidential Records." https://sgp.fas.org/congres/2002/041102reeves.html.

Resendez, Andres. (2016). *The Other Slavery: The Uncovered Story of Indian Enslavement in America.* Boston: Houghton Mifflin.

Richgels, R. W. (1980). "The Pattern of Controversy in a Counter-Reformation Classic: The Controversies of Robert Bellarmine."

The Sixteenth Century Journal, (*11*(2), 3–15.

Richgels, R. W. (1975). "Scholasticism Meets Humanism in the Counter-Reformation: The Clash of Cultures in Robert Bellarmine's Use of Calvin in the 'Controversies.'" *The Sixteenth Century Journal*, *6*(1), 53–66.

Ricoeur, Paul. (1967). *The Symbolism of Evil*. Boston: Beacon Press.

Risse, K., and Graziano, F. (2006). *Wounds of Love: The Mystical Marriage of Saint Rose of Lima*. *The Journal of Religion*, *86*(1), 121–122.

Roberts, Kyle. (2017). *A Complicated Pregnancy: Whether Mary Was a Virgin and Why It Matters*. Minneapolis: Fortress Press.

Robinson, R. (2000). "Taboo or Veiled Consent? Goan Inquisitorial Edict of 1736." *Economic and Political Weekly*, *35*(27), 2423–2431.

Robinson, R. (1997). "Cuncolim: Weaving a Tale of Resistance." *Economic and Political Weekly*, *32*(7), 334–340.

Robinson, R. (1993). "Some Neglected Aspects of the Conversion of Goa: A Socio-Historical Perspective." *Sociological Bulletin*, *42*(1/2), 65–83.

Rockett, W. (2008). "The Case against Thomas More." *The Sixteenth Century Journal*, *39*(4), 1065–1093.

Rockett, William. (2004). "Wolsey, More, and the Unity of Christendom." *The Sixteenth Century Journal*, *35*(3), 133–153.

Rohmann, Dirk. (2019). *Christianity and the History of Violence in the Roman Empire*. Stuttgart, Germany: CPI Press.

Rosenthal, S. F. (1990). "U.S. Policy in El Salvador." *Harvard International Review*, *12*(2), 38–42.

Roth, N. (1994). "Bishops and Jews in the Middle Ages." *The Catholic Historical Review*, *80*(1), 1–17.

Roth, Norman. (1995) Conversos, Inquisitors, and the Expulsion of the Jews from Spain. Madison: University of Wisconsin Press.

Rothman, Dirk. (2017). *Christianity, Bookburning, and Censorship in Late Antiquity*. Waco, TX: Baylor University Press.

Rowland, Ingrid. (2008). *Giordano Bruno: Philosopher/Heretic*. Chicago: University of Chicago Press.

Roy, F. (1958). "The Personality of Saint Bernadette." *The Furrow*, *9*(9), 584–588.

Rubenstein, Richard E. (2003). *Aristotle's Children*. New York: Harcourt, Inc.

Rubenstein, Richard E. (1999). *When Jesus Became God*. New York: Harcourt, Inc.

Rubios, Juan. (1513) El Requierimento. https://www.google.com/search?client=firefox-b-1-d&q=El+Requierimento.

Rudavsky, T. M. (2001). "Galileo and Spinoza: Heroes, Heretics, and Hermeneutics." *Journal of the History of Ideas, 62*(4), 611–631.Runciman, S. (1971). "The Decline of the Crusading Ideal." *The Sewanee Review, 79*(4), 498–513.

Runciman, S. (1964). "Islam and Christendom in the Middle Ages—the Need for Restatement." *Islamic Studies, 3*(2), 193–198.

Salisbury, Joyce. (2004). *The Blood of Martyrs*. New York and London: Routledge Press.

Samson, A. (2005). "Changing Places: The Marriage and Royal Entry of Philip, Prince of Austria, and Mary Tudor, July-August 1554." *The Sixteenth Century Journal, 36*(3), 761–784.

Sánchez, J. M. (2013). "The Spanish Bishops and Naziism During the Spanish Civil War." *The Catholic Historical Review, 99*(3), 499–530.

Sánchez, J. M. (1996). "The Spanish Church and the Second Republic and Civil War, 1931–1939." *The Catholic Historical Review, 82*(4), 661–668.

Sauer, Eberhart. (2009). *The Archeology of Hatred*. Gloucester, U.K.: Stroud Publishing.

Schenk, Christine. (2017). *Crispina and Her Sisters*. Minneapolis: Fortress Press.

Schmidt, Kelly L. (2022). "The Pervasive Institution: Slavery and Its Legacies in U.S. Catholicism." Cushwa Center for the Study of American Catholicism. 4-5.

Schneck, Stephen. (2022). "Should Catholics Serve in the Military?" *U. S. Catholic*. 6-25.

Schoffen, Elizabeth. (1917). *The Demands of Rome*. https://www.gutenberg.org.

Scholz, Susanne. (2017). *The Bible as Political Artifact*. Minneapolis: Fortress Press.

Schultz, Kai. (2016). "A Critic's Lonely Quest: Revealing the Truth about Mother Teresa." *New York Times.* 5-26.

Select Library of Nicene and Post Nicene Fathers and the Christian Church, A. Series II, Vol. 11: Socrates Scholasticus.

Scholasticus, Socrates. *Historica Ecclesiastic*a. https://www.documentacatholicaomnia.eu.

Scibilia, D. (1995). "The Christological Character of Labor: A Theological Rehabilitation of Mother Jones." *U.S. Catholic Historian, 13*(3), 49–61.

Severus, Sulpitius. (d. 425) *The Life of Martin of Tours.* https://cudl.lib.cam.ac.uk/view/MS-TRINITYHALL-00021/1.

Shaw, B. D. (2001). "Raising and Killing Children: Two Roman Myths." *Mnemosyne, 54*(1), 31–77.

Shaw, Brent D. (2015). "The Myth of the Neronian Persecution." *The Journal of Roman Studies.* (105), 73-100.

Shepherd of Hermas. (100-160) https://www.earlychristianwritings.com/shepherd.html.

Shepkaru, S. (2002). "To Die for God: Martyrs' Heaven in Hebrew and Latin Crusade Narratives." *Speculum, 77*(2), 311–341.

Shuger, D. (2008). "The Reformation of Penance." *Huntington Library Quarterly, 71*(4), 557–571.

Simpson, C. J. (1984). "The Stigmata: Pathology or Miracle?" *British Medical Journal (Clinical Research Edition), 289*(6460), 1746–1748.

Snaith, Norman. (1956). *Distinctive Ideas in the Old Testament.* London: Epworth Press.

Society of Friends. (1660). *The Quaker Peace Testimony.* https://quaker.org/legacy/minnfm/peace/

Society of Pius X. (2017) "Religious Liberty Contradicts Tradition." https://sspx.org/en/religious-liberty-contradicts-tradition.

Southwick, S. J. (1996). "Educating the Mind, Enlightening the Soul: Mission Schools as a Means of Transforming the Navajos, 1898–1928." *The Journal of Arizona History, 37*(1), 47–66.

Spinks, J. (2009). "Monstrous Births and Counter-Reformation Visual Polemics: Johann Nas and the 1569 Ecclesia Militans." *The Sixteenth Century Journal, 40*(2), 335–363.

Ste. Croix, G.E.M. (1954). "Aspects of the 'Great' Persecution." *The Harvard Theological Review, 47*(2), 75–113.

Stockman, Dan. (2022). "Research Shows Original Congregation of Sisters of Charity Owned Slaves." *Crux*, 2–16.

Strasser, U. (2004). "Early Modern Nuns and the Feminist Politics of Religion." *The Journal of Religion, 84*(4), 529–554.

Sullivan, K. (2009). "Disputations, Literary and Inquisitorial: The Conversion of the Heretic Sicart of Figueiras." *Medium Ævum, 78*(1), 58–79.

Sullivan, R. (1954). "Early Medieval Missionary Activity: A Comparative Study of Eastern and Western Methods." *Church History, 23*(1), 17–35.

Svrluga, Susan. (2024). "Loyola University Maryland Says It Has Ties to a 1838 Sale of Slaves." *Washington Post.* (January).

Swacker, B., and Deimling, B. (2000). "A Nineteenth-Century Church for the New Millennium: The Legacy of Pius IX and John Paul II." *The Massachusetts Review, 41*(1), 121–131.

Swarms, Rachel. (2019). "Nuns Who Bought and Sold Human Beings." *New York Times.* 8-2.

Sweet, D. G. (1978). "Black Robes and 'Black Destiny': Jesuit Views of African Slavery in 17th-Century Latin America." *Revista de Historia de América, 86,* 87–133.

Swiggett, G. L. (1936). "Conflict of Church and State in Mexico." *World Affairs, 99*(1), 40–42.

Szabo, J. (2002). "Seeing Is Believing? The Form and Substance of French Medical Debates over Lourdes." *Bulletin of the History of Medicine, 76*(2), 199–230.

Taylor, Justin. (2011). "Reading the Bible in the Time of the Curé of Ars." *Angelicum, 88*(4), 1103–1113.

Taylor, L. J. (2012). "Joan of Arc, the Church, and the Papacy, 1429–1920." *The Catholic Historical Review, 98*(2), 217–240.

Taylor, Quentin. (1998). "St. Augustine and Political Thought: A Revisionist History. Augustina, 48(4), 287-303.

Terrio, S. (1999). "Crucible of the Millennium: The Clovis Affair in Contemporary France." *Comparative Studies in Society and History, 41*(3), 438–457.

Testimony of Truth. (150-200). https://www.earlychristianwritings. com/truth.html.

Thompson, M. S. (1985). "Philemon's Dilemma: Nuns and the Black Community in Nineteenth-Century America—Some

Findings." *Records of the American Catholic Historical Society of Philadelphia, 96*(1/4), 3–18.

Throop, P. A. (1938). "Criticism of Papal Crusade Policy in Old French and Provençal." *Speculum, 13*(4), 379–412.

Tinker, T., and Freeland, M. (2008). "Thief, Slave Trader, Murderer: Christopher Columbus and Caribbean Population Decline." *Wicazo Sa Review, 23*(1), 25–50.

Traugott, Mark. (1988). "The Crowd in the French Revolution of February, 1848." *The American Historical Review, 93*(3), 638–652.

Trible, Phyllis. (1984). *Texts of Terror*. Philadelphia: Fortress Press.

Van der Lans,B. and Bremmen, Jan N. (2017). "Tacitus and the Persecution of the Christians: An Invention of Tradition?" *Eirene* 5, 299–331.

Varickayil, R. (1980). "Social Origins of Protestant Reformation." *Social Scientist, 8*(11), 14–31.

Verball, William. (2005). "The Council of Sens Reconsidered: Masters, Monks, or Judges?" Church History, 74(3), 460-493.

Vianney, John. (d. 1859) "Be Religious or Be Damned." https://www.ecatholic2000.com/cts/untitled-630.shtml.

Vianney, John. (d. 1859). Sermons of the Cure of Ars. https://www.theworkofgod.org/Library/Sermons/JdVianey/Sermons.htm

Volz, Carl A. (1997). *The Medieval Church*. Nashville: Abingdon Press.von

Vonnegut, Kurt. (2005) *A Man Without a Country*. New York: Dial Press.

Von Vacano, D. (2012). "Las Casas and the Birth of Race." *History of Political Thought, 33*(3), 401–426.

Wadsworth, J. (2004). "In the Name of the Inquisition: The Portuguese Inquisition and Delegated Authority in Colonial Pernambuco, Brazil." *The Americas, 61*(1), 19–54.

Walker, Mary. (2006). *Sovereign Ladies: Sex, Sacrifice, and Power*. New York: St. Martin's Press.

Walters, L. (1973). "The Just War and the Crusade: Antithesis or Analogies?" *The Monist, 57*(4), 584–594.

Warner, David. (2001) *Ottonian Germany: The Chronicon of Thietmar of Merseburg*. Manchester, U.K.: University of Manchester Press.

Watts, Edward. (2020). "Fiddling While Rome Converts." https://aeon.co/essays/pagan-complacency-and-the-birth-of-the-christian-roman-empire.

Waugh, Scott L., and Diehl, Peter. (1996). *Christendom and Its Discontents*. Cambridge: Cambridge University Press.

Wedgewood, C. V. (1960). *The Sense of the Past*. New York: Collier Books.

Weeks, A. (2005). "Between God and Gibson: German Mystical and Romantic Sources of 'The Passion of the Christ.'" *The German Quarterly, 78*(4), 421–440.

Weinstein, David, and Bell, Rudolph. (1982). *Saints and Society*. Chicago: University of Chicago Press.

Weisberger, Mindy. (2019) "Was Roman Emperor Nero's Evil Reputation Just 'Fake News'?" livestream/com/64812-nero-emperor-reign-pbs.

White, John. (1600) "The Fifth Voyage of Master John White in the West Indies and Parts of American Called Virginia." https://encyclopediavirginia/entries/john-white.html

White, L. Michael. (1998). "Magic, Miracles, and the Gospels." Lecture at Harvard University. https://www.pbs.org/wgbh/pages/frontline/shows/symposium/magic/html.

Wiering, Maria. (2022). "Troubling Past: The Church's Role in American's Boarding School Era." *The Catholic Spirit*, 4-26. Wilhite, David E. (2015). *The Gospel According to Heretics*. Grand Rapids, MI: Baker Academics.

Williams, Eric. (1944). *Capitalism and Slavery*. London: Andre Deutsch Publishing.

Williams, Gareth. (2015) "Charlemagne the Mass Murderer." *Medieval Warfare*, 5(2), 21-24.

Williams, James G. (1991). *The Bible, Violence, and the Sacred*. San Francisco: Harper Press.

Williams, Shannen. Dee. (2016). "The Color of Christ's Brides." *American Catholic Studies, 127*(3), 14-21.

Williams, Shannen Dee. (2020). "The Church Must Make Reparations for Its Role in Slavery." *National Catholic Reporter*, 6-1.

Wink, Walter. (1992) *Engaging the Powers*. Minneapolis: Fortress Press.

Wojcik, D. (1996). "'Polaroids from Heaven': Photography, Folk Religion, and the Miraculous Image Tradition at a Marian Apparition Site." *The Journal of American Folklore, 109*(432), 129–148.

Wolff, R. J. (1976). "Mediterranean Fascism and Diverse Catholic Responses: The Partito Popolare Italiano and the Opus Dei." *Records of the American Catholic Historical Society of Philadelphia, 87*(1/4), 33–50.

Woodward, Kenneth. (1990). *Making Saints*. New York: Simon and Shuster.

Wypustek, Andrzej. (1997). "Magic, Montanism, Perpetua, and the Severan Persecution." *Vigiliae Christianae, 51*(3), 276–297.

Xavier, Francis. *Life and Letters.* https://jesuitonlinelibrary.bc.edu.

Yardley, William. (2013). "Mary Ellen More-Richard: American Indian Memoirist Dies at Age 58." *New York Times*, 3-4.

Young, J. G. (2012). "Cristero Diaspora: Mexican Immigrants, the U.S. Catholic Church, and Mexico's Cristero War, 1926–29." *The Catholic Historical Review, 98*(2), 271–300.

Your Daily Martyr and the Precious Blood. (2016). https://devotion-to-our-lady.com-holy-martyrs.html.

Zabelka, George. (2022). " Bless the Bombs." *The Plough.*

Zarley, Kermit. (2019). "Should the Catholic Church Abolish the Priesthood?" *Patheos.* https://www.patheos.com/blogs/kermitzarleyblog/2019/05/the-catholic-church-should-abolish-the-priesthood/

Zapor, Patricia (2012). "Religious Liberty Under Attack." *The Arlington Catholic Herald.* https://www.catholicherald.com/cardinal-dolan-traces-historic-role-of-religious-freedom/

ABOUT THE AUTHOR

Eileen McCafferty DiFranco holds a Master of Divinity from United (formerly the Lutheran) Theological Seminary of Philadelphia. A lifelong student of history and theology, she has long experienced cognitive dissonance between the words of Jesus with the manner in which all Christian denominations, including the Catholic Church, have behaved in the world. The Cost of Sainthood grew out of her dissatisfaction with the various churches' elevation of right belief over right behavior.

DiFranco is a regular columnist for Southeastern Pennsylvania Women's Ordination Conference newsletter "Equal wRites" and the author of a 2017 book entitled How to Keep Your Parish Alive, which provides a blueprint for founding intentional Eucharistic communities when bishops close down a local parish.